Global Supply Chain Security

James R. Giermanski

THE SCARECROW PRESS, INC.
Lanham • Toronto • Plymouth, UK
2013

Published by Scarecrow Press, Inc.
A wholly owned subsidiary of The Rowman & Littlefield Publishing Group, Inc.
4501 Forbes Boulevard, Suite 200, Lanham, Maryland 20706
www.rowman.com

10 Thornbury Road, Plymouth PL6 7PP, United Kingdom

British Library Cataloguing in Publication Information Available

Library of Congress Cataloging-in-Publication Data

Giermanski, James R., 1939–
    Global supply chain security / James R. Giermanski.
        p. cm.
    Includes bibliographical references and index.
    ISBN 978-0-8108-8641-4 (cloth : alk. paper) — ISBN 978-0-8108-8642-1 (ebook)
    1. Freight and freightage—Security measures. 2. Ports of entry—Security measures. 3.
Customs inspection. I. Title.
    HE199.A2G54 2013
    363.12′064—dc23   2012033575

∞™ The paper used in this publication meets the minimum requirements of American
National Standard for Information Sciences—Permanence of Paper for Printed Library
Materials, ANSI/NISO Z39.48-1992.

Printed in the United States of America

Contents

Preface

In a living being, continued health and viability depend on the continuous flow of blood to the essential organs. So too does the continued well-being of our nation depend on the inbound and outbound trade flow of products such as energy, food, pharmaceuticals, and many more crucial components essential for our economic health and the generation of revenue. The global supply chain, however, can also be used to seriously damage and even destroy the nation's viability. The risk is generated by the millions of containers and trailers passing through our seaports and land ports of entry, which can serve as weapons systems and, if detonated, can close our ports and cut off the lifeblood of our nation: global trade. These containers and trailers also serve as the conveyance of counterfeit goods, drugs, and other illegal cargo into and through the United States. Like disrupting the blood supply and flow of the cardiovascular system or inserting bacteria or viral agents into that flow, introducing illegal or dangerous cargo into our homeland and its economy can result in serious or fatal consequences, an illness our nation cannot afford.

The purpose of this book is twofold: (1) to highlight the security elements involved in global trade and the potential vulnerabilities associated with them, and (2) to evaluate the level of competence our Department of Homeland Security has demonstrated in preparing for and treating the risks connected to vulnerabilities inherent in the global sea and land movement of products.

Acknowledgments

First, I would like to thank Don Philpott, writer and former editor of *International Homeland Security Journal*, without whose encouragement and continued advice and support I would neither have begun nor finished this project. I would also like to thank my son, Chris, director of international operations at Transportation Services Inc., for specific input on Mexican-U.S. supply chain security issues and my daughter, Dulce, for assistance in putting together the list of abbreviations used in this book. I'd also like to thank my wife, Maria, who kept me from giving up and put up with my grumbling during the research and writing process. Professorial colleagues also helped by contributing in certain chapters. Finally, I'd like to thank Denise Krepp, former senior counsel of the U.S. House of Representatives Homeland Security Committee, who put up with my ranting about congressional and administrative inaction on supply chain security.

Acronyms and Abbreviations

AAR	American Association of Railroads
ACAS	air cargo advance screening
ACC	American Chemical Council
ACE	Automated Commercial Environment
ACS	Automated Commercial System
AEO	authorized economic operator
AES	Automated Export System
AFOSI	Air Force Office of Special Investigations
AIS	automatic identification service
ALI	American Law Institute
AMS	Automated Manifest System
ANSI	American National Standards Institute
APIS	Advance Passenger Information System
ARRL	American Radio Relay League/National Association for Amateur Radio
ATA	American Trucking Associations
ATRI	American Transportation Research Institute
ATS	automated targeting system
B2A	business-to-authorities
B2B	business-to-business
BBWG	Beyond the Border Working Group
BTB ESC	Beyond the Border Executive Steering Committee
BTN	Brussels Tariff Nomenclature
BZPP	Buffer Zone Protection Program
CAMS	container automated monitoring system
CAS	Chemical Abstracts Service
CBP	Customs and Border Protection
CCC	Customs Convention on Containers

CERCLA	Comprehensive Environmental Response, Compensation, and Liability Act
CFR	Code of Federal Regulations
Chem-BZPP	Chemical Buffer Zone Protection Program
CISG	United Nations Convention of Contracts for the International Sale of Goods
CISLA	Cargo Intelligence, Security, and Logistics Association
COAC	Advisory Committee on Commercial Operations of Customs and Border Protection
CoC	chain of custody
COGSA	Carriage of Goods by Sea Act
CSD	container security device
CSI	Container Security Initiative
C-TPAT	Customs-Trade Partnership Against Terrorism
CVSA	Commercial Vehicle Safety Alliance
DEA	Drug Enforcement Agency
decaBDE	decabromodiphenyl ether
DHS	Department of Homeland Security
DOC	Department of Commerce
DOD	Department of Defense
DOE	Department of Energy
DOJ	Department of Justice
DOT	Department of Transportation
DTO	drug-trafficking organization
EDC	European Datacomm
EPA	Environmental Protection Agency
EPC	EPCglobal
ESI	electronically stored information
EU	European Union
FACA	Federal Advisory Committee Act
FAK	freight of all kinds
FAR	false accept rate
FAST	Free and Secure Trade
FBI	Federal Bureau of Investigation
FCA	free carrier
FCC	Federal Communications Commission
FCL	full container load
FDA OCI	Food and Drug Administration Office of Criminal Investigations
FEMA	Federal Emergency Management Agency
FIPS	Federal Information Processing Standards
FLETC	Federal Law Enforcement Training Center
FMCSA	Federal Motor Carrier Safety Administration
FMCSR	Federal Motor Carriers Safety Regulations
FOT	field operational test

FP7	Seventh Framework Programme for Research and Technological Development
FRR	false reject rate
G8	Group of Eight
GAO	Government Accountability Office
GDAIS	General Dynamics Advanced Information Systems
GPRS	general packet radio service
GPS	global positioning system
GSA	General Services Administration
GSM	global system for mobile communications
HEU	highly enriched uranium
HIDTA	high-intensity drug-trafficking area
HMR	Hazardous Materials Regulations
HSI	Homeland Security Investigations
HSI-IA	Homeland Security Investigations International Affairs
HTS	Harmonized Tariff Schedule
HTSA	Harmonized Tariff Schedule of the United States Annotated
HTSP	HAZMAT Truck Security Pilot
HTSUS	Harmonized Tariff Schedule of the United States
IBSGP	Intercity Bus Security Grant Program
ICC	International Commerce Commission
ICE	Immigration and Customs Enforcement
ICT	information and communication technology
IED	improvised explosive device
IEEE	Institute of Electrical and Electronics Engineers Standards Association
IIT	Instrument of International Traffic
IMO	International Maritime Organization
IPP	Infrastructure Protection Program
IPR	intellectual property rights
IPRSGP	Intercity Passenger Rail Security Grant Program
IRCA	Implementing Recommendations of the 9/11 Commission Act of 2007
ISO	International Organization for Standardization
ISPS	International Ship and Port Facility Security Code
IT	information technology
ITC	International Trade Commission
ITDS	International Trade Data System
LAN	local area network
LEO	low-earth-orbit
LOS	line of sight
MCA	mission critical assets
MKK	Radio Equipment Testing and Approval Association
MOU	memorandum of understanding

MSDS	material safety data sheets
NAFTA	North American Free Trade Agreement
NATAP	North American Trade Automation Prototype
NCCUSL	National Conference of Commissioners on Uniform State Laws
NCIC	National Crime Information Center
NII	nonintrusive inspection
NIPP	National Infrastructure Protection Plan
NIST	National Institute of Standards and Technology
NLETS	National Law Enforcement Telecommunications System
NOAA	National Oceanic and Atmospheric Administration
NSEERS	National Security Entry Exit Registrations System
NTC	National Targeting Center
NVOCC	non-vessel operating common carriers
OSHA	Occupational Safety and Health Administration
OTS	off-the-shelf
PACS	Programa Alianza para el Comercio Seguro/Program Alliance for Secure Commerce
PAPS	Pre-Arriving Processing System
PIP	Partners in Protection
PITEX	Program for Production of Articles for Exportation
PRD	personal radiation detector
PSA	prostate-specific antigen
PSGP	Port Security Grant Program
PTD	Physical Techniques Division
PTI	priority trade issue
RCC	Regulatory Cooperation Council
RCRA	Resource Conservation and Recovery Act
RF	radio frequency
RFI	request for information
RFID	radio frequency identification
RITA	Research and Innovation Technology Administration
RKC	Revised Kyoto Convention
ROI	return on investment
RSPA	Research and Special Programs Administration
S&T	Science and Technology Directorate
SAFECON	SAFE Container
SAIC	Science Applications International Corporation
SCAC	standard carrier alpha code
SEA	Safe Explosives Act
SEMARNAP	Secretaría de Medio Ambiente, Recursos Naturales y Pesca
SFI	Security Freight Initiative
SITC	Standard International Trade Classification
SMART-CM	Smart Container Chain Management

SSD	safe separation distance
STB	single transaction bond
STC	said to contain
T&E	transportation and exportation or testing and evaluation
TAPA	Transported Asset Protection Association
TECS	Treasury Enforcement Communications System
TEU	twenty-foot equivalent units
TREC	tamper-resistant embedded controller
TSA	Transportation Security Administration
TSCA	Toxic Substances Control Act
TSGP	Transit Security Grant Program
TSP	Trucking Security Program
TSSI	Total Security Services International
TSUS	Tariff Schedule of the United States
TTC	truck-tracking center
TWIC	Transportation Workers Identification Credential
UAT	user acceptance tests
UCC	Uniform Commercial Code
UN/DOT	United Nations Department of Transportation
USA Patriot Act	Uniting and Strengthening America by Providing Appropriate Tools Required to Intercept and Obstruct Terrorism Act
USCIB	United States Council for International Business
USDOT	United States Department of Transportation
USITC	U.S. International Trade Commission
USPIS	U.S. Postal Inspection Service
USTR	U.S. trade representative
WCO	World Customs Organization
Wi-Fi	Wireless Fidelity
WiMAX	Worldwide Interoperable for Microwave Access
WMD	weapon of mass destruction
WSC	World Shipping Council
WSN	wireless sensor networks

Chapter One

Genesis of Supply Chain Security

Its Origins, Its Transition, and Its Current Status

When did it leave? Where is it? When will it get here? What's its condition? If it left the port two days ago, why isn't it here now? These are familiar questions to any firm depending on a global supply chain. Governments have similar questions. Who's the shipper? Where is it coming from? Is it coming through a CSI port? What do we know about this container? With the incredible increase in the number of container volumes, seaport growth, and unpredictable seaport selection and usage, industry leaders and governments are looking for more knowledge faster. But paper knowledge in today's world is insufficient. The world's customs authorities and industry leaders recognize that only an automated electronic system can monitor these volumes and the security aspects surrounding them. Although the security and knowledge of cargo locations in the pipeline have always been concerns for industry, the events of September 11, 2001, or 9/11, increased the concern over unmonitored container movements as potential implements of terrorism.

In the United States, the common perception is that we have taken the leadership role in streamlining supply chain security. However, the reality is that the concept of supply chain security and container security has developed through three phases:

Phase 1. Harmonizing divergent customs practices;
Phase 2. 9/11 and port security; and
Phase 3. Origin to destination and a chain of custody.

Understanding these phases can best be explained by looking at the entities who led the development. These entities will be divided into worldwide organizations, U.S. legislation and programs and processes, and the European initiatives that were and are extensive and significant in developing supply chain security practices. There is no question that the world trading communities are now in Phase 3, the origin-to-destination or chain-of-custody stage.

WORLDWIDE ORGANIZATIONS

Revised Kyoto Convention of 1999

Phase 1, between 1999 and September 11, 2001, was the recognition of the need for cooperation and modernization among the world's customs authorities; the genesis for improving and modernizing customs practices around the world was the Revised Kyoto Convention of 1999.[1] However, the history and foundation for the worldwide movement to improve port and container security through the use of more efficient technology and control can be traced to its beginnings in the 1973 Kyoto Convention, where customs authorities from around the world met to harmonize tariffs. The Kyoto Convention specifically supported the application of new technology to customs practices. The Revised Kyoto Convention of 1999 had the goals of simplifying customs procedures with an emphasis on information technology and risk management involving automated systems to target and select high-risk shipments for inspection based on prearrival information. Specifically, the Kyoto Convention Information and Communication Technology Guidelines (ICT Guidelines) include the advance electronic transmission of information to customs computerized systems, including the use of the electronic exchange of information at export and import. They focus on simplifying customs procedures, information technology, automated targeting systems, maximum use of information technology, and e-commerce.

World Customs Organization (WCO)

Perhaps the foremost leader in supply chain security in Phase 3 was the World Customs Organization (WCO). The WCO grasped the opportunity to develop standards for enhancing global supply chain security by moving to automate and control global cargo movements. Furthermore, its efforts to develop standards of efficiency and security in this regard are being supported by governments around the world. Its push for automated systems and electronic transfers of data is critical in accommodating the worldwide growth of the container and port industry. The WCO adoption of the Revised Kyoto Convention of 1999 served as a baseline for the development of its SAFE Framework of Standards to secure and facilitate global trade. The SAFE Framework was approved and then officially adopted by the WCO in 2005.[2] Almost all member countries of the WCO followed by also adopting the SAFE Framework, including the United States. The SAFE Framework succeeded in pushing the security of cargo back to its stuffing or loading. It did so by involving the private sector and by requiring increased security at the point of origin or stuffing and as the container is moved point to point through the supply chain. The Framework clearly states that

Customs should use sophisticated methods to identify and target potentially high-risk cargo, including—but not limited to—advance electronic information about cargo shipments to and from a country before they depart or arrive; strategic intelligence; automated trade data; anomaly analysis; and the relative security of a trader's supply chain. For example, the Customs-Business Pillar certification and validation of point-of-origin security reduces the risk, and therefore, the targeting score.[3]

Furthermore, the customs administration should require advance electronic information on cargo and container shipments in time for adequate risk assessment to take place.[4] There are four core elements of the SAFE Framework:

1. Advance electronic manifest information requirements
2. Consistent risk-management approach
3. Inspection of certain containers by nonintrusive means
4. Benefits to businesses for cooperation

WCO proposed programs to "push the security of cargo and container further back into the supply chain by involving the private sector and by requiring increased security at the point of origin, e.g., the point of stuffing a container at a foreign manufacturer's loading docks, and as the container is moved point to point through the supply chain."[5] This was probably the most important element in promoting a chain-of-custody process applicable to the global supply chain. The appendix to Annex I of the SAFE Framework is entirely dedicated to the security of containers. The SAFE Framework and each of these core elements in particular are accommodated in the U.S. SAFE Port Act.

Kyoto Convention Information and Communication Technology Guidelines

The 2004 Kyoto Convention Information and Communication Technology Guidelines (ICT Guidelines) contributed to the origin-to-destination concept through guidelines on the electronic exchange of information at export and import, creating a chain of electronic data and a single global schema linked electronically. Specifically, the Kyoto Convention ICT Guidelines proposed the advance electronic transmission of information to customs services' computerized systems, including the use of the electronic exchange of information at export and import.

E-commerce can be broadly defined as the delivery of information, products, services, and payments using any kind of automated media, ranging from telephones to computers and beyond. While, in more technical terms, e-commerce can be seen as commercial activity conducted over closed or open networks linking electronic devices (usually computers), it has now acquired a wider sense of the use of electronic technology for all business needs.[6]

UN's "Single Window"

Phase 3, the origin-to-destination phase from 2004 to the present, can only be accomplished through a unified and efficient system of data transfer as envisioned in the Automated Commercial Environment (ACE). This idea of efficiency was crystallized in the UN Economic Commission for Europe's Recommendation 33 (approved September 2004), which was the proposal of a "single window" through which "trade-related information and/or documents need only be submitted once at a single entry point to fulfill all import, export, and transit-related regulatory requirements."

Transported Asset Protection Association (TAPA) and International Maritime Organization (IMO)

During this phase, there were also actions by international organizations such as the Transported Asset Protection Association (TAPA), which promoted its freight security requirements in 2001, and the International Maritime Organization (IMO), resulting in "Special Measures to Enhance Maritime Security," the International Ship and Port Facility Security Code (ISPS), which went into effect in 2004.

U.S. LEGISLATION

Trade Act of 2002

On September 11, 2001, everything seemed to change. Phase 2, between 2001 and 2004, focused on maritime issues. In response to the attack on the United States, the Trade Act of 2002 (as amended by the Maritime Transportation Security Act of 2002) was passed, requiring that Customs and Border Protection (CBP) promulgate regulations to begin collecting all manifests electronically. U.S. legislation like the Trade Act of 2002 addressed issues such as vessel identification systems, vessel security plans, port security assessments, and operational and efficiency matters such as the maritime intelligence system, all rooted in the electronic transfer of information.

SAFE Port Act of 2006

The SAFE Port Act was signed into law on October 13, 2006. Through this legislative action, the United States codified CBP's security programs such as the Customs-Trade Partnership Against Terrorism (C-TPAT) and the Container Security Initiative (CSI), U.S. programs that include and support WCO standards. U.S. programs were designed to develop and more quickly obtain more information and data connected to worldwide shipping and to improve the port and container security environment. The act included the requirement of scanning for radiation, automated targeting, and container security standards. The SAFE Port Act also mandated that the container security function be consistent with the law's definition of global supply chain, or from a good's foreign origin to its destination in the United States: "The term 'international supply chain' means the end-to-end process for shipping goods to or from the United States beginning at the point of origin (including manufacturer, supplier, or vendor) through a point of distribution to destination."[7] It also establishes "green lane" provisions in the form of tiers 1, 2, and 3. Tier 3 treatment, the greatest commercial incentive to importers and shippers, requires the use of a container security system: "utilization of container security devices, technologies, policies, or practices that meet standards and criteria established by the Secretary."[8] Green lanes are incentives for industry that help move containers through customs' control in an expedited fashion, increasing the competitive advantage of the user.

Implementing the 9/11 Commission Recommendations Act of 2007

In addition to the SAFE Port Act, Phase 3 also witnessed the passage of another U.S. legislative act called the Implementing the 9/11 Commission Recommendations Act of 2007, in which Title V addressed the "Security of Cargo Containers." The act requires breach detection and access prior to entering the economic zone of the United States. Additionally, the act requires electronic notification of any breach in the supply chain and requires the application of origin-to-destination security for all truck, rail, and vessel transit in international commerce with the United States. One issue in the act, however, is still connected to ports—the issue of scanning.

The act states that the secretary of the Department of Homeland Security (DHS) must ensure that container standards be developed and implemented that "identify the place of a breach into a container; notify the Secretary of such breach before the container enters the Exclusive Economic Zone [U.S. ports] of the United States; and track the time and location of the container during transit to the United States, including by truck, rail, or vessel." The law also requires 100% scanning of inbound containers to the United States in foreign ports. However, the 100% scanning requirement was not accepted by the rest of the trading world.

U.S. PROGRAMS AND PROCESSES

Customs-Trade Partnership Against Terrorism (C-TPAT)

C-TPAT is a cooperative voluntary program between industry and CBP. Its purpose is to strengthen the entire global supply chain by requiring its volunteer firms to meet minimum security standards established by CBP. It is an "inbound" program, easily recognized as such by both its security mandates and the type of business participants permitted in the program:

- U.S. importers of record
- U.S.-Canada highway carriers
- U.S.-Mexico highway carriers
- Rail carriers
- Sea carriers
- Air carriers
- U.S. marine port authority/terminal operators
- U.S. air freight consolidators
- Ocean transportation intermediaries
- Non-vessel operating common carriers (NVOCC)
- Mexican and Canadian manufacturers
- Certain invited foreign manufacturers
- Licensed U.S. Customs brokers

> What is most significant about C-TPAT is its consistency with the definition of the "international supply chain" contained in Section 2 of the SAFE Port Act, which requires security to begin at origin and end at destination: ". . . to provide reassurance that there are effective security procedures and controls implemented at the point of stuffing. . . . Container and trailer integrity must be maintained to protect against the introduction of unauthorized material and/or persons. At the point of stuffing, procedures must be in place to properly seal and maintain the integrity of the shipping containers and trailers."[9]

Rail was singled out as having to provide tracking information. Additionally, C-TPAT participants must move toward electronic transmission of information consistent with the new e-Manifest, a component of the ACE system, the U.S. CBP's single window.

U.S. security programs like C-TPAT clearly reflected the movement to control the supply chain from its beginning to its ultimate destination. What is most significant is C-TPAT's consistency with the definition of "international supply chain" contained in Section 2 of the SAFE Port Act, which requires the security rules for C-TPAT participants to begin at origin and end at destination. As an example, as of 2007, C-TPAT standards for Mexican long-haul carriers included the following:[10]

- Security beginning at stuffing
- Tracking and monitoring
- Nine areas of security

In compliance with the SAFE Port Act, some C-TPAT participants like rail must even provide tracking information. All C-TPAT participants must move toward electronic transmission of information consistent with the new e-Manifest. Now, through mutual recognition of companion customs programs, there is a worldwide movement of major trading nations' customs authorities to recognize the need for origin-to-destination security and the concept of supply chain security beginning at stuffing. All of the following programs demonstrate, in one way or another, the concept that supply chain security begins at stuffing:

* Secure Exports Scheme Program (New Zealand)
* Partners in Protection Program (Canada)
* Golden List Program (Jordan)
* Authorized Economic Operator Program (Japan)
* Authorized Economic Operator Program (Korea)
* Secure Trade Partnership Plus Program (Singapore)
* Authorized Economic Operator Program (European Union)

Container Security Initiative (CSI)

In the United States, the CSI program, an initiative set in motion by the U.S. Commissioner of Customs after 9/11, supports cooperative Group of Eight (G8) action on transport security. CSI addresses the threat to border security and global trade posed by the potential for terrorist use of a maritime container to deliver weapons of mass destruction (WMD). It proposes a security regimen to ensure that all containers that pose a potential risk for terrorism are identified and inspected at foreign ports before they are placed on vessels destined for the United States. CSI's core elements are the following:[11]

Identify high-risk containers. CBP uses automated targeting tools to identify containers that pose a potential risk for terrorism, based on advance information and strategic intelligence. Containers are prescreened and evaluated before they are shipped; they are screened as early in the supply chain as possible, generally at the port of departure.

Use technology to prescreen high-risk containers. This presumes that screening can be done rapidly without slowing down the movement of trade.

Use smart containers or tamper-evident containers.

Through CSI, CBP officers work with host customs administrations to establish security criteria for identifying high-risk containers. Those administrations use nonintrusive inspection (NII) and radiation detection technology to screen high-risk containers before they are shipped to U.S. ports. CSI, as a reciprocal program, also offers its participant countries the opportunity to send their customs officers to major U.S. ports to target oceangoing, containerized cargo destined for their countries. Likewise, CBP shares information on a bilateral basis with its CSI partners. Japan and Canada currently station their customs personnel in some U.S. ports as part of the CSI program.[12] CSI's program is anchored in the 24-hour manifest rule, which requires that all manifest information be electronically provided 24 hours before U.S.-bound containers are laden into a vessel at a foreign port. CBP officers are only allowed to physically inspect containers in the participating foreign country ports when authorized to do so by that nation's customs authorities. The CSI program is more dependent on data acquisition and analysis.

Automated Commercial Environment (ACE)

ACE is the commercial trade processing system being developed by CBP to facilitate trade while strengthening border security. The ACE secure data portal connects CBP, the trade community, and participating government agencies by providing a single, centralized, online access point for communications and CBP information, providing users with the capacity to monitor daily operations and identify compliance issues through access to more than 125 reports, and to electronically update account data, merge accounts, access multiple accounts via one username, create a new importer identification record (CBP Form 5106), and ensure the accuracy of all account information.[13]

As of May 2011, the number of ACE account types now includes practically every entity doing business with CBP, and there are more than 17,000 ACE portal accounts, including more than 3,000 importer and broker accounts and more than 14,000 carrier accounts. The use of ACE was mandated of all carriers and U.S. Customs brokers. ACE manifest filing has a strong national security purpose. All shipments, without exception, must include complete bill of lading information, electronically entered into the ACE system.

e-Manifest

The e-Manifest is the key electronic format that facilitates the use of the ACE system and will be applicable to all vessel carriers entering and leaving the United States. It is applicable at the time of this writing to U.S. cross-border movements through ports of entry on both the southern and northern borders. Examples of required entries include driver's identification, product code, shipper and consignee, all bill of lading data, package type, value, and country code, to name a few. The e-Manifest is a requirement for all modes of carriage, and the electronic instrument for moving toward an electronic system of data transfer.

While the beginning for logistics and customs efficiency may be Kyoto, the security genesis is certainly 9/11, which became the catalyst speeding up the movement to the generation and use of electronic information. These data may include all types of information, depending on unique government requirements, circumstance of product, mode of carriage, country of origin, history of shipper and consignee, and more. They may be secured or unsecured, depending on the players. While there are many sources of logistics and security data, the nexus of both becomes evident. From the generic bill of lading and/or booking confirmation or dray order, one can obtain information such as the following:[14]

- Identity of person supervising stuffing and arming the system at origin
- Document number
- Booking number
- Shipper/exporter
- Forwarding agent and license number
- City or point of origin (stuffing)
- Date of departure from origin, if known
- Consignee
- Notify party
- Place of receipt by land carrier
- Exporting carrier (vessel line)
- Seaport of loading (origin seaport)
- Loading pier or terminal, if known
- Seaport of discharge (destination seaport)
- Declared value
- Container ID number
- Gross weight in pounds or kilograms or other measurements
- Description of goods (six-digit tariff number)

Required customs forms may add to this list by requiring the following and more:

- International Maritime Organization (IMO) number
- Nationality of ship
- First port or place where carrier takes possession
- Name of vessel
- Name of master
- Last foreign port before the United States
- Marks and container numbers
- Bill of lading number
- Driver's identification

Secure Freight Initiative (SFI)

Another program initiated was the Secure Freight Initiative (SFI), a joint effort by the DHS and the Department of Energy (DOE) designed "to scan containers for nuclear and radiological materials overseas and to better assess the risk of inbound containers."[15] Announced in 2006, the program was implemented in 2007 in six foreign ports to gather information on potential carriage of nuclear material and report the information found. This data will be combined with other available risk assessment information, such as currently required manifest submissions, to improve risk analysis, targeting, and scrutiny of high-risk containers overseas.

International Trade Data System (ITDS)

The SAFE Port Act also requires the establishment of an electronic trade data interchange system to be known as the International Trade Data System (ITDS), which must be implemented as soon as the CBP's ACE system is fully implemented. The National Performance Review by the vice president of the United States recommended the creation of the ITDS in 1995. Codified in the SAFE Port Act, the ITDS establishes a single portal system, operated by the CBP, for the collection and distribution of standard electronic import and export data required by all participating federal agencies. It will become the repository of electronic trade information generated by the ACE system and the e-Manifest.

Nonintrusive Inspection (NII) Program

NII is mobile gamma-ray imaging technology. It is deployed at seaports and at land ports of entry, permitting officers to detect and interdict contraband (such as narcotics, weapons, and currency) hidden within conveyances and/or cargo, while simultaneously facilitating the flow of legitimate trade and travel. The mobile gamma-ray imaging system employs a gamma-ray source that permits officers to quickly see inside tankers, commercial trucks, cargo containers, and other conveyances without having to physically open the conveyance and/or container. NII machines can scan vehicles up to 125 feet in length in one pass. One version of the system is mounted on a truck chassis and is operated by a three-man crew. NII operates by slowly driving past a parked vehicle with a boom extended over the target vehicle.[16] NII is smaller in scale and is used at U.S. ports of entry, directed at individuals coming into the country. The use of NII at ports of entry and Border Patrol checkpoints is based on a requirements analysis of the individual conditions at each location.

Container Security Device (CSD) Beginnings

From Kyoto to the e-Manifest, there is a global consistency in the collection, storage, and electronic transmission of trade and manifest data, from the stuffing of the container at origin to the opening of the container at destination. These electronic data must be generated at the shipper's site and transmitted, at times to different locations, as soon as the container begins its initial travel to its destination. This chain-of-custody concept can be easily implemented through the use of current container security devices (CSDs), which serve to implement the control from origin to destination. Although the United States has progressed into the container security area, it has done so based on not only its own initiative, brought about by 9/11, but also because of international standards to which it subscribes. Phase 3 captures and exceeds the vision contained in the Revised Kyoto Convention of 1999 of improving and modernizing customs practices around the world. It specifically supported the concept of applying new technology to customs practices. The revised Kyoto Convention had the goals of simplifying customs procedures, emphasizing information technology and risk management, and using automated systems to target and select high-risk shipments for inspection based on prearrival information. CSDs employing an array of sensors allow for multiple types of logistics data to be collected and transmitted while a container is moving from origin to destination. These areas of detection and control include the following:

- Geofencing and reporting path diversions
- Remote locking and unlocking
- Radiation detection (including shielded enriched uranium)
- Temperature detection (remote sensing and adjustments)
- Vibration detection (vibration differentiation, e.g., from gantry, drayage, drilling)
- Light detection
- Infrared detection
- Drugs/chemicals detection
- Humans

Changes to Federal Rules of Civil Procedure

Phase 3 also saw a new legal development in the United States that is extremely important for supply chain and container security.[17] Trade terms and (obviously) logistics data began to be electronically transmitted throughout the global supply chain. Electronic information has become essential not only to governments but also to the exporters and importers who must comply with the electronic mandates. Changes in the Federal Rules of Civil Procedure took effect on December 1, 2006, specifically to six rules: 16, 26, 33, 34, 37, and 45.

These changes in rules asserted that electronically stored information (ESI) is a class of evidence and equal to paper or any other type of physical evidence. Each rule is distinct but related. Rule 16 allows pretrial meetings to discuss discovery issues regarding ESI. Rule 26 clarifies the need to disclose information about holders of ESI and its description before a discovery request, and it allows the safeguarding of privileged information to be withheld or returned. Rule 33 makes it clear that ESI includes business records. Rule 34 defines computer-based and other digitally stored data as ESI and its format as a separate category, subject to production and discovery. Rule 37 addresses the destruction of ESI and when it can or cannot be destroyed. The strongest rule alteration probably occurred in Rule 45, which recognizes ESI as a distinct category of discoverable information, allowing for it to be subpoenaed in the same way as paper documents. Subpoenas may also be executed on individuals or companies not directly involved in the litigation.

ESI is all-inclusive. It can be found in e-mail, voicemail, instant messages, text messages, documents, spreadsheets, databases, file fragments, metadata, digital images, and digital diagrams. It can be stored in every type of electronic media, including hard drives, thumb drives, computers, handheld devices, backup tapes, and optical disks. The bottom line is that the U.S. Supreme Court now allows for the use and admission of electronic data in court and as potential evidence in civil matters upon discovery. Up until 2007, only electronic information involving criminal proceedings could be seized and used in court. This new allowance involving civil, noncriminal, electronic data for use in court is exciting news for those involved in both law enforcement and civil litigation involving supply chain and container security matters.

EUROPEAN LEADERSHIP THROUGH THE SEVENTH FRAMEWORK PROGRAMME FOR RESEARCH AND TECHNOLOGICAL DEVELOPMENT (FP7)

European Union Regulations

European Union (EU) actions such as EC Regulation No. 1935/2004, dealing with origin-to-destination and traceability controls for the safety of foodstuffs, and EU Report No. 40008032-6-2-2005, declaring that security was essential to the supply chain from origin to destination, contributed to moving into the origin-to-destination control or the chain-of-custody system era.

EU Commission's Initiative

The complete name of FP7 is the Seventh Framework Programme for Research and Technological Development. It was created by the EU Commission to last for seven years, from 2007 until 2013. The program has a total budget of more than €50 billion and responds to Europe's needs in terms of jobs and competitiveness and maintaining leadership in the global knowledge economy.[18] Within FP7, four separate research programs have been specifically examining the idea of supply chain and container security: CONTAIN, INTEGRITY, CASSANDRA, and SMART-CM.

CONTAIN

CONTAIN will specify and demonstrate a European shipping container surveillance system that will encompass regulation, policy, and standardization recommendations, new business models, and advanced container security management capabilities.[19]

INTEGRITY

INTEGRITY targets door-to-door container transport, focusing on safe, secure, and efficient transport. INTEGRITY will develop procedures and technologies allowing for supply chain visibility, security, and predictability.[20] It has used actual private sector players in the global supply chain and has tested sophisticated equipment, including scanning and CSD offerings and attributes.

CASSANDRA

CASSANDRA focuses on intermodal container logistics, developing a common solution for "supply chain visibility, where data for visibility can be shared between business and government using visualization tools and an open architecture to monitor data and cargo flow and container integrity."[21]

SMART-CM

Smart Container Chain Management (SMART-CM) focuses on using advanced technology and research

> to overhaul the complete container door-to-door transport chain so that it is more efficient, secure, market driven, and competitive. It systematically analyses current processes and systems, produces new innovative concepts for processes and technologies, and demonstrates all these in a set of 2 world scale Demonstrators covering 4 supply chain corridors.[22]

SMART-CM involves all types of large global participants in container trade, such as K&N, DHL, COSCO, PSA, and DPW, as well as smaller firms and international organizations involved in setting standards and promoting transport and container security. Its objectives are clear:

- Stimulate interoperable B2B (business-to-business) cooperation in door-to-door container transport security
- Develop compliant application of B2B and B2A (business-to-authorities) container security data solutions with international customs operations
- Develop a neutral approach and service platform for secure and interoperable data communications

- Define added-value services and chain visibility–enabling techniques for fulfilling operational requirements of the actors
- Develop prototypes of advanced applications in global container management, such as dynamic scheduling at the containers
- Assess large applicability of the above-mentioned project solutions by considering costs and benefits
- Analyze existing business models in global container chain management and operation and study e-business models
- Contribute to standards development for advancing of interoperability of technologies

U.S. NATIONAL STRATEGY ON SUPPLY CHAIN SECURITY

In January 2012, DHS released its strategy on supply chain security. Contained in the six-page document are two goals:

Goal 1. Promote the efficient and secure movement of goods.

Goal 2. Foster a resilient supply chain.

Specifically, to achieve goal 1 we will enhance the integrity of goods as they move through the global supply chain. We will also understand and resolve threats early in the process and strengthen the security of physical infrastructures, conveyances, and information assets, while seeking to maximize trade through modernizing supply chain infrastructures and processes.[23]

This goal includes the need to verify the accuracy of the container's cargo so that it is not misdirected or compromised. Additionally, there must be a limiting of access to cargo, cargo conveyances, and port infrastructure while maximizing cargo flow within the supply chain. To implement this strategy, DHS listed the following priority actions:[24]

- Align Federal activities across the United States Government to the goals of the Strategy.
- Refine our understanding of the threats and risks associated with the global supply chain through updated assessments.
- Advance technology research, development, testing, and evaluation efforts aimed at improving our ability to secure cargo in air, land, and sea environments.
- Identify infrastructure projects to serve as models for the development of critical infrastructure resiliency best practices.
- Seek opportunities to incorporate global supply chain resiliency goals and objectives into the Federal infrastructure investment programs and project assessment process.
- Promote necessary legislation that supports Strategy implementation by Federal departments and agencies.

- Develop, in concert with industry and foreign governments, customized solutions to speed the flow of legitimate commerce in specific supply chains that meet designated criteria and can be considered low-risk.
- Align trusted trader program requirements across Federal agencies. We will consider the potential for standardized application procedures, enhanced information-sharing agreements, and security audits conducted by joint or cross-designated Federal teams.

CONCLUSION

Without question, global supply chain security has not been an overnight phenomenon, nor has it been a product of or led by the United States. Clearly, the prime mover of global supply chain security, visibility, and efficiency has been the World Customs Organization, the European Union's Commission, and the private sector itself. If anything, the U.S. role has not produced standards or practices accepted worldwide. The U.S. influence, if any, has been in its C-TPAT program and its assistance to other nations in developing their own security programs and in the size and economic importance of the United States in international trade and government-to-government cooperation.

NOTES

1. http://www.wcoomd.org/ie/en/Topics_Issues/FacilitationCustomsProcedures/facil_wco_instruments.htm.

2. "WCO Framework of Standards to Secure and Facilitate Global Trade," Global Facilitation Partnership for Transportation and Trade, http://www.gfptt.org/entities/ReferenceReadingProfile.aspx?id=4f81474a-e598-44cb-9e6f-00e830124618.

3. *WCO SAFE Framework of Standards*, World Customs Organization, June 2011, p. 15.

4. *WCO SAFE Framework of Standards*, Standard 6, "Advance Electronic Information," p. 16.

5. *WCO Framework of Standards to Secure and Facilitate Global Trade*, Version 2.0, World Customs Organization, April 2005, p. 12.

6. *Guidelines on the Application of Information and Communication Technology*, Kyoto ICT Guidelines, World Customs Organization, June 2004, p. 7.

7. SAFE Port Act, Section 2, "Definitions," 10.

8. SAFE Port Act, Section 216(b.3).

9. "C-TPAT Security Link Portal—Questions and Answers," CBP, http://www.cbp.gov/xp/cgov/trade/cargo_security/ctpat/ctpat_members/implement_portal/portal_qa.xml.

10. Customs-Trade Partnership Against Terrorism (C-TPAT) Minimum Security Criteria and Guidelines: Long Haul Carrier in Mexico, CBP, August 2007.

11. "Fact Sheet, Container Security Initiative," CBP, Media Services, March 8, 2004, www.cbp.gov.

12. "Container Security Initiative (CSI)," World Trade Ref, http://www.worldtraderef .com/wtr_nl/WTR_site/csi.asp.

13. "ACE at a Glance Fact Sheet," CBP, http://www.cbp.gov/xp/cgov/newsroom/ fact_sheets/trade/ace_factsheets/ace_glance_sheet.xml.

14. As an example, see Customs Form 1302, *Inward Cargo Declaration 06/09.*

15. http://www.nnsa.energy.gov/aboutus/ourhistory/timeline/secure-freight-initiative -launched-secure-u.s.-nuclear-and-radiological-.

16 http://www.cbp.gov/xp/cgov/newsroom/news_releases/05292008.xml.

17. James Giermanski, "Protection in the Electronic Age," *Journal of Commerce Online Commentary*, June 15, 2009.

18. "The Main Objectives of FP7: Specific Programmes," Seventh Framework Programme (FP7), European Commission Cordis, http://cordis.europa.eu/fp7/understand_ en.html.

19. "Container Security Advanced Information Networking," European Commission Cordis, http://cordis.europa.eu/search/index.cfm?fuseaction=proj.document&PJ _LANG=EN&PJ_RCN=12286721&pid=0&q=80B534907F7016A7C7BA8D9A4186AD FE&type=sim.

20. "Intermodal Global Door-to-Door Container Supply Chain Visibility," European Commission Cordis, http://cordis.europa.eu/search/index.cfm?fuseaction=proj.document &PJ_LANG=EN&PJ_RCN=10453442&pid=1&q=80B534907F7016A7C7BA8D9A418 6ADFE&type=sim.

21. "Common Assessment and Analysis of Risk in Global Supply Chains," European Commission Cordis," http://cordis.europa.eu/search/index.cfm?fuseaction=proj .document&PJ_LANG=EN&PJ_RCN=12209664&pid=5&q=80B534907F7016A7C7BA 8D9A4186ADFE&type=sim.

22. "Smart Container Chain Management," European Commission Cordis, http:// cordis.europa.eu/search/index.cfm?fuseaction=proj.document&PJ_LANG=EN&PJ_RCN =10453167&pid=3&q=80B534907F7016A7C7BA8D9A4186ADFE&type=sim.

23. *National Strategy for Global Supply Chain Security*, Department of Homeland Security, January 2012, p. 1.

24. *National Strategy for Global Supply Chain Security*, p. 5.

Chapter Two

Maritime and Port Security

Ultimately, the foundation of American strength is at home. It is in the skills of our people, the dynamism of our economy, and the resilience of our institutions. A diverse modern society has inherent, ambitious, entrepreneurial energy. Our strength comes from what we do with that energy. That is where our national security begins.[1]

This chapter will focus on the issue of global supply chain security, specifically maritime-related security. It will, when appropriate, link truck and rail to the global supply chain. Since, for the most part, international agencies and governments have focused primarily on the passenger transport component of air security, this chapter will not concentrate on air cargo security because of the paucity of laws, programs, and systems in the air component dedicated to air cargo security.

Perhaps Robert W. Kelly made the clearest point of all about the inevitability of another terrorist attack and its impact on the nation's infrastructure:[2]

There is a widely held opinion within the Intelligence Community of the United States that future terrorist activities against U.S. interests at home and abroad are a virtual certainty. Experts also believe that a future attack is likely to target the U.S. economy and critical infrastructure. Further, intelligence estimates indicate that Al Qaeda planned the 9/11 attacks for five years. We are living on borrowed time. If a WMD were to be detonated at a major U.S. port (LA/LB, NY/NJ, Houston, Miami) we could expect the following immediate consequences:

- Substantial loss of life, property damage and the potential threat of hazardous substances to population areas;
- Immediate closure of all air, rail and sea ports;
- A protracted (and probably futile) search for the "other bomb/s" that would likely go on for weeks . . . if not months;
- The gradual reopening of airports and selected border crossings;

- The continued closure/restriction of sea ports, resulting in a worldwide backup of goods and materials; and
- Within weeks—a global recession and a severely damaged U.S economy.

Since 9/11, the global supply chain has become a potential means of introducing weapons of mass destruction (WMD), affecting all worldwide cargo movements to and from trading nations, but especially those of nations more vulnerable to terrorism, like the United States. This potential threat is made worse by the supply chain's use of the container, which is normally sealed when it arrives at its port of departure. In addition to not really knowing the true contents of the container or the quantity of containers at any given time or place, afloat or in port, moving on the highway or on a railcar, means an incredible security nightmare for those nations expecting or having already experienced terrorist attack. Theft; contamination of pharmaceuticals, food products, and sensitive material; and speed in providing a competitive edge are additional issues beyond terrorism that require a controlled global supply chain. Therefore, the international supply chain must be managed safely and, to the degree possible, controlled. The following will give one an appreciation of the seriousness of this problem:

- Approximately 90% of all cargo moves are by container.[3]
- At any given time, there are 100 million containers in circulation globally.[4]
- In the United States, 9 million containers arrive at U.S. seaports annually, nearly 30,000 per day.[5]
- In 2004, 23.5 million containers, trailers, and railcars entered the United States with cargo.[6]

Nassim Nicholas Taleb, author of *The Black Swan*, warns of the unthinkable that really can happen. This is particularly poignant when applied to the security of our seaports and what a disruption could do:[7]

> Globalization creates interlocking fragility while reducing volatility and giving the appearance of stability. In other words, it creates devastating Black Swans. We have never lived before under the threat of a global collapse. Financial institutions have been merging into a smaller number of very large banks. Almost all banks are interrelated. So the financial ecology is swelling into gigantic, incestuous, bureaucratic banks—when one fails, they all fall. The increased concentration among banks seems to have the effect of making financial crises less likely, but when they happen they are more global in scale and hit us very hard. We have moved from a diversified ecology of small banks, with varied lending policies, to a more homogeneous framework of firms that all resemble one another.

Professor Taleb was clearly talking about the potential for a catastrophic collapse of the global financial community that would affect the entire world. But what about the possibility of the collapse of just the global supply system?

Could that also be a black swan? Could the predicted disruption of the supply chain, in Professor Taleb's words, constitute the "warnings that the imbeciles chose to ignore"? I think so.

RISK AND SEAPORT AND LAND PORT SIGNIFICANCE

In 2006 the Rand Corporation did a study for the Department of Homeland Security (DHS) using a fictitious nuclear explosion at the Port of Long Beach and considering what the likely impact would be. Rand concluded the following outcomes:[8]

- Sixty thousand people might die instantly from the blast itself or quickly thereafter from radiation poisoning.
- An additional 150,000 people might be exposed to hazardous levels of radioactive water and sediment from the port, requiring emergency medical treatment.
- The blast and subsequent fires might completely destroy the entire infrastructure and all ships in the Port of Long Beach and the adjoining Port of Los Angeles.
- Six million people might need relocation, because fallout will have contaminated a 500-kilometer area.
- Gasoline supplies might run critically short across the entire region because of the loss of Long Beach's refineries—responsible for one-third of the gas west of the Rockies.

In May 2005, the Government Accountability Office (GAO) published its Maritime Security report that referenced a Booz Allen Hamilton report estimating that a discovered undetonated WMD would result in the port's closing for 12 days at the cost of $58 billion.[9] Considering that, according to the GAO Maritime Security report, there are over three hundred seaports and 3,700 cargo and passenger terminals, what would happen if they all closed simply to inspect the containers in the port facility? In March 2006 the Congressional Budget Office said, while cautioning about potential overstatements in the original research done for the Pacific Maritime Association, that a 10-day shutdown of West Coast ports would cost the economy $1.9 billion per day.[10] And the Brookings Institution estimated that the use of WMD in a shipping container would cost the United States $1 trillion.[11]

Although what government agencies, research entities, and consultants say about the role and importance of seaports and their value to the economy is enlightening, perhaps their value is best expressed by the 2005 testimony of Bethann Rooney, manager of ports security for the Port Authority of New York and New Jersey:[12]

Ninety-five percent of the international goods that come into the country come in through our nation's 361 ports; twelve percent of that volume is handled in the Port of New York and New Jersey alone, the third largest port in the country. The Port generates 229,000 jobs and $10 billion in wages throughout the region. Additionally, the Port contributes $2.1 billion to state and local tax revenues and $24.4 billion to the U.S. Gross Domestic Product. Cargo that is handled in the Port serves 80 million people or thirty-five percent of the entire U.S. population. In 2004, the port handled over 5,200 ship calls, 4.478 million twenty-foot equivalent units (TEUs), which is approximately 7,300 containers each day, 728,720 autos, and 80.6 million tons of general cargo. Today, international trade accounts for 30 percent of the U.S. economy. Considering all this, it is easy to see how a terrorist incident in our nation's ports and along the cargo supply chain would have a devastating effect on our country and its economy.

Land ports of entry are also critical infrastructure for this nation and, indirectly, the global economy. The United States has 163 land ports. Of those 120 (75%) are managed by the General Services Administration (GSA), with 43 ports directly under the control of DHS. "On an average day, about $2 billion in trade cross the nation's 163 border crossings, along with more than 350,000 vehicles, 135,000 pedestrians and 30,000 trucks."[13] Merely looking at Laredo, Texas, the largest land port of entry on the southern border, one can see the enormity and criticality of the amount of cargo and its conveyances crossing that border port. Laredo is the second busiest land port by value of imports and exports, and the sixth largest gateway compared with all U.S. land, air, and sea freight gateways. The trade merchandise crossing through Laredo in 2008 was $116 billion, about 14% of the value of U.S. total land trade. It was the major gateway for both exports and imports, with inbound shipments accounting for 53% of the value of freight handled by U.S. land ports in 2008 and outbound shipments accounting for 47%. Its World Trade Bridge and its Columbia Bridge handled more than 1.5 million incoming commercial trucks and 329,000 rail containers from Mexico in that year alone.[14]

The cargo entering and exiting these ports is critical for the economy. Take, for example, 2008 exports and imports for which data are available. U.S. exports amounted to $1.283 trillion (U.S. as origin price) in the following categories:[15]

- Industrial supplies, 29.8%
- Production machinery, 29.5%
- Nonauto consumer goods, 12.4%
- Motor vehicles and parts, 9.3%
- Food, feed, and beverages, 8.3%
- Aircraft and parts, 6.6%
- Other, 4.1%

Imports were equally significant and amounted to $2.115 trillion (U.S. as destination price):

- Non-auto consumer goods, 23.0%
- Fuels, 22.1%
- Production machinery and equipment, 19.9%
- Nonfuel industrial supplies, 14.8%
- Motor vehicles and parts, 11.1%
- Food, feed, and beverages, 4.2%
- Aircraft and parts, 1.7%
- Other, 3.2%

On September 25, 2006, DHS released its Fiscal Year 2006 Infrastructure Protection Program (IPP), "an important component of the Administration's larger, coordinated effort to strengthen the security of America's critical infrastructure." The IPP is awarding $400 million to protect this critical infrastructure. The $400 million is divided into seven programs:

1. Port Security Grant Program (PSGP), $168,052,500
2. Transit Security Grant Program (TSGP), $135,998,093
3. Buffer Zone Protection Program (BZPP), $47,965,000
4. Chemical Buffer Zone Protection Program (Chem-BZPP), $25,000,000
5. Intercity Bus Security Grant Program (IBSGP), $9,530,000
6. Intercity Passenger Rail Security Grant Program (IPRSGP), $7,242,855
7. Trucking Security Program (TSP), $4,801,500

Since surface transportation through our land ports of entry carried goods valued at $55.9 billion in the first seven months of 2006,[16] one would assume that land ports of entry would be included in U.S. critical infrastructure and be eligible to apply for funds. The Port Security Grant Program listed only seaports identified by the U.S. Coast Guard as eligible to apply. Thus, one assumes that land ports of entry would be included in the BZPP program. However, with respect to the BZPP, DHS says, "The list of eligible sites within each State will remain classified for security purposes." State agencies will administer these funds. Land ports of entry are not included in the remaining five IPP programs. So where are they? Are land ports the secret sites referenced in the Buffer Zone program and therefore, in fact, critical infrastructure? In an attempt to determine whether land ports were classified as critical infrastructure, I examined the National Infrastructure Protection Plan (NIPP). In it are 13 critical infrastructure sectors:

1. Defense industrial base
2. Telecommunications
3. Drinking water and water treatment systems
4. Public health and health care

5. Chemical production and distribution
6. Energy
7. Banking and finance
8. National monuments and icons
9. Information and technology
10. Emergency services
11. Agriculture and food
12. Postal and shipping
13. Transportation

There are four other key resources: government facilities, commercial facilities, dams, and nuclear power materials. Nowhere in the 17 categories are land ports of entry listed. Consequently, I reviewed some associated plans:[17] the National Plan to Achieve Maritime Domain Awareness, the Maritime Transportation System Security Plan, the Maritime Commerce Security Plan, the Maritime Infrastructure Recovery Plan, and the International Outreach and Coordination Strategy. Nowhere in these plans was there mention of land ports.

Was the seeming omission of land ports merely a matter of definition? To find out, I went to the Maritime Transportation Security Act of 2002. Section 70101, Definitions, contained the following: "The term 'facility' means any structure or facility of any kind located in, on, under, or adjacent to any waters subject to the jurisdiction of the United States." That could explain why Detroit is eligible for PSGP funds. But it doesn't explain why Laredo is ineligible. Again, land ports of entry were nowhere to be found. Are they less important to our economy than seaports? I followed up by reviewing the 2008 NIPP and the latest, 2009. The words "land port" or "land port of entry" are not included. In fact, while waterways are critical, not even the word "seaport" was found in the latest NIPP.

It is crystal clear that the U.S. ports of entry are the sine qua non of economic growth and health. The taking out with WMD of just one seaport or one land port of entry would, as 9/11 did with airports, close *all* U.S. seaports and land ports, for no other reason than to inspect containers in all other ports. Because of consequential sympathy explosions,[18] the container blast would not only kill and injure port personnel but also affect people and infrastructure for miles beyond the port. Land ports and their surrounding populations are obviously clearly at risk.

Imagine taking out one seaport and one land port. Since over 90% of our international trade moves by vessel and truck, essentially all trade would stop. If, during the examination of existing containers within the port's area, WMDs are discovered, it would be necessary to move, isolate, and disarm the container away from any population and trade infrastructure, creating further delays in resuming port operations. Given the state of the U.S. economy and the health of the global economy, one simply cannot deny the consequences of a foreseen but practically unaddressed black swan. Besides no imports, there would be no exports, no manufacturing to make those exports, no foreign energy, and so on. Where will those vessels afloat discharge their cargo? Even if their cargo was discharged in Canada or Mexico, it could not enter the United States by land, since U.S. land ports of entry would also be closed. What would happen to the world's vessel container carriers? What about the truck and rail carriers? What happens to their revenue and workforce? And what happens to port-related jobs? If taking out a port included the use of nuclear waste, what would be the expected timeframe for use of that port area? I think even Professor Taleb's imbeciles would understand this. The black swan would shut down this economy, impact all citizens without exception, and likely created chaos, lawlessness, and violence.

RELIANCE ON PROGRAMS AND PRACTICES IN THE MARITIME PORT SECTOR

The real question is, can this catastrophe happen? And the real answer is yes![19] There are two primary scenarios: WMD in an inbound container from a f,oreign location, or WMD in an outbound container leaving the United States, placed there and executed by a homegrown terrorist. Can those scenarios be easily accomplished? Unfortunately, given DHS's policies, again the answer is yes. Here's why. Probably the most reasonable and politically acceptable treatment of port and maritime security is contained in the publications of the Homeland Security and Defense Business Council. In its Port and Maritime Security monograph, the council cites three initiatives, two of which have now worked their way into federal legislation: the 2001 Customs and Border Protection supply chain security program called the Customs-Trade Partnership Against Terrorism (C-TPAT) and its 2002 Container Security Initiative (CSI). The third is the Transportation Worker Identification Credential (TWIC) program.

However, the government and port authorities rely on more than these three programs. They also rely on scanning, radio frequency identification (RFID) tags and container seals, and the content of in-bond shipments. I will not spend time on container seals since we all know that all the current mechanical seals can be bypassed without disturbing the seal, and I have video evidence to demonstrate that. RFID and in-bond management by Customs and Border Protection (CBP), however, are so misused that I have devoted a full chapter to each. (RFID can be used as an improvised explosive device—and I have scientific video evidence to demonstrate that—and in-bonds constitute the Trojan horse of port security.) Finally, I will treat the maritime vulnerability posed by transshipments in chapter 10. Therefore, in this chapter I will treat only C-TPAT, CSI, TWIC, scanning, and the outbound container treatment—all virtually unrealistic programs.

C-TPAT

Of the three programs, the Customs-Trade Partnership Against Terrorism (C-TPAT) is a positive and reasonably successful attempt at supply chain security. Its participants are all voluntary; therefore, CBP knows them well and audits them for compliance. Of course, that is a key weakness of the program—membership is voluntary and only those who want to be secure and subject themselves to audit will participate, exactly the firms the United States is likely not to worry about in the first place. Terrorists are unlikely members of C-TPAT, and terrorists who work for firms participating in C-TPAT will likely be discovered and prevented from using a legitimate shipment as a WMD through a C-TPAT system. Up until December 2011, there was no interest in or comment about the outbound threat of containers leaving the United States. It appeared that only my writing about this vulnerability was ever in the public eye. So, whether true or not, I'm taking a little credit for some of this change to move to apply C-TPAT to U.S. exporters.

If this happens, it would signal that the United States is becoming more like the European and other nations in adopting authorized economic operator (AEO) programs following the World Customs Organization (WCO) SAFE Framework. According to a *Journal of Commerce* article in December 2011, 31 WCO members have AEO programs in various stages of development. Japan and Costa Rica have AEO programs and agreed to pilot-test export C-TPAT with the United States:[20]

> Now Customs and its Advisory Committee on Commercial Operations are taking the first steps to formally secure the outbound supply chain. The objective is a mirror of the Customs-Trade Partnership Against Terrorism, but for exporters. Since 2002, importers, customs brokers and carriers have made efforts to secure their import supply chains. Now, the same best practices may apply to the outbound supply chain.

Sean Doherty, acting C-TPAT director, confirmed CBP's intention to include exporters by announcing a pilot program with Japan, Colombia, and Costa Rica.

CSI

The Container Security Initiative (CSI) is a *mandatory* program covering all vessel shipments from a foreign port to the United States. CSI addresses the threat of a terrorist weapon contained in a shipping container destined for the United States, and it seeks to target and prescreen containers from foreign ports to identify those that are high risk. CSI requires notification to CBP by vessel carriers of manifest information of all containers 24 hours prior to stowing the containers onto the vessel. It asked for cooperation of foreign ports in allowing the presence of CBP inspectors at those ports. Now codified by the U.S. SAFE Port Act, CSI is a weak program at best. Its weakness is in its core component: the 24-hour manifest.

A manifest is like a tally sheet of what the vessel is carrying. Except for visible cargo, the carrier has *never* known for sure what is in a locked and sealed container that it receives for carriage. This has been recognized ever since we have had locked containers. Prior to CSI, the vessel carrier was forced to use honest terms such as FAK (freight of all kinds) or STC (said to contain), which accurately explained that this or that was supposed to be in the container. The reality is no different today under CSI, except that CSI does not permit carriers to use those phrases. Therefore, the carrier must put on the manifest what the shipper or shipper's agent says the contents are. In essence, nothing has really changed. It is an information-based system that depends on the vessel carrier's manifest to identify the cargo in a container that the vessel is carrying. Unfortunately, the vessel carrier makes and files the manifest and, consequently, is 100% dependent on the shipper (consignor) or the shipper's freight forwarder for information about contents. As such, the vessel carrier really serves as a third party in verifying the contents of the container—the equivalent of hearsay.

Unless changed, in CSI, the details and accuracy of cargo information will always be linked to the person or firm who provides the cargo information to the carrier, who then uses that supplied information to complete the 24-hour manifest. The vessel carrier has no firsthand knowledge of the container's contents. CSI's 24-hour rule places the responsibility of sending the manifest to CBP with the shipping line, specifically the liner that loads the container into the vessel at the foreign port for movement to the United States. Essentially, the carrier is still filing what the container is said to contain. Only now, instead of using the term STC, the carrier will use at least a six-digit harmonized tariff number of the products furnished by the shipper or shipper's agent to identify the cargo. Ultimately, we still don't really know what is in the container being carried to the United States. For this to begin to change, the U.S. Senate would have to ratify (and the president sign) the new Rotterdam Rules, which so far it has refused to do. Or DHS would have to mandate the use of container security devices (CSDs) that would provide the identity of the individual who inspected and verified the contents at the time of sealing and arming the container.[21] Combining the use of CSDs with the Rotterdam Rules would accomplish two objectives. It would identify the person who verifies the container's content at its stuffing, thus pinpointing the initial link in the supply chain, while supporting the new responsibility of the vessel carrier in taking liability for the contents at origin.

TWIC

The last area of port and maritime security seems to rest with the Transportation Worker Identification Credential (TWIC) program. Under this program, "DHS was required to issue a worker identification card that uses biological metrics, such as fingerprints, to control access to secure areas of ports or ships. Responsibility for developing the card was placed with the TSA (Transportation Security Administration), with a preliminary deadline of having cards for 6 million maritime workers by August 2004."[22] The TWIC for maritime industry workers was mandated in the Maritime Transportation Security Act of 2002, and after slow progress and missed deadlines, the TSA finally began issuing TWIC cards in October 2007. However, there are still problems with adequate card readers. Take for instance the most recent event. Recently, according to the TSA, a system error caused a federal code number to be incorrectly embedded on the TWIC card's microchip, affecting approximately 26,000 cardholders. Their cards may not be usable because of encoding error problems with the electronic reader. In an incredibly perplexing statement, TSA said that while the errors were fixed in April 2011, it did not notify the users until November.[23] Since only a few ports have electronic readers working, apparently TSA was not concerned. What does that mean for port security? All told, TSA has issued some 1.8 million TWICs. The agency has published a list of card serial numbers that may have the encoding problem. The agency will replace cards free of charge. However, if the credential is being used at locations without a reader, the holder does not have to replace it right away. It is clear that this program is simply not functional.

There are also rumors on the docks that the port workers are refusing to renew the $132 TWIC cards. As one mariner stated: "They are angry, and many, like me, had to drive seven hours twice to access the TWIC office in order to get one. Two days of work lost for nothing. One chief engineer is sending them a bill for his lost time. Maybe in small claims court nobody will show up to defend TWIC and he would have a judgment." Others provide evidence that this official identification card is not even recognized and usable for identification at airports. Below are the direct comments of an experienced and respected ship's captain about the TWIC program:

> Presently I hold five U.S. Master's Licenses and three foreign Master's and have been a professional Mariner since 1972. I am ex–Coast Guard and NOAA [National Oceanic and Atmospheric Administration]. I am familiar with dealing with governmental agencies. The TWIC program is the biggest boondoggle to date. It has been written up numerous times in the *Professional Mariner*, stating the flaws in the system, but it continues down its path.

His comments also reflect firsthand knowledge of how easy it is to simply bypass the system, exchange cards, and continue to do what was always done before the existence of the TWIC card and program. He cited numerous problems and said that the bottom line was that the TWIC program does not improve port or maritime security and is essentially a joke. It's probably best summed up with his following statement:

9/11 has changed our lives forever, but we still do not have fidelity in our training or in the management. The laws governing our vessels and port security are changing so fast. I feel people have become more lax instead of more aware. I believe people want to do a good job and take pride in their position, but trying to keep up with the bureaucratic red tape and changes can't let them. They don't have time to learn a system before it changes again.

Besides these three programs, CBP has developed others such as the 10+2 Program and technological systems for scanning containers in foreign and domestic ports. The 10+2 Program seems to be a good program, but its fundamental weakness is the reliability of the shipper's statement of content. However, the use of scanning has not reached its objectives. In-container detection of radiation, explosives, drugs, and more is currently available. The European Union (EU) and even DHS know this, but neither has mandated its use. The United States still relies on scanning as a defensive technique.

Scanning

Congress legislated 100% scanning, and the president signed the legislation. The requirements to scan containers were contained in the SAFE Port Act, signed into law in October 2006, and in the Implementing Recommendations of the 9/11 Commission Act of 2007, signed into law in August 2007. The SAFE Port Act says this about scanning at U.S. seaports:

SCANNING CONTAINERS.—Subject to section 1318 of title 19, United States Code, not later than December 31, 2007, all containers entering the United States through the 22 ports through which the greatest volume of containers enter the United States by vessel shall be scanned for radiation. To the extent practicable, the Secretary shall deploy next generation radiation detection technology. (Section 121)

The new Implementing Reecommendations of the 9/11 Commission Act of 2007 go further by amending the SAFE Port Act to say:

IN GENERAL.—A container that was loaded on a vessel in a foreign port shall not enter the United States (either directly or via a foreign port) unless the container was scanned by nonintrusive imaging equipment and radiation detection equipment at a foreign port before it was loaded on a vessel. (Section 1701)

The standard Congress is using is this: the United States can mandate that other sovereign states obey our law. How can we as a nation mandate other nations to provide the means for or perform the scanning of containers inbound to the United States in their ports? There is a clear question of sovereignty and a foreign nation's right to decide what steps to take within its sovereign territory. The

EU's taxation commissioner, Laszio Kovacs, said 100% scanning would not only not improve security but cost EU exporters. Even Ralph Basham, the U.S. commissioner of CBP, said on July 11, 2007, in a speech to the Center for Strategic and International Studies, that 100% scanning is "fundamentally flawed" and "just does not make sense" because it would impede the flow of commerce. Supporting Commissioner Basham's position are Christopher Koch, president of the World Shipping Council (WSC), and Janet F. Kavinoky, director of transportation infrastructure for the U.S. Chamber of Commerce.[24] In April 2009, Acting Commissioner of CBP Jayson P. Ahern affirmed that the United States simply cannot compel other nations to scan containers for us. He testified: "CBP is currently taking a close look at what will be possible and useful and will come back to the Congress soon with a clear path forward."

Given the objections of our trading partners and even the WCO, the scanning requirement in foreign ports has already failed, and the scanning in domestic ports is simply not reliable, according to a retired CBP supervisor responsible for scanning in one of our seaports. Furthermore, in May 2005, three scientists, Devabhaktuni Srikrishna, A. Narasimha Chari, and Thomas Tisch, released a paper on detecting nuclear materials in transport. Their conclusions were clear and compelling. First, terrorists are most likely to use highly enriched uranium (HEU) rather than plutonium, because the assembly of the HEU bomb is not as technically complex as the assembly of a plutonium bomb. Second, terrorists can circumvent a network of fixed detectors. Fixed detectors not only lack sufficient proximity and exposure to the vehicle in transit but also do not screen many types of vehicles. Third, research and development breakthroughs cannot change the physics of detection: passive detection of HEU will continue to be limited by its natural rate of radioactivity, and the attenuation of radioactivity is sharp with distance/shielding.

According to the paper's authors, the physics of detection are fairly simple. Gamma rays and neutrons from shielded HEU are detectable at only short distances and only when there is adequate time to count a sufficient number of detected particles. The closer a detector is to the source of emission and the longer it "sniffs," the greater the probability of detecting HEU.[25] In-container radiation detection and transmission through CSDs that can solve this problem is simply not promoted by DHS.

Based on these factors, the only reasonable conclusion is that the United States does not know what is in inbound containers, and its programs, scanning technologies, and systems do not prevent WMD from entering the United States in containers shipped from abroad, especially if those containers were transshipped through smaller transshipment ports where scanned containers are discharged from the vessel and remain in a smaller port's container facilities waiting for restowing aboard a vessel bound for the United States.

PORT VULNERABILITIES: THE SWAN'S FINAL FEATHER

Let us assume that all DHS programs work perfectly to prevent inbound containers from entering U.S. ports. Could we still have a black swan event? The answer is, absolutely. DHS has refused to admit or take steps to control perhaps the greatest threat to our port system: the outbound container. Yet for DHS, the focus is on TSA patdowns or X-rays for adult air travelers, and the CSI and C-TPAT focus only on inbound traffic—imports. DHS and its CBP seem oblivious to security vulnerability to our ports posed by containers *leaving* the United States. Each of CBP's major container security programs has one focus: inbound cargo. Other nations, however, recognize the security importance of outbound containers. The EU's AEO security program, a counterpart to C-TPAT, recognizes and acknowledges the outbound risk as equal to inbound, requiring documentation and information about exporters of products through its ports. C-TPAT does not, even in the face of growing concern over homegrown terrorism, as recently demonstrated by the arrest of Pvt. Naser Jason Abdo, a 21-year-old AWOL soldier from Kentucky's Fort Campbell. Recent comments by Rep. Bennie Thompson (D-MS), ranking member of the House Homeland Security Committee, support the concern for homegrown terrorism when referring to the recent domestic terrorist attack in Norway: "Although we are awaiting a preliminary investigation, this incident unfortunately reminds us that we must remain vigilant against the threat of homegrown terrorism, especially the threat posed by lone wolves."[26]

In demonstrating this U.S. vulnerability, a firm from Belmont, North Carolina, without any existing record of exporting or being in the international trade business, but involved in supply chain and container security business, intentionally shipped an empty 20-foot dry container from North Carolina to Germany through the Port of Charleston. The container was never opened by CBP or anyone else, and nobody outside the firm knew for sure what was in the container. While absolutely accurate in its declared contents, it could have contained WMD. If that firm had wished to use that container as a WMD, it could have done so with ease. This same firm has also demonstrated, with a neighboring municipal police bomb squad, how easy it is to blow up a container in our ports of entry using the same electronic technology required for use in our ports and used by CBP (see chapter 9). The outbound threat begs the question: if 100% of adult airline travelers *are* a security risk and each has to be examined for what each can attach to his or her body, then what is the risk of exported containers, which are apparently *not considered* a security risk and are *100%* excluded from a security inspection? DHS's current practice of inspecting all adult airline travelers is about as distorted as deciding to inspect all domestic tractor-trailers moving from one city to another because a trailer could explode en route to or at its destination city. There is a gross miscalculation of critical risk, which should be a matter of serious concern about government competence in meeting its obligation to keep us free and safe.

CONCLUSION

Even Professor Taleb's imbecile must admit that this scenario must constitute a black swan possibility. What is necessary now is a serious, comprehensive empirical study by a nonprofit, nongovernment research institution or university to determine the potential consequences of temporarily closing *all* our U.S. ports as a result of the detonation of WMD in any one or more of them. Daily loss of pass-through cargo such as oil, job loss in all the industries affected by imports and exports, and all related business linkages such as trucking and rail business loss should be measured. The findings would make this government understand the critical nature of really knowing and controlling what enters our ports, whether from foreign inbound shipments or domestic outbound shipments. A study of this nature would force, one hopes, DHS and CBP to require the use of in-container devices that would detect and report unauthorized access, monitor movement, and report contents such as radiation and explosives. But most important in any mandate to use CSDs would be the requirement of communicating the identity of the actual, authorized person who verifies the cargo at container stuffing, arming, and sealing at origin and the identity of the authorized person accessing the container at destination, in effect creating a virtual chain of custody. Short of this, there should be no question that a black swan event could literally destroy the economy of the United States for a significant period, if not permanently, and injure other global economies. It is time now to mandate the use of CSDs that currently exist as off-the-shelf products. All the black feathers are there.

NOTES

1. *National Security Strategy of the United States of America*, 2002, p. 31.
2. Robert W. Kelly, "Chain of Perils: Hardening the Global Supply Chain and Strengthening America's Resilience," The Reform Institute, March 6, 2008, p. 3.
3. *Customs Today*, Office of Public Affairs, March 2005.
4. *Customs Today*, Office of Public Affairs, March 2005.
5. *The National Strategy for Maritime Security*, September 2005.
6. *CBP Performance and Annual Report*, CPB, fiscal year 2004.
7. Nassim Nicholas Taleb, *The Black Swan: The Impact of the Highly Improbable* (New York: Random House, 2007); *"The Black Swan*: Quotes and Warnings That the

Imbeciles Chose to Ignore," Nassim Nicholas Taleb, http://www.fooledbyrandomness. com/imbeciles.htm.

8. Charles Meade and Roger C. Molander, *Considering the Effects of a Catastrophic Terrorist Attack*, RAND Center for Terrorism Risk Management Policy (Santa Monica, CA: Rand Corporation, 2006), p. 9.

9. *Maritime Security*, GAO-05-448T, Government Accountability Office, May 17, 2005, p. 5.

10. As reported in *The Economic Costs of Disruptions in Container Shipments*, Congressional Budget Office, in an attachment to a letter to Rep. Ron Coleman, Permanent Subcommittee on Investigations, Committee on Homeland Security and Government Affairs, March 29, 2006, p. 15.

11. Michael E. O'Hanlon, Peter Orsgaz, Ivo H. Daalder, I. M. Destler, David L. Gunter, James L. Lindsay, Robert E. Litan, and James B. Steinberg, *Protecting the Homeland One Year On* (Washington, DC: Brookings Institution Press, 2002), Table 1-2, p. 7, http://www.brookings.edu/fp/projects/homeland/newhomeland.pdf.

12. Bethann Rooney, "Detecting Nuclear Weapons and Radiological Materials: How Effective Is Available Technology?" before the Subcommittee on Prevention of Nuclear and Biological Attacks and Subcommittee on Emergency Preparedness, Science, and Technology, House Committee of Homeland Security, June 21, 2005.

13. "Fast Facts, Land Ports of Entry Tool Kit," U.S. General Services Administration, http://www.gsa.gov/portal/content/103603.

14. "Laredo, Texas—Land Gateway," Research and Innovation Technology Administration (RITA), Bureau of Transportation Statistics, http://www.bts.gov/publications/americas_freight_transportation_gateways/2009/highlights_of_top_25_freight_gateways_by_shipment_value/port_of_laredo/index.html.

15. "What Are USA Major Exports and Imports Today?" Answers.com, http://wiki.answers.com/Q/What_are_USA_major_exports_and_imports_today.

16. "Moving the American Economy," U.S. Department of Transportation, BTS 45-06, September 29, 2006, p. 1.

17. http://www.dhs.gov/dhspublic/interapp/editorial/editorial_0608.xml.

18. "Sympathy explosions" is a term often used by law enforcement bomb squads. They occur when flammable or explosive cargo is ignited by an explosive blast sufficient to set off a chain reaction of explosions in a commonly shared area, as in a seaport or customs facilities at land ports of entry.

19. For a comprehensive treatment of the development of container security standards, see Jim Giermanski, "The Development and Globalization of Container Security," *Defense Transportation Journal*, September 2008, pp. 16–22.

20. R. G. Edmonson, "C-TPAT Eyes Exports," *Journal of Commerce*, December 23, 2011, http://www.joc.com/government-regulation/c-tpat-eyes-exports.

21. For a comprehensive treatment of this area, see Jim Giermanski, "Container Security: Lead, Follow, or Get Out of the Way," *Maritime Professional*, First Quarter 2011, http://www.maritimeprofessional.com.

22. The 9/10/11 Project, "Port and Maritime Security," Homeland Security Defense Business Council, April 10, 2011, p. 2, http://homelandcouncil.org/pdfs/digital_library_pdfs/hsdbc91011projectportmaritimesecurity.pdf.

23. R. G. Edmonson, "Error Could Cause Thousands of TWIC Cards to Be Rejected," *Journal of Commerce Online*, December 6, 2011.

24. *Florida Shipper*, August 27, 2007.

25. Devabhaktuni Srikrishna, A. Narasimha Chari, and Thomas Tisch, "Nuclear Detection: Portals, Fixed Detectors, and NEST Teams Won't Work for Shielded HEU on a National Scale, So What Next?" May 16, 2005, p. 1, http://iis-db.stanford.edu/evnts/4249/disarm.pdf.

26. Mickey McCarter, "US Officials Emphasize Dangers of Lone Wolf Terrorists after Norway Attacks," HSToday.US, July 25, 2011, http://www.hstoday.us/briefings/today-s-news-analysis/single-article/us-officials-emphasize-dangers-of-lone-wolf-terrorists-after-norway-attacks/2c6b7eb7a84a2366847c860a604bbbfd.html.

Chapter Three

The Supply Chain and U.S. Border Security with Mexico

With respect to the North American Free Trade Agreement (NAFTA), the United States has two partners: Canada and Mexico, the nations sharing U.S. borders. However, there is a significant difference between them in sharing security concerns. Canada supports its U.S. partner's concern over homeland security and agrees to help. After a February 4, 2011, meeting in Washington, President Barack Obama and Canadian Prime Minister Stephen Harper released a declaration outlining a shared vision for security. Mexico has done little to cooperate with the United States in improving cross-border commercial truck traffic. Therefore, the thrust of this chapter will be on Mexico-U.S. commercial border crossing practices and the vulnerabilities they pose to the United States.

I have written much about the U.S. southern border, Mexican truck access to the United States, the blatant weaknesses in the in-bond carriage across borders and through the United States, the e-Manifest and the knowledge it provides about what really comes into the United States, and the need to address a cross-border security vulnerability that does *not* relate directly to individuals crossing our border illegally. The Department of Homeland Security (DHS), Customs and Border Protection (CNP), and Immigration and Customs Enforcement (ICE) know about the commercial crossing vulnerability, but they seem not to care, or disagree, or are unable for unknown reasons to take action to address the problems. Even the U.S. Department of Justice was made aware of the legal issues of current border-crossing protocols but refused to take action.[1] I have also testified in Congress on the southern border commercial vulnerability, and no congressional action was ever taken. In this chapter, I will present an analysis of the Mexico-U.S. border issue, showing the vulnerability posed by current supply chain protocols. I will show

- Why the southern border is unique with respect to commercial truck traffic
- Who really controls commercial truck crossings (75% of it)

33

- The vulnerability posed by this control
- Why DHS, CBP, and ICE have not addressed it
- The potential or real role of the Mexican drug cartels in intensifying the vulnerability allowed to grow by some of our Homeland Security agencies

COMMERCIAL OPERATIONS AT THE SOUTHERN BORDER

There is no place in North America like our southern border with respect to cross-border carriage of imported and exported products by commercial trucks.[2] In volume alone, in 2009, there were 4,291,000 incoming truck crossings through the southern border.[3] Almost 100% of those trucks were not permitted to enter the United States directly. The Mexican long-haul carriers drop their trailers and containers in drop lots, often unsecured, for days and weeks on the Mexican side of the border to wait for a certain class of Mexican businessmen to release or give permission for the containers and trailers to cross into the United States. What is perhaps even more amazing is that this class of Mexican businessmen, who are Mexican Customs brokers, also stop all U.S. cargo entering Mexico on the U.S. side of the border until these brokers give the cargo permission to cross. However, if one were to export a product to Mexico by air, the U.S. exporter would not need the goods to be released or permitted entry into Mexico by a Mexican businessman before the plane took off from the United States. Nor would a seagoing vessel have to wait until its Mexican-bound cargo was released for entry before sailing to Mexico. Furthermore, with respect to air and vessel carriage, the U.S. freight forwarder or U.S. air cargo agent, should one be used, would be federally regulated. However, for some reason, exclusive forwarding agents of the Mexican Customs brokers on the border, in spite of the legal requirement of having to be registered and regulated under the International Commerce Commission (ICC) Termination Act of 1995 (P.L. 104-88), are not registered or federally regulated. Of course, there are nationally and internationally recognized freight forwarders and third-party logistics companies on the southern border that are registered and regulated.

So why do we have a system of foreign controls delaying cargo and using unregistered U.S. freight forwarders? Simply, this is the means to force the Mexican exporter to pay the Mexican Customs broker upfront to send the good across the border, essentially creating a guaranteed cash business. This process is known and has been known by the U.S. government. To remove all doubt about this control, one merely needs to look at NAFTA.

One of the main tenets of NAFTA was to eliminate barriers to trade and facilitate the movement of goods among Mexico, Canada, and the United States. This is stated in chapter 1's objectives.

Article 102: Objectives

1. The objectives of this Agreement, as elaborated more specifically through its principles and rules, including national treatment, most-favored-nation treatment and transparency, are to:
   a) eliminate barriers to trade in, and facilitate the cross-border movement of, goods and services between the territories of the Parties;
   b) promote conditions of fair competition in the free trade area

However, to the contrary, U.S. negotiators of NAFTA allowed Mexico to reserve the right to use Mexican citizens exclusively to forward freight into or out of the United States, supporting the monopoly that one of Texas's Customs brokers associations attempted to prevent by asking the Department of Justice (DOJ) to change the wording prior to NAFTA's implementation. Not only did our federal government refuse to take action against this Mexican Customs brokers' monopoly, but it also allowed Mexico to institutionalize it through the NAFTA treaty. The leading U.S. Department of Transportation (USDOT) NAFTA negotiator was asked how USDOT's NAFTA negotiating representatives could have agreed to a monopoly by Mexican citizens for controlling cross-border commercial movements. She responded, "I didn't know it was in there." Here is what the U.S. negotiators didn't know was negotiated:[4]

Cross-Border Services
A shipper's export declaration must be processed by a Mexican national licensed as a customs broker ("agente aduanal") or by a representative ("apoderado aduanal") employed by the exporter and authorized by the Secretaría de Hacienda y Crédito Público for this purpose.
   Phase-Out: None. Subject to discussion by the Parties five years after the date of entry into force of this Agreement.

In effect, the United States negotiated an agreement giving Mexican nationals exclusive rights to an area of international commerce that directly impacts our security and largely takes place on U.S. soil.

For a U.S. exporter sending goods to Mexico, it is the same except that the U.S. goods remain on the U.S. side at a Mexican "exclusive forwarding agent," avoiding the definition of freight forwarder contained in the ICC Termination Act of 1995. Like the Mexican outbound goods, the U.S. outbound goods ultimately wait in the U.S. forwarding agent's lot or distribution area until the Mexican importer pays the Mexican Customs broker to cross the cargo; pays the duty, if any; and, of course, pays the Mexican Customs broker's fees. Additionally, the carrier that crosses the cargo into Mexico is usually a Mexican drayage or transfer trucking company, often owned or controlled by the Mexican Customs broker—another means of revenue in the controlled process.

CONTROL OF THE CROSSING PROCESS

Essentially, all crossings into and out of Mexico are in the hands of Mexican Customs brokers, a cartel of business enterprises that influences costs, speed of movement, integrity of the cargo, and, ultimately, the security of our border as it relates to commercial crossings. At the present time, in order to export goods from the United States into Mexico, Mexican regulations require that the Mexican inward manifest ("relación de entrada") be submitted at the time of entry and have the relevant commercial invoice attached thereto. This "relación de entrada" and another entry summary document ("pedimento de importación") must be prepared and processed by a licensed Mexican Customs broker ("agente aduanal"). This process involves a series of functions, including appraisement, classification, inspection, inventory, and others. These take place on the U.S. side of the border.

Mexico allows only Mexican citizens who were born in Mexico to be licensed Customs brokers. U.S. Customs brokers and freight forwarders who are citizens of the United States are therefore not allowed to perform these services, although they must be performed in the United States. U.S. citizens may not forward freight to Mexico in their own names, even though the work is performed within the national territory of the United States, and, as already settled in NAFTA, U.S. citizens are not allowed to forward freight from Mexico to the United States. However, the exact reason for the requirement that a Mexican Customs broker arrange to forward exports from the United States *into* Mexico is unclear. There seems to be something of a conspiracy of silence from the parties benefiting from the present scheme. Only Mexican citizens can facilitate cargo crossing into Mexico by land. (Air and vessel carriage are not controlled in the same fashion.)

This control of northbound commercial traffic is dangerous and expensive because it necessitates the use of drayage or transfer firms (carriers that merely cross cargo from one side of the border to the other) and drop lots where Mexican long-haul truckers leave and store trailers and containers to wait for the drayage or transfer carrier to pick them up for movement into the United States. Again, all is controlled by the Mexican Customs brokers. No U.S. citizen can affect or complete the forwarding process. These Customs practices that are reserved exclusively for Mexican citizens have continued because the United States has avoided taking action. The following examples illustrate 20 years of inaction in addressing this situation.

If one divides the crossing practice of commercial trucks into four segments of revenue generation (first, outbound from Mexico on the Mexican side; second, inbound into the United States on the U.S. side; third, outbound from the United States on the U.S. side; and fourth, inbound to Mexico on the Mexican side), it is clearly evident that 75% of revenue and 75% of control are exclusively in the hands of the Mexican Customs broker. Only the portion (25%) of the inbound U.S. side is in the hands of a U.S. Customs broker, who has no knowledge of whether the drayage driver came directly from the CBP's facilities or stopped somewhere else where cargo could be removed or added before arriving at the U.S. Customs broker's facilities. The U.S. Customs broker who has already arranged to clear the goods through CBP may never actually check the contents of the trailer or container.

This Mexican control is equivalent to a monopoly and amounts to a cartel of Mexican businessmen who can act in a fashion to not only control the process, but also create and maintain a system that becomes a vulnerability in our security. Because this control is also present on the U.S. side of the border at the forwarding agent facilities of the Mexican broker, there is clearly a U.S. legal issue about the registration of the forwarders, who claim that they are exempt from regulation because they are "exclusive agents" for the Mexican broker. This is especially important with respect to in-bond shipments crossing from the United States into Mexico that are opened and manipulated at some forwarding agents' facilities.

It doesn't take much imagination or profound thinking to realize that the very nature of this system surrenders control of trailer content of both inbound and outbound shipments to a foreign nongovernment entity about which, in most cases, we know very little. This process and the lack of knowledge of those who control it become a serious risk.

THE VULNERABILITY OF THE PROCESS

The vulnerability of the process consists of:

- Lack of knowledge of container contents, beginning at the origin of the shipment
- Access to cargo waiting at drop lots
- Limited or no knowledge about and control of drayage firms
- Control of exclusive forwarding agents on the U.S. side

Knowledge of Contents at Mexican Origin

Due to the evolution of the transportation industry in North America, certain practices have become commonplace. Because of this, there is actually less knowledge of what is being moved into and even out of the United States. It used to be common for shippers to request the pick-up of a load, which meant a driver would take an empty container or trailer to the shipper's location and verify freight and piece count as it was loaded. This was done for liability purposes because the carriers assumed full responsibility for damages or missing freight. However, because of the time commercial drivers are allowed to drive in the United States, due mostly to hours-of-service regulations of the Federal Motor Carrier Safety Administration (FMCSA), the time it takes to load the conveyance is considered on-duty time and counted against the driver's allowed daily working limit. Therefore, the shipper now ensures that the cargo is loaded and ready to be carried when the driver arrives.

Also because of the need for increased efficiency, shippers have requested equipment pools at these locations, which allow the shipper to preload cargo and store it at their facility until the carrier has a driver ready to pick it up. As a by-product of this increased efficiency, much of the cargo liability of the carrier and the carrier's ability to verify freight are lost. This means that the shipper, instead of the motor carrier, fills out a bill of lading (the contract for carriage) certifying that the information contained in it is correct. The driver simply signs the bill of lading, acknowledging receipt of the cargo and agreeing to carry it to a location.

In Mexico, this standard practice has continued,[5] not because of any hours-of-service issue there but because of the lack of liability coverage and the abundance of U.S. carrier-based equipment in the region. Mexican carriers utilize U.S.-based trailers for the majority of all international freight moves. Because of the influx of trailers, many Mexican carriers use the pool system to provide efficiency and also to control the Mexican shipper's costs of housing the foreign trailer pool. As a result of the increase of trailer pools and the elimination of the carrier's right or responsibility to verify and count freight, there is little, if any, real knowledge of actual cargo. In many cases, major carriers only conduct audits and verify the integrity of shippers to ensure that the cargo bound for the United States is legitimate. That said, the only person who can really verify what was loaded at the point of origin is the person or persons loading the trailer.

Unlike in the United States, where we have information and knowledge of contents, carrier, and even driver, in Mexico cargo identity is really unknown to the Mexican long-haul carrier or driver when it is picked up at origin in Mexico. Additionally, the U.S. authorities know very little about the Mexican manufacturer or carrier. Consequently, except for Mexican manufacturers and carriers who are members of Customs-Trade Partnership Against Terrorism (C-TPAT), CBP has little or no knowledge of what is actually in the trailer or container. Even with the use of the automated commercial environment system and the e-Manifest on the southern border, CBP only knows what the container is "said to contain" and doesn't know that the trailer is even the same trailer that left the place of origin in Mexico. The level of what is known about the cargo coming from Mexico through our land ports of entry can best be explained through the actual words of a major U.S. Customs broker. I asked him, "How do you know that what is said to be in the conveyance is, in fact, in the conveyance?" His answer was, "We don't. It is all on good faith."

Access to Cargo Waiting at Drop Lots

Probably the greatest opportunity to access a trailer and remove or add cargo is at the location where the trailer is dropped by the Mexican long-haul carrier to wait for the permission of the Mexican Customs broker to cross into the United States. Unless it is a "hot" or specially treated shipment, *all* trailers with cargo bound for the United States are dropped and stored at a trailer yard of some type until the Mexican Customs broker executes a "pedimento de exportación," which releases the goods for movement into the United States. Many, if not most, of these lots are unsecured. Therefore, drugs, contraband, illegal human traffic, or even weapons of mass destruction (WMD) can be placed into these trailers.

Additionally, there is no law or regulation by the Mexican government over these drop lots or even this system of control by the Mexican Customs brokers. Drop lot usage provides an opportunity for the drug cartel and for terrorists to manipulate the contents and even use the trailer as a weapons system.

Knowledge of the Drayage Firm, the Driver, and Activity

The e-Manifest requires information on the drivers and passengers bringing cargo into the United States, their conveyances, and equipment used. There are problems, however. The first problem is driver information. The truck e-Manifest is not linked to the other driver-connected CBP program, Free and Secure Trade (FAST). FAST uses an ID card for Mexican drayage drivers coming into the United States. To a degree, the FAST card authenticates and approves drivers entering U.S. ports of entry. However, although the truck e-Manifest mandates driver information, it does not require all drivers to have FAST cards. Therefore, duplicate information must be transmitted, actually causing the expedited entry process to be diminished. The second problem is that the regulations implementing truck e-Manifest (19 CFR [Code of Federal Regulations] 123.92) require any inbound truck with commercial cargo to report its arrival to CBP electronically. But only those authorized to report electronically can do so.

Unfortunately, the motor carrier that crosses cargo into the United States is a transfer or drayage carrier, and, in most cases, would not even have access to a computer because the transfer company is essentially a mom-and-pop short-haul carrier, merely shuttling trailers from one side to the other. As one Mexican motor carrier told me, "The control of the drayage crossing is often done by someone with a cellular phone while shopping at the grocery store." Nonetheless, CBP has defined the carrier as the one entering the import lot or compound. The transfer carriers have two options. They can report to CBP themselves or they can hire a third party, such as a U.S. Customs broker or the Mexican Customs Brokers' Association—or, as of March 15, 2007, they can hire another truck carrier who already has an Automated Commercial Environment (ACE) portal account. Anyone with a valid ACE account may transmit in the portal or through an electronic data exchange.

Whether long-haul or drayage, CBP needs information on the driver and the cargo. The core problem, however, is that the use of drop lots mandated indirectly by the Mexican Customs broker cartel's crossing system necessitates the use of a drayage firm about which we know little if anything, and the use of drop lots that provide access to the trailer as it awaits crossing—typically for more than a week, depending on the Mexican broker and the port at which he operates.

Exclusive Forwarding Agents on the U.S. Side

The Mexican broker cartel also avoids U.S. federal law covering freight forwarders by defining freight forwarders as "exclusive forwarding agents," instead of using the legal term. Surface freight forwarders provide essential services like transportation, break-bulk or deconsolidation, warehousing, and even Customs brokerage. Because of freight forwarders' growth and essential role in global trade and cross-border operations, the U.S. Congress reregulated them under the ICC Termination Act of 1995. The act clearly defined the forwarder:[6]

FREIGHT FORWARDER—The term "freight forwarder" means a person holding itself out to the general public (other than as a pipeline, rail, motor, or water carrier) to provide transportation of property for compensation and in the ordinary course of its business—

(A) assembles and consolidates, or provides for assembling and consolidating, shipments and performs or provides for break-bulk and distribution operations of the shipments;
(B) assumes responsibility for the transportation from the place of receipt to the place of destination; and
(C) uses for any part of the transportation a carrier subject to jurisdiction under this subtitle.

Section 13906 of the act requires the freight forwarder to carry liability and cargo insurance and to comply with requirements related to service of process and court proceedings. To register, the applicant must complete Operating Authority form OP-1 (FF), which requires the applicant to provide proof of insurance; type of business structure; owner of business identification; business partners, if in a partnership; agent address; and whether the applicant or principals have been convicted of a federal or state offense involving the possession or distribution of a controlled substance. In other words, in the United States much is known about surface freight forwarders—except, of course, many of those working the southern border.

Since most forwarders along the southern border claim *not to be* freight forwarders under U.S. law but exclusive forwarding agents of the Mexican Customs broker, the USDOT and even the IRS know very little about those intermediaries working for *foreign business entities* in the control of inbound and outbound cargo. The obvious question is, why hasn't DHS or USDOT addressed this issue?

WHY DHS, CBP, AND ICE
HAVE NOT ADDRESSED THE PROCESS

Having lived on the Mexican border, worked extensively on border crossing issues, and testified in the U.S. Senate and House and in the Texas House, I can say with absolute certitude that CBP is aware of the issue. Even ICE is aware of the vulnerabilities posed by cross-border trailer and container movement. In fact, in 2009, ICE made a video in Laredo, Texas, about how easy it is to bypass the required seals used on containers and trailers entering through our ports. While I have a copy of that video, it seems not to have garnered the attention of those in DHS nor those on the House and Senate Homeland Security Committees. In fact, I have been told by CBP in Laredo, Texas, that there is nothing it can do, and it is a matter for the U.S. Department of State and the administration to confront. According to CBP, it's a political issue. I agree with CBP.

Unfortunately, this "political issue" is a genuine security issue for all of us, especially those living in U.S. port cities along the border. It is a political issue far above the level of CBP. Why, with Congress knowing that there are terrorists using Mexico for entry into the United States, is there no apparent interest in Congress or in the administration in fixing it, especially now when the border is getting more dangerous?

ROLE OF THE MEXICAN DRUG CARTELS

It is undeniable that the Mexican drug cartels are a serious issue not only for Mexico but also for the United States. It is also undeniable that the Mexican Customs brokers operate as a business cartel in controlling the commercial crossings at our southern border. Is it possible that there could be cooperation between the Mexican Customs brokers and the Mexican drug cartels? So far there is no evidence, at least available to the public, that there is cooperation. It makes sense, however, that there is a relationship or *could be* a relationship. What is more disturbing is that information from current informants of drug cartel activities indicates the presence of Middle East entities now connected to the cartels in one of the biggest transcarriage ports on the southern border. Also disturbing is the current problem of pay-offs having to be made by Mexican truck companies to the drug cartels. So far, the cartels have been reluctant to target large Mexican long-haul carriers with U.S. roots. And while many smaller Mexican long-haul truck lines have been targeted by the drug cartels, U.S. companies have been relatively unaffected to this point. Operationally, all carriers have had to review and reconsider loading, transit, and crossing times to avoid cartel violence. Many carriers are no longer allowing freight over the road or for shuttle service after dark. Others are utilizing convoy operations and secondary GPS trackers to increase security and avoid pilferage or introduction of contraband into northbound shipments.

If there is opposition to or trouble in collecting these payments, serious and deadly results follow. Recently, two Mexican males connected to Transportes Elola, SA de CV, a Mexican truck company doing business with U.S. firms, were kidnapped. At the request of U.S. individuals connected to these men, contact was made with informants in Mexico. It was confirmed that they were kidnapped, but there was nothing that could be done, as they were now "cooking," an expression meaning that these men were dead and now in acid. To further verify the situation, the car driven by those who were kidnapped was located in Mexico, and the license plate number was given to me to confirm the accuracy of the information provided. During the discussion with contacts, it was also confirmed that now *most* Mexican trucking companies, especially in one trans-carriage port, are, in fact, paying off the drug cartel. One merely has to look at the growth exhibited in the two drug cartel maps from 2008 and 2012 (see figures 3.1 and 3.2) to see that *all* U.S. land ports on our border are presently subject to cartel influence. This is supported by the U.S. DOJ in this statement: "Moreover, Houston is a major hub for the trucking industry; tractor-trailers are commonly used by DTOs (Drug Trafficking Organizations) to smuggle large drug shipments from Mexico through the HIDTA (High Intensity Drug Trafficking Area) region to markets throughout the United States."[7]

I have also been told, by a significant Mexican Customs broker, of interference by one drug cartel in certain high-value shipments, and it is well documented that drug cartels insert drugs into trailers bound for the United States. Additionally, my own intelligence gathering of drug cartel activities indicates that there are at least three Middle East entities now connected to the cartels in Nuevo Laredo, Mexico, directly across from Laredo, Texas. I have passed on that information, among other intelligence, to the U.S. Drug Enforcement Agency (DEA) and received a thank-you from them. I also passed it along to CBP with no response.

Is there a connection between the apparently uncontrollable Mexican Customs brokers and the apparently uncontrollable drug cartels? I do not know as of the time of this writing. But here is the problem: the Mexican Customs brokers are not willing to change their business practices. Why would they? Their practices are tantamount to a pay-first, cash-only business. But their practices are the reason for the drop lots, the use of drayage, and the use of many unregulated U.S. freight forwarders. The United States knows very little, if anything, about the background of these businessmen. The Mexican Customs brokers are also not part of our C-TPAT program, so we don't know much about their security measures, if anything, or their business partners or business relationships. However, C-TPAT allows Mexican manufacturers and motor carriers to participate in the C-TPAT program and even be audited to ensure C-TPAT compliance. Finally, while it is a

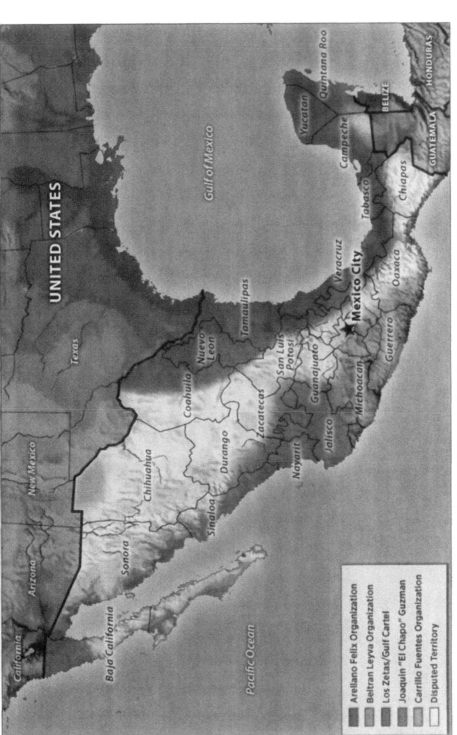

Figure 3.1. Areas of cartel influence, 2008. Courtesy of Stratfor: www.Stratfor.com.

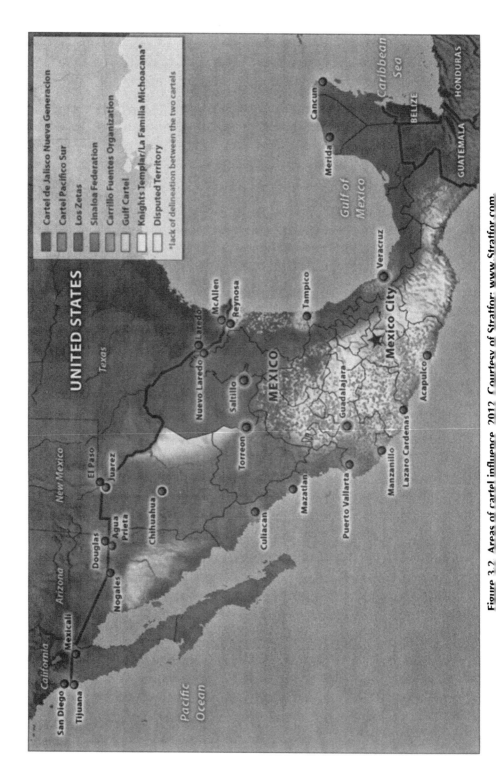

Figure 3.2 Areas of cartel influence, 2012. Courtesy of Stratfor; www.Stratfor.com.

foreign seaport program, it is also important to recognize that Mexico is not part of the U.S. Container Security Initiative (CSI) even though they are a NAFTA partner. Our other NAFTA partner, Canada, is a member and has developed its own supply chain security program called Partners in Protection (PIP) that, along with C-TPAT, is mutually recognized by both the United States and Canada. However, to be fair, Mexico has launched the Program Alliance for Secure Commerce (PACS), modeled on the World Customs Organization's SAFE Framework of Standards.[8] While PACS has not yet qualified for mutual recognition, it is a positive step in attempting to improve cross-border supply chain security.

One could reasonably conclude that the drug cartels may be using and even promoting the current illegal alien crossing furor to divert attention from their main movement of guns, money, drugs, and terrorists enabled to cross both ways through a Mexican-controlled commercial system using a massive number of container and trailer crossings that could serve as the most efficient, effective, and safe means of continuing the life-blood flow necessary to sustain them. While this cannot be shown at this time, it is difficult to believe that the cartels, as I learned recently, are only bringing in munitions hidden in cars that smell so bad from the deliberate application of foul-smelling garbage and worse that Customs and Aduana inspectors make only a cursory examination, if any at all.

CONCLUSION

A simple, but true, example will serve to illustrate my contention. An inbound container passed through the southern border into the United States. At its destination in the interior of the United States, it was opened. The U.S. firm discovered a plastic jug of urine, a plastic bag of urine, a backpack, a can of sardines (unopened), a hat, a fanny pack, and a white tank top. Who entered the country? What was their purpose? What if there had been a bomb instead of people? The real threat of terrorism, drugs, or illegals in commercial conveyances crossing the southern border will not be solved by ACE, the e-Manifest, or C-TPAT. There is an essential need for a comprehensive reform in southern border-crossing practices and a change in commercial culture. Security begins at stuffing at origin and must be maintained through unloading at destination.

The current operating and institutional crossing environment along the southern border is inefficient, expensive, and above all, a serious security risk and vulnerability that can only be fixed by those above the level of CBP. Only high-level administration action, likely through the coordinated efforts of the U.S. Department of State, the U.S. Trade Representative's Office, and DHS, can fundamentally change the current system and improve our security. Until that is done, it is only a matter of time . . .

NOTES

1. James Giermanski and David Neipert, "Government Acquiescence and Inaction on Our Southern Border: The Commercial Border-Crossing Threat," *Supply Chain Digest*, November 21, 2011.

2. Verification of the border-crossing process can be found in "North American Free Trade Agreement (NAFTA) Implementation: The Future of Commercial Trucking across the Mexican Border," *CRS Report for Congress*, updated September 22, 2004.

3. BTS State Transportation Statistics, *Research and Innovative Technology Administration*, USDOT, 2009, p. C-14.

4. NAFTA, Annex I, *Reservations for Existing Measures and Liberalization Commitments*, http://www.international.gc.ca/trade-agreements-accords-commerciaux/agr-acc/nafta-alena/texte/anx1b-mex.aspx?lang=en&view=d.

5. For an expanded treatment of this issue, see Jim Giermanski, "ACE, the E-Manifest, C-TPAT and the Southern Border," *Homeland Defense Journal*, April 2007.

6. Public Law 104-88, 104th Congress, ICC Termination Act of 1995, Section 13102, Definitions, No. 8.

7. *Strategic Drug Threat Developments*, http://www.justice.gov/ndic/pubs32/32771/strateg.htm.

8. Eric Kulisch, "Mexico to Start Trusted Shipper Program," *American Shipper*, March 10, 2011, http://www.americanshipper.com/NewWeb/news_page_SNW2.asp?news=185676.

Chapter Four

The Supply Chain and
U.S. Border Security with Canada

There is really no comparison between the U.S.-Mexico southern border and the U.S.-Canada northern border. It is a day-and-night comparison. Drayage on the southern border is a serious security risk, and it is a system that the United States has refused to address. Since drayage is a problem on many fronts, at least the state of Texas has addressed the truck-safety issue and tries to enforce safety standards on Mexican drayage trucks. Drayage is not a major issue on the northern border, nor is it a security risk. On the southern border, Mexican long-haul carriers are still engaged with the U.S. government to be allowed to service the interior of the United States as agreed upon in the North American Free Trade Agreement (NAFTA). On the northern border, Canadian long-haulers have been officially allowed to provide service to the U.S. interior since 1982 as a result of Canada's Brock-Gotlieb Understanding, which confirmed that U.S. carriers would have continued access to the Canadian market.[1] A presidential memorandum from President Ronald Reagan from September 20, 1982, lifted the moratorium with respect to Canadian trucking companies, allowing them to access beyond-the-border commercial zones into the U.S. interior.

The biggest distinction, however, is the control of the Mexican Customs brokers who have a monopoly on commercial cross-border practices, as detailed in chapter 3. The most serious distinction is the role of the Mexican drug cartels. Canada has no equivalent on our northern border. Until 2011, Mexico had no Customs security program. Canada, however, has had the Partners in Protection (PIP) security program, which is similar to the U.S. Customs-Trade Partnership Against Terrorism (C-TPAT) program, and has been officially designated by the United States as a mutually recognized program. Mutual recognition signifies that both countries apply similar security standards and similar site validations when approving companies for membership in their respective programs and that both countries recognize each other's members and may grant them similar benefits.[2]

Mexico recently established a Customs security program called Programa Alianza para el Comercio Seguro (PACS), which is just beginning to take shape as a pilot program.[3]

A SECURE TRADING PARTNER

President Barack Obama and Canadian Prime Minister Stephen Harper, following their December 7, 2011, meeting, announced an action plan demonstrating shared security and economic competitiveness. This plan was generated from a meeting between the leaders on February 4, 2011, which resulted in the issuance of a joint declaration titled "Beyond the Border: A Shared Vision for Perimeter Security and Economic Competitiveness." The principle of the joint declaration is clear:

> We intend to work together in cooperation and partnership to develop, implement, manage, and monitor security initiatives, standards, and practices to fulfill our vision. We recognize that our efforts should accelerate job creation and economic growth through trade facilitation at our borders and contribute directly to the economic security and well-being of both the United States and Canada.

Its key areas of cooperation are:

- Addressing threats early
- Trade facilitation
- Economic growth and jobs
- Integrated cross-border law enforcement
- Critical infrastructure
- Cybersecurity
- Managing our new long-term partnership

The joint declaration of February 4, 2011, also created a Canada–United States Regulatory Cooperation Council (RCC). Whereas the action plan aims to enhance security and economic competitiveness through measures taken at the shared perimeter and border, the RCC aims to better align mutual regulatory approaches to protect health, safety, and the environment while supporting growth, investment, innovation, and market openness. The following sections attempt to capture the essence of this joint declaration.

Addressing Threats Early

Addressing threats at the earliest possible point is essential for strengthening the shared security of both countries while at the same time improving the free flow of legitimate goods and people across the border. Efforts will be made to develop a common understanding of the threat environment; to align and coordinate security systems for goods, cargo, and baggage; and to support the effective identification of people who pose a threat, which will enhance safety and facilitate the movement of legitimate travelers. To achieve this end, there will have to be a common approach and a shared understanding of the threat environment through improving intelligence operations and sharing appropriate information.

Both nations admit that they will have to develop and implement processes, procedures, and policies to enable an effective, shared understanding of activities, threats, and criminal trends or other consequences in the air, land, and maritime environments. They agree to

- Create an inventory of American and Canadian domain awareness capabilities at the border by May 31, 2012, and identify gaps and vulnerabilities in capabilities by October 31, 2012
- Prioritize coverage of gaps by April 30, 2013, to create a vision for jointly deploying new technology to address identified gaps
- Establish a process by April 30, 2013, to coordinate the joint procurement and deployment of technology along the border

This effort will enhance the security of supply chains, starting at the earliest possible point in the supply chain and ensuring the integrity of the screened cargo through to its destination. Both countries will make better informed risk-management decisions due to advance information sharing for inbound offshore cargo shipments, harmonization of advance data requirements, sharing of real-time preload screening and examination results, and the harmonization of targeting and risk assessment methodologies and results that are key elements to the success of this initiative. Canada and the United States will develop

- By June 2012, a common set of data elements required for in-bond (United States)/in-transit (Canada) shipments arriving from offshore and for domestic shipments that transit through the other country
- A process to identify and evaluate options by September 2012 under which trusted traders could use alternate processes and approaches to submit advance data elements, including examining whether and how existing program flexibilities can be enhanced
- By December 2013, a common set of required data, as well as any alternate processes and approaches for trusted traders

Trade Facilitation and Economic Growth and Jobs

The declaration clearly states, "The free flow of goods and services between the United States and Canada creates immense economic benefits for both countries."

Strengthening security of the border will create more openness for legitimate travel and trade. Therefore, Canada and the United States are to work on creative ways of improving traffic flows, including infrastructure and technology enhancements. This will mean that both nations will strive to ensure that border crossings have the capacity to support the volume of commercial and passenger traffic inherent to economic growth and job creation on both sides of the border. Mutual planning and coordination in planning, building, funding, and, in general, modernizing border facilities will be important to enhancing risk management practices.

Another important aspect will be the harmonization of existing programs and processes in an attempt to lessen costs. One method will be to streamline Customs programs and facilitate regulatory compliance in working toward an integrated cargo security strategy. One strategy will use compatible screening mechanisms at foreign ports before the goods are shipped to Canada or the United States.

There are two tiers to securing the supply chain under the declaration. Tier 1 will focus on supply chain security, and tier 2 will focus on trade compliance and expedited border and accounting processes. Under tier 1, the goals will be to

• Harmonize the U.S.-based C-TPAT program and the Canada-based PIP program and offer new benefits, including an automated enrollment system. Canada will develop an interoperable communication portal similar to that of the United States by December 2013
• Extend Free and Secure Trade (FAST) benefits to members in these programs at agreed locations beginning in mid-2012

There is also a proposed "single window" through which importers can electronically submit all information to comply with Customs and other participating government agency regulations. Tier 2 relates more to trusted travelers than to supply chain security.

Integrated Cross-Border Law Enforcement

By building on existing bilateral law enforcement programs, there will be an effort made to integrate cross-border law enforcement operations through leveraging law enforcement officers and resources designated to jointly identify, assess, and interdict persons and organizations involved in transnational crime. It is interesting to note that though there is transnational and organized crime on the southern border, Mexico has no objectives similar to Canada's, where there isn't any drug cartel influence. Canada and the United States also agree to improve the sharing of relevant information to reduce criminal activity where possible.

The United States and Canada have already developed successful models for preventing criminals from crossing the border. The Shiprider pilot program, for example, employs cross-designated officers to patrol the maritime areas between the two countries, while Integrated Border Enforcement Teams and Border Enforcement Security Task Forces support joint investigations and law enforcement action at and between ports of entry. The U.S. Department of Justice, the Department of Homeland Security, the Royal Canadian Mounted Police, Public Safety Canada, and Justice Canada will complete this scope of operations and program architecture for the next-generation pilot projects by spring or summer 2012. There will also be two pilots deployed simultaneously by summer 2012.

Critical Infrastructure and Cybersecurity

The United States and Canada benefit from shared critical and cyber infrastructure. Therefore, both countries agree to strengthen cybersecurity and protect vital government and critical digital infrastructure of national importance in making cyberspace safer. Joint efforts will be made to prevent, respond to, and recover from both physical and cyber disruptions and to implement comprehensive cross-border measures to strengthen the critical and cyber infrastructure with strong cross-border engagement. Each nation will enhance an already strong bilateral cybersecurity cooperation to better protect vital government and critical digital infrastructure and increase both countries' ability to respond jointly and effectively to cyber incidents. This will be achieved through joint projects and operational efforts, including joint briefings with the private sector and other stakeholders and the enhancement of real-time information sharing between operation centers.

Managing the Partnership: Implementation and Oversight

The United States and Canada intend to establish a Beyond the Border Working Group (BBWG) composed of representatives from the appropriate departments and offices of the respective federal governments. While the responsibility of coordinating interagency falls on the president and prime minister and their administrations, the BBWG will be instrumental in that coordination, and it created a plan of action appropriate for both nations' border-related entities to implement.

Additionally, Canada and the United States will form an assistant secretary/assistant deputy minister–level Beyond the Border Executive Steering Committee (BTB ESC) that will hold annual meetings to discuss the management of the shared border, progress on identified initiatives, and areas of further work. It will oversee the implementation of the goals of the action plan and declaration. To ensure continued transparency and accountability, Canada and the United States will generate a joint, public Beyond the Border Implementation Report, which will be issued yearly during the three-year period set out in the February 4, 2011, declaration, with the expectation of continuation. The report will be submitted to the president of the United States by the secretary of state in coordination with the secretary of homeland security, the secretary of commerce, and the attorney general; and to the prime minister of Canada by the minister of public safety and the minister of international trade.

CURRENT PRACTICES

If there were any doubts about the distinction between the Canadian and Mexican borders, the following, in almost verbatim terms, reveals the *current* Ontario Ministry of Transportation Canada-U.S. Border Crossing Checklist.

All Carriers

- Participation in programs such as C-TPAT, FAST, and Pre-Arrival Processing System (PAPS) is one way to expedite the clearance of legitimate travelers and goods across the border.
- Ensure that drivers are aware of and follow the instructions for required documentation when they arrive at the border.

All Drivers

- Drivers should have the required personal identification (including photo ID, driver's license, and/or passport—see below) ready for presentation at primary inspection before arriving at the booth. U.S. Customs officials advise that drivers searching for these documents when they arrive for inspection add to the time taken for clearance.
- Drivers must turn on interior cab lights and open all interior drapes/blinds to the sleeper area for easy inspection. Unnecessary personal belongings should not be carried by drivers, as they can lead to questions from Customs officials about where these items were obtained.
- Drivers should ensure that all Customs paperwork is completed and ready for presentation to Customs officials at primary inspection before arrival. Port directors at all major border crossings report that about 35% of drivers show up at primary inspection without having properly completed paperwork, such as the carrier manifest and shipper's documentation. This is a major problem.
- Drivers should be prepared to clear Customs and Border Protection at primary inspection. One of the easiest ways to be prepared is to communicate in advance with the shipper and the U.S. Customs broker so that the information on the shipment is transmitted to Customs before the truck arrives at the border point (PAPS).

- Drivers should be prepared to communicate with U.S. border officials in clear understandable English. This is the law in the United States under CFR (Code of Federal Regulations) 49, Part 391.11(b)(2).

Canadian Citizen Drivers

- At a minimum, a driver should carry photo identification (driver's license) and birth certificate or citizenship card, and have them ready for presentation at primary inspection. It is recommended that Canadian citizen drivers obtain and carry a valid passport.

Non-Canadian/U.S. Citizen Drivers

- Individuals who are not citizens of Canada or the United States must carry a valid passport and will be required by Immigration officials to complete an I-94 card, even if the driver qualifies under the visa waiver program. I-94 cards are only available on-site at border crossings into the United States. If the driver requires an I-94 card, the driver will be instructed by officials at primary inspection to report to Immigration to complete the documentation. The cost of the I-94 is $6 (U.S.) payable by cash in U.S. funds (U.S. officials will not accept Canadian funds).
- If drivers clear Customs at primary inspection and require an I-94 card, they must report to Immigration to fill out the I-94 and receive verbal clearance from a U.S. Immigration official to proceed into the United States.

   If drivers require an I-94 card, do not clear Customs at primary inspection, and are referred to secondary inspection to see their brokers, they must first go to Immigration before presenting their paperwork for Customs clearance at secondary inspection.

   Remember—clearance from U.S. Customs is a verbal clearance or verbal release. There is no stamp or receipt indicating that shipments have cleared Customs. Drivers should only proceed after being told by a U.S. Customs official that their shipment(s) has cleared.
- In addition, some individuals may require a U.S. nonimmigrant visa. Drivers should not proceed to the border unless they know whether this requirement applies to them.
- If travel documents are required (e.g., nonimmigrant visas or passports), drivers should ensure that they are in order, easily accessible, valid, and ready to be presented before arriving at primary inspection.
- If a driver is refused entry into the United States for reasons related to U.S. immigration law, the driver must report to Canada Customs as well as Citizenship and Immigration Canada on the return trip to Canada. U.S. Immigration officials have also indicated that if one is refused entry at one border

point, the practice of "port shopping" will not be tolerated and individuals will be subject to penalties under U.S. law (which can include vehicle seizure and permanent banishment from the United States).

CONCLUSION

I must end this chapter as I started it. Both the Mexican and the Canadian borders are important to our security and economy, but one is dangerous and expensive to cross, and the government is uncooperative. The other is not dangerous and not expensive to cross, and the government is cooperative. Why the difference?

NOTES

1. North American Free Trade Agreement Arbitral Panel Established Pursuant to Chapter Twenty, in the Matter of Cross-Border Trucking Services (Secretariat File No. USA-MEX-98-2008-01), February 6, 2001, p. 9.

2. "Partners in Protection," Canada Border Services Agency, http://www.cbsa.gc.ca/security-securite/pip-pep/menu-eng.html#c03.

3. "The Alliance for Secure Commerce—Mexico's AEO Program," *Global Trade News*, May 12, 2011, http://www.integrationpoint.com/globaltradenews/index.php/2011/05/the-alliance-for-secure-commerce-mexicos-aeo-program/.

Chapter Five

Container Security and the Smart Container

The world is trying to ensure that global container traffic is controlled and secure, reducing the vulnerability containers could pose for nations and their ports. Governments and nongovernment organizations are constantly debating and demanding that certain protocols be adopted to achieve this security, for instance, the demand by the United States for scanning. Unfortunately, these organizations do little to demonstrate that they understand the business needs of the private sector. Securing the supply chain actually provides business benefits to the private sector, specifically in that it makes money for those who secure the supply chain. There really don't have to be opposing sides to this issue. It is time for both industry and government to understand the value of smart containers: protect the homeland and make a profit!

SMART CONTAINERS TODAY: HOW ARE THEY DEFINED?

First, how do we define smart containers? Second, what do they detect? Third, how smart is smart? Fourth, how do they know when to begin and end working? Fifth, what are the benefits? Sixth, who pays? And finally, does their usage meet the requirements of Customs security programs?

How Do We Define Smart Containers?

Smart containers are smart because they can carry on a conversation, and the user or their international control center ("platforms") can communicate with them, depending on the programming, sensors, and technology used, in real time or close to real time. Smart containers can be defined by what they do—more specifically, what they are programmed to do. Their sophistication ranges from simple reporting of location only to a chain-of-custody system from origin to destination. Some containers are simply more intelligent than others because of how they are equipped and programmed.

What Can Be Detected and Reported besides Location?

The easy response is that it depends! Each type of cargo provides a different benefit for varying users. If you are Coca-Cola and you are shipping syrup from Puerto Rico to the U.S. mainland, you are probably not worried about theft—how does a thief move stolen syrup, and is it worth stealing? Coca-Cola is likely more worried about contamination or perhaps the fallout of one of its containers being a host for a nuclear device destined for detonation when it arrives in the United States. If you are a pharmaceutical company like Pfizer, you will have a fear of contamination. Therefore, you might need to have additional information about the container's internal environment, like temperature. And because of their high value, medicines like Viagra make perfect targets for theft.

But government needs are likely to be more comprehensive. If you are the government, you want to know about breaches in the container and the presence of substances like biological agents, chemical agents, shielded enriched uranium, humans, explosives, drugs, and more. In one incident mentioned in chapter 3, a major U.S. trucking firm opened a container of products originating in Mexico and found evidence of human nonpaying passengers: food, plastic containers of urine, and items of clothing, along with a hole in the roof of the container that hadn't been discovered en route to the United States.

Although what to detect varies by the type of shipper, there is some agreement. One must first detect any unauthorized breach into a container/trailer through *any* portion of the container, not just through the doors. Second, one must detect the internal environment of the container for the safety of the product being carried. And third, one *must* detect the presence of substances like weapons of mass destruction (WMDs), human cargo, and illegal drugs. But what if you are Home Depot? You might just want to know where the container is because of looming sales on the products that are in the container, which is still moving through in the global supply chain. Thus, the core detection requirements of contamination, theft, WMD, drugs, and humans can be supplemented with detecting positioning of the container on its journey. Another detection option is called geofencing. In essence, the container detects a variance between where it should be and where it is, as a result of a hijacking, for instance, or having simply been sent to the wrong consignee or the wrong location. Vibration and heat can also be detected in the case of cutting through container walls. What we *should be* able to detect, however, may not be what we *can* detect, given the level of technological sophistication at this time.

How Smart Is Smart?

Tracking and tracing functions, traits of a mentally challenged smart container, merely monitor location by RFID (radio frequency identification), by fixed antennas, or by satellite or cellular communication, depending on the level of communication latency the user is willing to accept. The very smart containers can electronically tell one the following: the contents of the container, who supervised loading the cargo and who is accountable for the accuracy of the contents at origin, the time the container was sealed, when it left its origin, its route, its internal environment, its progress, whether it deviated from its course, its arrival at port of embarkation, when it was loaded aboard the vessel, whether it was breached, when it arrived at the destination port, and who opened it and verified the cargo. The costs of some of these sensors are high, and some of them are just being developed. Companies out there can provide smart containers now. The Department of Homeland Security (DHS) is taking a role in promoting their development through programs like SAFE Container (SAFECON), which offers funds to refine sophisticated sensing of "WMD, explosives, contraband, or human cargo in maritime shipping containers."[1] Furthermore, government programs of this nature have encouraged small firms to do the research and development needed for patent development in the sensor and container security–related areas. Although the development of sophisticated sensors is ongoing, some high-tech sensors for use in containers are already available. For instance, although we do not yet have the technology for nonintrusive portal machines to scan containers for shielded enriched uranium,[2] we do have in-container sensors that, because of the nature of a container voyage, which offers time to "sense," coupled with the in-container close proximity of the sensor to the potential uranium source, offer the ability to detect the presence of shielded uranium, without nonintrusive portal machines.[3] New applications of electrochemical and electromagnetic technology and other technologies (about which I know very little) all suggest the continued development and production of sophisticated sensors that are capable of detecting the presence of WMD, drugs, and humans in containers and trailers.

When Does Smart Start and Stop?

Everything depends on the security program and software utilized. At present, the smartest container has a sophisticated, comprehensive chain-of-custody system that begins at the stuffing (loading) of the container at origin, maintains monitors, and reports its integrity to the end of the global supply chain path at destination. Its process includes the human element in the supply chain and the electronics of the system. No system is 100% effective, and one cannot depend on technology alone. However, technology often overshadows the role of humans in security systems.

Container systems have to include the identification of the party responsible and personally accountable for final inspection of the cargo prior to its sealing and dispatch and subsequent international movement to destination. Someone must take responsibility for confirming the cargo on the bill of lading or booking sheet, for activating the smart container system, and for locking the doors. This responsible party must be vetted with respect to integrity and competence. Equally, there must be a counterpart at destination. Both parties are electronically connected by a unique identifier to the smart container to complete the system. This can be done with an electronic activation key, cellphone, or an equivalent, that is used at stuffing to load data such as origin with the bill of lading and booking information, information needed by customs authorities, and other data such as the identity of the supervising and arming agent at origin and the final agent deactivating the system at destination. This secure electronic key protocol is then used to insert the data from the company's logistics system into the device affixed in the container and carried to destination. At activation, the accountable party becomes an integral element in the smart container security system.

Once the container is activated by using an electronic key protocol inserted in the electronic memory of the container, the device can be read at almost any time during the voyage through satellite communication. When a smart container is opened at destination by an equally accountable person and cargo is missing and there were no breaches detected, recorded, and reported, the accountable person at origin can face disciplinary or, worse, criminal action by appropriate authorities. Worldwide control centers offer the capacity to serve as a third-party electronic record of the transaction recorded automatically in its servers. The smartest container offers an electronic receipt of delivery, accomplished through the opening of the container by a person at destination approved and authorized to open the container, which is provided by another specialized electronic key protocol usable only with and by an authorized individual at the point of destination. European Datacomm (EDC) and GlobalTrak in the United States can today provide these smart containers.

HOW DO SMART CONTAINERS TRANSMIT WHAT THEY DETECT?

There is a risk of focusing too much on detection and not enough on its usage. Information present but unknown is quite useless. To provide information about breaches, contraband, WMD, and so on, a smart container must be capable of reporting the detection. At this time, there are several generally accepted methods of transmitting data discovered by in-container sensors: RFID, satellite, cellular, and now even magnetic transmissions (see chapter 15). The users of each extol the benefits of the application they employ. However, a closer look at these alleged benefits needs to be taken. It seems that while the larger companies in the smart container market are committed to RFID, their commitment will be short-lived. The problems of RFID are many.

RFID Technology

In this chapter I will treat RFID in a general way, covering only its major features as they relate to smart containers. See chapter 9 for detailed ramifications of RFID use. Here I will only cover, in a cursory way, its technical applications, infrastructure, timeliness, features, costs, and risks.

Technical Applications

RFID is critically impaired for global usage because there is no worldwide agreement on frequencies. The RFID frequency on which data are carried in Germany is not the same RFID frequency approved for use in the United States, nor the one approved by China for use there. Since frequencies vary, so do the equipment requirements, making it impossible to use everywhere in the world—but shipping containers go everywhere in the world. Additionally, protocols differ. Protocols are like someone speaking French and the other English at different speeds, stopping and starting at different times. In other words, there are no global rules for RFID communication.

Infrastructure

RFID, since it is radio frequency, needs antennas in every location where one wants to read or talk to the RFID unit of the container. Antennas must be placed on property owned by, leased by, or provided to the RFID user. Acquisition, then, is both a legal and operational issue, especially when RFID signals have limited distance and direction. Antennas also require maintenance and control. Furthermore, other users of RFID can select locations for their units that interfere or distort another RFID user's signals—a footprint problem. It also seems that fixed antennas are not very practical given legal access rights and costs. Therefore, handheld transceivers must replace the fixed antennas—creating another problem of equipment, the need for increased personnel to interrogate each container, and the high cost of handheld units.

Timeliness

RFID can only make use of chokepoints or physical areas through which the container must pass. Similar to the transceivers used at department store doors that sound an alert if the RFID tag is not removed for the product just purchased, no alert is given until one passes through the chokepoint. In other words, RFID is land-based and historical in nature. The container reports what happened to it before it reached the chokepoint only at the time it passes through the chokepoint where there is an antenna and transceiver to interrogate it. Of course, if the container were breached and goods stolen or an explosive device inserted prior to the chokepoint, it would be too late to respond to the breach, assuming the RFID unit could detect breaches into the container other than through its doors.

Features

RFID can utilize different sensors for different purposes. It can be electronically linked to sensors such as light, vibration, and temperature. The problem is that it lacks the capacity to report what it detects until it reaches a chokepoint. An RFID user only knows something when and if the container reaches the chokepoint.

Costs

Both RFID and satellite require hardware, and both RFID and satellite require the installation of an antenna into the container. However, the use of RFID means costs of infrastructure acquisition, antennas for fixed sites, handheld transceivers, staff to use them, and maintenance. Once an antenna is installed in the container, satellite costs are limited to the cost of message traffic. And since satellite message traffic involves short bursts of data, it is less expensive, especially when compared to infrastructure, maintenance, handheld readers, and corresponding personnel costs for RFID.

Risks

In my opinion, RFID connected to container interrogation should not even be allowed in U.S. ports. It can actually serve as the means to detonate an explosive device. Because of its radio frequency characteristics and the legal requirement to use a frequency established and mandated by government regulations, anyone who knows the frequency can design a dirty bomb to explode when the container is interrogated in the U.S. seaport—in effect, acting as the trigger for the detonation. With RFID, it is, however, possible to listen for the correct frequency signal and trigger a device based on the presence of such a signal. Such a signal will, for instance, be present in a port when interrogating a container using RFID.

In summary, RFID is inadequate for global container security in almost every way. Then why do the giants seem to be committed to it? Its use is certainly understandable for retail, warehouse control, and in any situation where one can control infrastructure and location. The GEs, Maersks, and IBMs of the world may have simply prematurely jumped on the RFID bandwagon and now want the U.S. government to support the RFID investment that they have foolishly made. The more one knows about global supply chain security, the more one has to accept the inevitable: the future of global container security is not RFID. It is satellite.

Satellite Communication

In addition to RFID, there is satellite communication. In general, there are two broad categories of satellite systems. The first and most widely known is geostationary or high-orbit satellites in equatorial orbit that appear to be stationary. Geostationary or geosynchronous satellites are approximately 36,000 kilometers (23,320 miles) above the earth and rotate along with the earth. Inmarsat is an example of a geostationary satellite firm that offers voice, broadband, and satellite phone service. The second category is a low-earth-orbit (LEO) satellite approximately 800 kilometers (496 miles) above the earth; these do not rotate with the earth. The advantages of LEO applications include inexpensive, narrow-band data transmission in frequencies similar to FM signals. Some LEO systems allow for voice and visual signals. Regardless, both LEO and geosynchronous systems offer logistic advantages by tracking and identifying the location of containers and trailers throughout the supply chain. Additionally, firms such as Iridium or ORBCOMM (LEO constellation owners) provide 24-hour communication service at multiple gateway control centers that receive, manage, and forward communications from their satellites to locations worldwide. Yet geostationary satellite communication systems such as Inmarsat may have advantages over LEO systems because of better real-time reporting. There is significant use of satellites in a geosynchronous orbit for monitoring the location of containers and trailers, mostly for asset management purposes.

It is important to remember, though, the distinction between satellite tracking and satellite communications. Tracking may be perfectly fine for asset management but inadequate for container security and control. Tracking means that the satellite pings the container that has a GPS (global positioning system) antenna. For the container to send its location to those who want to know it, it must have another antenna to use. Two-way sophisticated satellite communications require a modem, and this additional antenna, along with other electronic circuitry, will allow the container to talk to its satellite provider under certain conditions. GPS systems are not without weaknesses—for instance, dead spots and visible antennas on the conveyance. Having a visible antenna, while seemingly harmless, allows those who intend to hijack or breach a container or trailer for the purpose of terrorism to do so without detection. Second, the capacity to sense what is going on inside the container and its reporting require greater electronic sophistication than tracking alone. Sensors that can detect and, through satellite communication, report the breach or change in container status in real time or almost real time virtually extend the U.S. borders to foreign locations. Finally, satellite communication can make use of worldwide 24-hour-call centers. EDC, for example, has 100 24-hour global call centers, allowing it real-time transmission and response capability for just about anywhere in the world, clearly avoiding the landlocked antenna infrastructure necessary for RFID operations at chokepoints.

Cellular Communication

Although cellular communication is known by many acronyms, it is most commonly called GSM (global system for mobile communications). There are different channels or bandwidths, and different areas of the world use different bands. While there are roaming capabilities and connectivity between different areas of the world, cellular communication has not made any significant inroads into the smart container world. There are dedicated bands for radio LANs (local area networks), and industrial, scientific, and medical bands—for instance, between 2400 and 2483 MHz. As with RFID, there are government issues and set-asides designated by the Federal Communications Commission (FCC) in the United States and MKK (Radio Equipment Testing and Approval Association) in Japan. One reason is the disparate levels of cellular communication development and sophistication. As wireless broadband is adopted, worldwide networks vary. There are issues similar to RFID with respect to frequencies and bandwidths, protocol, and infrastructure such as network gateways, subnetwork gateways, towers, and base stations; and there are different systems—cellular; Wi-Fi, utilizing hot spots; and WiMAX (Worldwide Interoperable for Microwave Access). So far there has not been any notable progress toward universal acceptance of these cellular technologies as an answer to container communications, especially in light of competing applications and levels of development and sophistication worldwide. Finally, there are fundamental security issues like interoperability, authentication, tampering, and eavesdropping or access to information transmitted in the clear as opposed to encrypted transmissions. Cellular communication in many ways simply mirrors RFID issues and problems.

WHEN DOES SMART START AND STOP?

So far, the literature on this subject has focused not on a solution to the problem of security but on the sensors and communication hardware that are part of the solution. The security solution requires a complete system of end-to-end coverage, a solution from origin to destination.

At the present time there is a patented container security system that begins at the stuffing (loading) of the container at origin and maintains, monitors, and reports its integrity to the end of the global supply chain path at destination. Its process adds the human element in the supply chain to the electronics of the system. No system is 100% effective, and one cannot depend on technology alone. However, technology often overshadows the role of humans in security systems. Container systems have to include the identification of a party responsible for final inspection of the cargo prior to its dispatch and subsequent international movement. Someone must take responsibility for confirming the cargo on the bill of lading or booking sheet, for activating the smart container system, and for locking the doors. This responsible party must be vetted with respect to integrity and competence. Equally, there must be a counterpart at the destination. Both parties must be electronically associated by a unique identifier to the smart container to complete the system. This can be done with an electronic activation key that is loaded at origin with bill of lading and booking information, or information needed by customs authorities, and other data such as the identity of the supervising and arming agent at origin and the final agent deactivating the system at destination. This secure electronic key is then used to transport and insert these data from the company's logistics system into the device affixed in the container. Therefore, at activation the responsible party becomes an integral element in the smart container security system. Once the container is activated by inserting the electronic key, data contained in the electronic memory of the container device can be read at almost any time during the voyage through satellite communication. The activation also allows the smart container to notify appropriate parties of an unauthorized breach or to report the condition of the container or, depending on the sensors used, to report the condition of the cargo within the container and even to report its own hijacking all the way from origin to destination. This process becomes, in effect, the equivalent of a chain of custody. It treats the container as if it were a certified and registered letter. The smart container provides a unique identifier for tracking that allows the consignee or consignor to query the container and also allows the container to independently report any movement off its intended journey. It offers the capacity to serve as a third-party record of the transaction, recorded automatically by a worldwide call center. A smart container offers an electronic receipt of delivery, accomplished by the opening of the container by a person at the destination approved and authorized to open the container, which is provided by another specialized electronic data key usable only with and by the authorized individual at the point of destination. And it exceeds the security of Registered mail by offering breach detection into the container not just through the doors, but through any part of the container; by offering off-course alerts; and by offering other sensory information as needed by the user. A smart container system, therefore, is not just a locked door. It is a system that must[4]

- Electronically identify the authorized personnel stuffing and securing the container, and accept and report information like container/trailer number and booking data;

- Detect a breach in any part of the container;
- Report the breach in real time (or close to real time);
- Track the container through the supply chain;
- Identify the authorized personnel unsealing the container; and
- Be software-friendly to accommodate disparate logistics programs in communicating critical data.

WHAT'S IT WORTH, AND WHO PAYS?

The short answer is that we all pay one way or another, and industry has few options. The government does not mandate in-container security devices. Their use is encouraged in the SAFE Port Act of 2006, with the tease benefit of the special tier 3 Green Lane provisions if a firm uses an in-container security system. But so far only government programs, not smart containers, seem to be used as incentives, and these programs are voluntary. C-TPAT is one of them. While now codified into U.S. law, C-TPAT is still a voluntary program that allows and encourages companies involved in international trade to become members. By becoming members, the firms must meet security obligations. At the present time, C-TPAT is open to air carriers; sea carriers; land (rail and truck) carriers, including foreign truck carriers; air freight consolidators; U.S. marine ports/terminals; foreign manufacturers (Mexico); warehouses; U.S. licensed Customs brokers; and importers.

It is quite clear that none of these entities is government. But all of these must incur expenses to be a member. For instance, the U.S. importer must mandate and ensure that its foreign supplier meets the same requirements that it does. The U.S. importer must spend money on security measures at its facilities. It must spend money on security training and education, and it must spend money on technology. All of these expenditures make the government's job easier, specifically the job of CBP. The cost burden is, thus, shifted. In return, C-TPAT participants receive benefits. Although each category has unique costs, the alleged benefits represent a one-size-fits-all approach.

Of course, the private sector pays for all of this. In fact, CBP in March 2006 boasted about how the U.S. zone of security is being pushed back to the point of origin and how participation in C-TPAT "allows for better risk assessment and targeting, freeing CBP to allocate inspectional resources to more questionable shipments." The conclusion seems obvious: let private enterprise spend its money to push back our border and free up CBP for something else. In return, here's what a C-TPAT importer participant gets as incentives: a good feeling about pushing back the border to the shipment's origin; expedited shipments through Customs (tier 1 treatment; tier 2 treatment; and tier 3, also called Green Lane treatment); lower probability of inspections;[5] and having a designated manager at CBP for one's account. The problem is that pushing back the border is not Target's or Home Depot's duty. It's the duty of Congress and the administration. Additionally, expedited shipments, while ostensibly connected to qualifying as tier 1, tier 2, or tier 3 participants, seem more artificial than real or significant.

Tier 1

In essence, within 90 days of being accepted into C-TPAT, an importer can expect to receive a 20% reduction in one's score used in connection with the automated targeting system (ATS).

Tier 2

After being a validated tier 1 participant, an importer may become a tier 2 participant and receive benefits that may include[6]

1. reduced scores in the Automated Targeting System;
2. reduced examinations of cargo; and
3. priority searches of cargo.

Tier 3

The importer must have achieved tier 2 and must employ smart container technology that uses systems or sensors to detect entry into the container along its international supply chain from origin to destination and be able to report it. Qualifying criteria for tier 3 benefits may include[7]

1. compliance with additional guidelines . . . particularly with respect to controls over access to cargo throughout the supply chain;
2. submission of additional information regarding cargo prior to loading . . . ;
3. utilization of container security devices, technologies, and practices; . . . and
4. compliance with any other requirements established by the Secretary.

Benefits *may* include[8]

1. the expedited release of a Tier 3 participant's cargo in destination ports within the United States during all threat levels designated by the Secretary;
2. further reduction of examination of cargo;
3. priority for examination of cargo;
4. further reduction in the risk score assigned pursuant to the Automated Targeting System; and
5. inclusion in joint incident management exercises, as appropriate.

However, Green Lanes do not exist at U.S. seaports, and in reality benefits are few in number. In a 2007 cost/benefit survey report, CBP reported the following with respect to benefits of participation:[9]

Fewer examinations (34.4% decrease)
Better supply chain visibility (29.4% better)
Improvements in predicting lead-time (24.3% better)
Improvements in tracking orders (22.2% better)
Fewer disruptions in supply chain (28.9% decrease)

Genuine expedited service will rest with the implementation of Green Lanes, which should give a return to the shipper or importer. Green Lanes depend on the use of smart boxes, among other criteria. Unfortunately, it seems that the return is either not known to, appreciated by, or significant enough to the beneficiary to use smart containers. Or the beneficiary is simply focusing on the costs involved in using smart container technology, not weighing the bottom-line benefits of expedited shipments. What does that cost in inventory and cycle time? Some claim that C-TPAT benefits are, in fact, costing the importer money. So far, there is really no incentive for the private sector when it knows that C-TPAT benefits are not guaranteed, but the upfront costs are.

So far there are varying claims of benefits to the private sector for using sophisticated smart container technology, GPS tracking, RFID devices, and government programs like C-TPAT. A recent study from Stanford University reveals quantifiable benefits. It included the following examples:[10]

- Improved product safety—38% reduction in theft/loss/pilferage, 37% reduction in tampering;
- Improved inventory management—14% reduction in excess inventory, 12% increase in reported on-time delivery;
- Improved supply chain visibility—50% increase in access to supply chain data, 30% increase in timeliness of shipping information;
- Improved product handling—43% increase in automated handling of goods;
- Process improvements—30% reduction in process deviations;
- More efficient Customs clearance—49% reduction in cargo delays;
- Speed improvements—29% reduction in transit times;
- More resilience—30% improved response time; and
- Higher customer satisfaction—26% reduction in customer attrition and 20% increase in new customers.

Other sources offer different but compelling benefits to using smart container technology. A 2003 BearingPoint study showed benefits varying from $600 to $700 per container per move; a 2005 A. T. Kearney report showed a benefit of $1,150 per move; and the Congressional Budget Office in March 2006 suggested a benefit of 0.8% of the value of the container contents. In a 2006 A. T. Kearney survey report, respondents stated that "they need real-time data for accurate visibility into their supply chains."[11] And accurate data do not exist within the current logistics industry. Smart boxes, then, can provide the missing data deemed important to shippers. The report further revealed that the U.S. Department of Defense is now utilizing smart boxes. These smart boxes have "reduced overall losses (military supplies) to less than 8 percent."[12] There is a favorable bottom line to using smart boxes based on speed alone. The A. T. Kearney, BearingPoint, Stanford, and Congressional Budget Office reports all, in one way or another, acknowledge that control and speed through the supply chain and especially through ports pay off. If we take the average of savings estimates, $1,000, and subtract the cost of a smart box used for that voyage of between $50 and $100, the immediate bottom-line benefit for that one container is a savings of $900 to $950.[13]

Until Congress offers something besides a voluntary program with unreliable benefits, paying for and using a smart container will be an industry decision for industry-recognized benefits—better supply control, lower costs, faster movement, and security with respect to theft, contamination, and product quality during shipment—not the detection of WMD, explosives, contraband, and human cargo. It is not that WMD and the rest are not important to all of us. It is that the private sector does not want to pay for it because it has no direct payoff to their owners. The private sector wants Congress to at least provide some form of incentive that pays off for the private sector, which ultimately pays off for all of us.

CUSTOMS TREATMENT OF SMART CONTAINER DEVICES

What seems an obvious benefit to smart container adoption and use is still negatively impacted by government action in some cases, particularly here in North America by the government of Mexico. The issue is that container security devices for Mexico seem to be dutiable or treated on a fee basis for entry into Mexico, impairing and almost eliminating their use. However, smart containers, those with container security devices (CSDs), are covered internationally by Customs authorities.

Customs Convention on Containers, 1972

The definitive international guidance and basis for CBP decisions on this question is provided by the Customs Convention on Containers (CCC) of 1972. The CCC of 1972 went into effect in 1975, terminating and replacing the 1956

Container Convention and setting new rules for the treatment of containers moving in global commerce. The CCC became the worldwide standard for the Customs treatment of containers by those nations signing, ratifying, accepting, or adhering to it. Additionally, and without garnering any attention in doing so, the CCC was very specific with respect to signaling the tariff treatment of CSDs well before CSDs were manufactured and utilized. The obvious rationale for a treaty on containers is for nations to be consistent in their definition and treatment of containers as instruments that merely carry the goods to a nation, not to be classified or entered as products themselves into the domestic commerce of that nation to which they merely carry the cargo. Article 1, Section C, of the CCC defines a container as:

> an article of transport equipment (lift-van, movable tank or other similar structure);
>
> (i)   fully or partially enclosed to constitute a compartment intended for containing goods;
> (ii) of a permanent character and accordingly strong enough to be suitable for repeated use;
> (iii) specially designed to facilitate the carriage of goods, by one or more modes of transport, without intermediate reloading;
> (iv) designed for ready handling, particularly when being transferred from one mode of transport to another;
> (v)   designed to be easy to fill and to empty; and
> (vi) having an internal volume of one cubic metre or more.

It also indirectly defines a CSD that is a part of the inbound container:

> the term "container" shall include the accessories and equipment of the container, appropriate for the type concerned, provided that such accessories and equipment are carried with the container. The term "container" shall not include vehicles, accessories or spare parts of vehicles, or packaging. Demountable bodies are to be treated as containers.[14]

Article 10, paragraph 1, also provides that "temporary admission shall be granted to component parts intended for the repair of temporarily admitted containers."[15] Containers, then, as defined by the CCC are unmotorized holders of substantial cargo. In the United States, containers are specified as instruments of international traffic (IIT) by DHS, which uses the CCC as its source and basis for this classification. However, each nation can include other definitions of containers and still be consistent with the CCC. In fact, the secretary of the Department of Homeland Security may except the applications of Customs law on "lift vans, cargo vans, shipping tanks, skids, pallets, caul board, and cores for textile fabrics . . . which have all been . . . explicitly classified as Instruments of International Traffic."[16] CSDs, although not classified as IITs, can be classified as accessories of IITs.

Furthermore, Article 11 of the CCC allows products like CSDs to be admitted separately as a container accessory as long as they are to be used on an inbound container or an outbound container in international commerce: "The Contracting Parties agree to grant temporary admission to accessories and equipment of temporarily admitted containers, which are either imported with a container to be re-exported separately or with another container, or imported separately to be re-exported with a container."[17] CBP cites the CCC in its Headquarter Rulings regarding CSDs as a container accessory. In the United States, then, there is precedent for the classifying of CSDs for special Customs treatment. Therefore, firms typically ask for clarification from CBP through what is known as a binding ruling to protect themselves from subsequent Customs decisions that would later classify the CSD in a way that would make it dutiable retroactively. Two such rulings again clarify the appropriate treatment of CSDs in relation to IITs: the IBM case in 2007 and the Bose Corporation case in 2008.

U.S. Government Rulings Regarding IITs

IBM attempted to obtain a reconsideration of a CBP decision that IBM felt was an inappropriate tariff treatment of its imported tamper-resistant embedded controller (TREC), which is "an enhanced container security, monitoring and tracking device which when installed, collects, analyzes and reports data as to the status, condition and location of the container and its contents."[18] Headquarters confirmed the original CBP decision that the imported TRECs were subject to declaration and entry filings unless they were attached to and imported as part of the container, which is defined in the CCC as declared in CBP Headquarters Ruling Letter 116684 of August 2006. In short, the ruling stated that if the container meets the standard as an IIT and the TREC is attached to the container as a "container accessory," the device is free from separate entry declaration. However, TRECs are not IITs and importing them for entry into the commerce of the United States would subject them to tariff treatment.

In the case of Bose in 2008, Bose asked that its PT100-C Tracker, using GPS satellite technology and employed in its containers carrying Bose products produced around the world, be considered as IITs and not subject to duties, since the PT100-C Tracker was an accessory of a shipping container, which is already designated as an IIT by CCC and DHS Headquarters. In this case, CBP made it very clear that PT100-C tracking devices constitute accessories or equipment of IITs pursuant to 19 C.F.R. § 10.41a(a)(3) and are therefore designated as instruments of international traffic pursuant to 19 C.F.R. § 10.41a(a)1.[19] However, it noted that CSDs not attached to the container cannot be classified as an IIT. Mexican treatment, however, is still unclear.

Treatment within the North American Free Trade Agreement (NAFTA)

With respect to North America, the United States and Canada are original signatories, and each ratified CCC, Canada in 1975 and the United States in 1984.[20] Mexico has not. That does not mean that Mexico cannot accept or apply CCC standards. Mexico can if it so chooses. However, often firms now beginning to use these CSDs are concerned about how Mexican Customs (Aduana) will treat the CSD with respect to tariff classification and duties, given that NAFTA generates significant trade. That trade volume also suggests linked security questions. NAFTA has no reference to tariff treatment of IITs. In fact, the tariff schedules of the United States, Canada, and Mexico constitute three separate volumes of the agreement. The commonality of Customs process among the three nations is linked to the World Customs Organization (WCO) standards and to other treaties into which all three nations have entered. This means that while the United States and Canada are signatories and follow the articles of the CCC, Mexico has not ratified or accepted the CCC and is not compelled to follow its guidelines. Therefore, while IITs are treated similarly in both Canada and the United States, they are not treated the same way by Aduana.

Attempts have been made to obtain the official guidelines from Mexico regarding the Customs treatment of IITs without success. However, opinions from respected Mexican Customs brokers suggest that IIT tariff treatment is similar. As long as the CSD is attached to the container for use as a container monitoring and security accessory, it will not be subject to duties. One broker's opinion is this:

> In theory, if the device is attached to the trailer, from my perspective it will not have to [be] declared independently, for it is a part of the trailer's security overall devices and thus it is not to be used for any other purpose but to bring security to the products contained inside of the cargo bay. . . . If it is by itself then it will have to be declared and potentially pay duties and taxes, and I say "potentially" for if the importer has a temporary import scheme in place then these duties could be evaded.

Another Mexican broker's opinion is this:

> The short of it is that for MX Customs purposes and the commercial cargo, there is no declaration. *But* for MX Customs for the temporary bond that the MX carrier will post, the GPS equipment will be listed on there as part of the container/van. That way when the trailer is returned to the USA and the bond is cancelled on the MX Export side, the GPS unit will show up and the bond will be cancelled with the GPS unit by the MX carrier with MX Customs.

The GPS unit has nothing to do with the admissibility of the cargo and the commercial invoice declaration. In many countries in the world, CSDs will not have to be declared or duties paid on their entry when they are used as accessories attached to the container, an IIT. However, it appears that Mexico is a little different. The CSD is likely to have to be covered by the carrier's, importer's, or Customs broker's bond as a temporary entry. There may even be a small cost if it is treated as a temporary entry. Mexico is simply different. Because it is, the use of a very good Mexican Customs broker is essential.

Postscript

On December 11, 2010, I asked the Mexican Embassy for comment on the situation or any assistance it could give to resolve this question. Subsequent telephone conversations with the embassy resulted in a request that I should not write anything about this situation until the embassy had the opportunity to obtain a clarification from Aduana (Mexican Customs). With the understanding and concurrence of the embassy, I agreed not to write anything until the end of January 2011, giving sufficient time for Aduana to publish or make available an official determination. It appears that the Mexican Embassy did all it could do to help clear up the issue. Despite the cooperation of the Mexican Embassy, as of January 31, 2011, the embassy was unable, perhaps because of new leadership in Aduana, to obtain any determination or ruling as to the official Mexican Customs treatment of CSDs, thus freeing me to write about this situation.

CONCLUSION

Smart containers know when they are breached or entered, when their internal environment changes, where they are, how to talk, when to start and stop talking, what to say, and when to begin and end being smart. They exist now, they are getting more sophisticated, and they offer to the world knowledge of where any given product is and its condition. They are even smart enough to generate revenue for the user while offering protection to all of us. What is missing is government's support for them. Their increased use will ultimately depend on government incentives and benefits, in spite of possibly being smarter than the governments that want them.

NOTES

1. Broad Agency Announcement (BAA), HSARPA BAA07-02A, SAFE Container (SAFECON) Program, February 1, 2007.
2. James Giermanski, "No More Excuses or Delays," *American Shipper*, October 2006, pp. 2–4; GAO-07-347R, *Combat Nuclear Smuggling*, April 2007.

3. Devabhaktuni Srikrishna, A. Narasimha Chari, and Thomas Tisch, "Nuclear Detection: Portals, Fixed Detectors, and NEST Teams Won't Work for Shielded HEU on a National Scale, So What Next?" May 16, 2005, p. 1, http://iis-db.stanford.edu/evnts/4249/disarm.pdf.

4. Robert W. Kelly, *Containing the Threat: Protecting the Global Supply Chain through Enhanced Cargo Container Security,* The Reform Institute, October 3, 2007, pp. 8–9.

5. Currently, if CBP examines a container, all others listed on the entry are held in the port until the initial inspection is completed. In April 2007, CBP claimed to be developing a new procedure for C-TPAT participants that would require only the container(s) targeted for exam to be held, thereby reducing demurrage fees. Under this procedure, trusted C-TPAT importers would be allowed to move the remaining containers to their premises, keeping the container(s) and seals intact, until Customs lifted the hold on the entire shipment.

6. SAFE Port Act, Section 215(b).

7. SAFE Port Act, Section 216(b).

8. SAFE Port Act, Section 216(c).

9. Abdoulaye Diop and David Hartman, *Customs-Trade Partnership Against Terrorism Cost/Benefit Survey Report of Results*, Weldon Cooper Center for Public Service, University of Virginia, August 2007, p. 47.

10. Barchi Peleg-Gillae, Gauri Bhat, and Lesley Sept, *Innovators in Supply Chain Security*, The Manufacturing Institute, Stanford University, July 2006, p. 4.

11. A. T. Kearney, *Smart Boxes*, July 28, 2006, p. 1.

12. Kearney, *Smart Boxes*, p. 2.

13. James Giermanski, "Security Worth the Cost, of Course," *American Shipper*, June 2007, p. 4.

14. Customs Convention on Containers, 1972, Customs Cooperation Council, United Nations/International Maritime Organization, Geneva, December 2, 1972, p. 4.

15. Customs Convention on Containers, 1972, p. 7.

16. HQ H044900, December 18, 2008 BOR-4-07OT:RR:BSTC:CCI H044900, p. 1.

17. Customs Convention on Containers, 1972, p. 8.

18. HQ H005096, March 12, 2007 BOR-4-07-RR:BSTC:CCI H005096, p. 1.

19. HQ H044900, December 18, 2008 BOR-4-07OT:RR:BSTC:CCI H044900.

20. Pacific Islands Treaties Series Status Report, http://www3.paclii.org/pits/english/status_pages/1972-3.html.

Chapter Six

The Need for a Global Chain of Custody

Tracking, tracing, and custody are all generally accepted concepts involving the control of movement, and we often hear from the major logistics service providers about how good their tracking services are. And, in fact, they are pretty good. These tracking, tracing, and custody concepts have in their fundamental cognitive structure the idea of path, corridor, multiple parts, flow, coordination, and ultimate union control: "the union of connected sets whose intersection is not empty is still connected."[1] However, what is often omitted or overlooked is the fundamental sine qua non, the core principle, of "beginning." What is the beginning of a chain of custody (CoC)? A CoC must start at the beginning of the connective custody and control process. In this chapter, I will address the significance of cargo stuffing, the concept of authorized or trusted agent, the means of connectivity, the legal role of that authorized agents, and the consequences of a connected and visible supply chain.

What tracking and tracing do not provide is a genuine chain-of-custody system, even though some carriers claim they do. They cannot provide that beneficial service because of two essential reasons. First, their shipping containers are not sealed and monitored for access from origin to destination, and second, the signature of the person who verifies the cargo and its quantity and seals the container is not present. Without the identity of the person and the person's signature attesting to the contents, there cannot be a chain of custody, but only a system of tracking—if, in fact, the movement of the container or trailer is actually monitored. The distinction is extremely important with respect to the global supply chain and its use, especially in the distribution of counterfeit products, drugs, and even WMDs (weapons of mass destruction).

LOADING THE CONTAINER

Establishing and maintaining cargo integrity begins with stuffing the container at origin. A chain of custody involves "the movement and location of physical evidence from the time it is obtained until the time it is presented in court."[2] As in a criminal case, a supply chain CoC needs three types of essential assertions: (1) that the cargo is what it purports to be and in the quantity stated; (2) that the cargo was in the continuous possession or control of the carrier who took charge of the cargo from the time it was loaded in the container at origin until the time it was delivered at its final destination; and (3) that there is evidence of the identify of each person or entity who had access to it during its movement and that the cargo remained in the same condition from the moment it was sealed in the container for transfer to the carrier that controlled possession until the moment the carrier released the cargo into the receipted custody of another. All elements of cargo information, container identification, and identification of the person verifying the cargo and all who had access to it during movement will be maintained electronically in secure servers of the container security device (CSD) provider's control system.

The Trusted Agent

From its beginnings in the Revised Kyoto Convention (RKC) of 1999, there began a clear move to simplify customs procedures, maximize the use of electronic information technology, automate targeting, and change from a paper trail to e-commerce, not only to ensure proper tariff revenue collection but also to facilitate trade to make international movement of cargo through customs more efficient and less expensive for the global trading community. As a result of the RKC agreement and the initial U.S. development of its supply chain security program the Customs-Trade Partnership Against Terrorism (C-TPAT), the World Customs Organization (WCO) developed its SAFE Framework of Standards. The SAFE Framework then became the source of the European Union's authorized economic operator (AEO) supply chain security program and the genesis for the concept of an "authorized person."[3] Following these movements, the new Incoterms® 2010 published by the International Chamber of Commerce went into effect in January 2011. These commercial rules are linked to the United Nations Convention on Contracts for the International Sale of Goods (CISG), which are the international rules of commercial contracts and contain and demonstrate a new focus on the security role of the shipper and its obligation and legal liability to ship what was ordered. There is also international movement to ratify the new Rotterdam Rules, which, when ratified, will place the responsibility and liability for cargo content on the vessel carrier. These three private-sector responsibilities are treated later in a single chapter.

In the United States the "trusted agent" concept comes from the Federal Information Management Act and relates not to the supply chain but to information technology (IT) security. According to a recent e-mail from a senior Department of Homeland Security (DHS) manager, the trusted agent concept "is very broad, in that it can be other DHS government agents, other country customs or regulatory agents, could be a security officer for the shipper, person that is submitting the cargo data to ACE (Customs broker, freight forwarder, etc.), even the person closing the door and arming the devices." This broad U.S. interpretation, however, completely misses or distorts the essence of the concept—knowing what was loaded in the container.

Without knowing the cargo, the initial point of connectivity is essentially inoperable as the starting point. Even the following customs programs discuss, in one way or the other, the concept that the supply chain security begins as "stuffing":

- Secure Export Scheme Program (New Zealand)
- Partners in Protection Program (Canada)
- Golden List Program (Jordan)
- Authorized Economic Operator Program (Japan)
- Authorized Economic Operator Program (Korea)
- Secure Trade Partnership Plus Program (Singapore)
- Authorized Economic Operator Program (European Union)

Thus, it is imperative that the initial point of a connectivity process begin *at the beginning*! Loading cannot take place without a human agent. The human agent could be the company's forklift driver, the dispatcher, the loading dock supervisor, or even an authorizing manager who has a specific duty to verify the cargo and its quantity. It could even be a third party hired by the shipper—for instance, SGS or Cotecna, which currently provide inspection services around the world. Regardless of agent type, the agent must attest to the conveyance's contents and be identified as the one who verifies the cargo, arms the CSD, and seals the container for its global movement—the essential beginning of a connective chain of custody maintained to destination.

The Means of Connectivity

Maintaining connectivity in the chain-of-custody system depends on the security program, software, and hardware utilized. While no system is 100% effective and one cannot depend on technology alone, there are "off-the-shelf" CSDs that provide connectivity through a sophisticated, comprehensive CoC system that begins with the loading of the container at origin, monitors it, and reports its integrity to the end of the global supply chain path at destination. CSDs can include the identity of the trusted agent verifying the cargo at loading and the agent's counterpart at destination. Both parties are electronically connected by a unique identifier to the smart container system, along with bill of lading or booking information or data needed by customs authorities. Therefore, at CSD activation, the accountable party becomes the initiating element in the smart container security system that provides a legal chain of custody.

THE CONSEQUENCES OF A SOUND CHAIN OF CUSTODY

Security, Law Enforcement, and Compliance to Commercial Standards

If a smart container is opened at destination by an equally accountable person and cargo is missing, and there were no breaches detected, recorded, or reported, the accountable person at origin can face either disciplinary or criminal action by appropriate authorities. In effect, the chain-of-custody treatment of cargo can be the mirror image of the treatment of evidence for prosecution—for instance:

- Evidence found by the law enforcement officer = cargo that was actually loaded
- Identification of the officer who found the evidence = identification of the accountable individual verifying the cargo
- Officer's signature as the first component of or link in the evidence chain = electronic signature of the person verifying that the proper cargo and quantity was loaded
- Control of evidence by a third party in the evidence room awaiting use in trial = third-party command center's control of cargo movement, breach detection, and notifications
- Receipt and removal of evidence for trial = receipt and unloading of the cargo by an identified, accountable person at destination

Thus, like the chain of evidence, supply chain risk management is fundamentally an issue of control. What is absolutely clear is that the human element is the essential core of that issue. Global supply chain and container security systems are inextricably linked to detailed personnel selection, competence, and performance. Controlling risks in any international supply chain system must begin, be executed by, and end with the human component. Therefore, the combination of direct control in personnel selection and indirect control of intermediaries through systems—human quality combined with system quality—is or should be the main focus of risk management within the global supply chain. Additionally, with the use of CSDs, this kind of information will be maintained in worldwide control centers in the CSD provider's computer servers, which serve as repositories of electronically stored information (ESI) of any CSD transactions recorded during movement. This ESI becomes a source of evidence, should legal action follow.

A chain-of-custody process from origin to destination also supports Incoterms 2010, a publication of the International Chamber of Commerce that provides the playbook of international rules involving international sale of goods. These new terms now contain security requirements for the shipper, making a chain-of-custody system essential for compliance.

There are also changes coming for shippers, consignees, and vessel carriers with respect to carriage of goods by sea: the new Rotterdam Rules. According to the UN General Assembly, the Rotterdam Rules are a "uniform and modern global legal regime governing the rights and obligations of stakeholders in the maritime transport industry under a single contract for door-to-door carriage."[4] The new door-to-door liability places the vessel carrier directly in a CoC. Instead of the vessel carrier filing what the shipper says is in the container, the vessel carrier will be automatically and "actually be responsible to know" what is in the container.

This chain requires security throughout its carriage from stuffing, verification, and sealing at origin confirmed by an authorized agent who arms a container's security system and seals the container. All elements of cargo information, identification of the container in which it was sealed, identity of person verifying the cargo, all who had access to it during movement, and related dates and times will be maintained electronically in secure servers of the CSD provider's control system.

THE ROLE OF THE HUMAN ELEMENT

Whatever the chain of custody, the individual is the key component. The human factor is obvious in C-TPAT's core components, which include the following:[5]

1. Business partner security
   a. Written and verifiable process for the selection, including manufacturers, product suppliers, vendors
2. Procedural security
   a. Protection against unmanifested material being introduced into a shipment
   b. Record keeping
   c. Internal controls—inventories
   d. Manifest procedures
   e. Documentation verifications—quantity, quality, marking
3. Physical security
   a. Surveillance and lighting
   b. Proper communications systems
   c. Signage considerations
   d. Monitoring program for sensors and alarms
   e. Facilities—fencing, guards, alarms

    f. Shipping and receiving controls

    g. Theft prevention—limited access to shipping areas, back dock procedures

4. Access controls

    a. Identification requirements—entry and exit logs, photo ID, escorts, package scans

5. Personnel security

    a. Background checks—criminal, credit, driving, employment history

    b. Employment screening—background, drug screening

    c. Code of conduct—distributed and acknowledged

6. Education, training, and threat assessment

    a. Employee requirements, incentives

7. Information technology security

    a. Passwords, usage accountability

8. Container security

    a. Stuffing and destination controls

    b. Breach detection devices

    c. Monitoring shipment progress

9. Container inspection

    a. Seven-sided inspection (right and left sides, ends/doors, ceiling/floor, undercarriage)

While personnel security is directly focused on the individual, each core component is dependent on the human factor. The remaining eight components are extensions of personnel security and confirm the importance of the individual in executing C-TPAT requirements. Therefore, in the global supply chain, custody begins with the identity of the person who verifies the cargo, its quantity, its conveyance, and all else necessary under the contract for carriage. From the time of loading, transferring, or allowing access, there must be a signature or identification of anyone allowed proper access. That signature today can be electronic in nature and as legal as a pen and paper signature, as allowed by recent changes to the Federal Rules of Civil Procedure. The new changes to the federal civil procedure rules prevent the fraudulent manipulation of paper documentation and facilitate the use of "single window" concepts of electronic data interchange, which expedite and improve efficiencies in the international movement and control of cargo.

APPLICATION TO CONTAINER OR TRAILER MOVEMENT

The reality of global trade necessitates the use of containers and trailers that today can be secured and monitored throughout their international movement by the use of CSDs. These devices, in turn, can necessitate the use of unique identification codes to identify the particular person who certifies the container's content and its quantity at origin. Their use impacts both security and efficiencies. For instance, a person who certifies the container's contents at origin and seals the container at the time of certification can become an obvious target of investigation if the container arrives with cargo other than that certified and the container had custodial care from origin to destination capable of detecting and reporting any unauthorized access during its global movement. All elements within this chain of custody are stored and available for law enforcement and company officials evaluating a potential criminal act or merely the competency of the individual verifying the cargo at origin. Specifically, a chain-of-custody system provided by the software of the CSD itself creates the following benefits:

- It provides a unique code identifying the accountable person, confirming container contents, activating the CSD, and sealing the container at origin.
- The transport container carries data to include contents and logistics and shipping data regarding the container number, shipper, consignee, vessel (if carried by vessel), master, ports of lading and discharge, and other analogous data.
- It detects a breach into the container, and communicates date, time, location, and duration of access into the container to interested parties, including the owner, U.S. government agencies or equivalent foreign agencies, and so on.
- It offers various sensors such as infrared motion sensors, sound sensors, location sensors (such as GPS, or global positioning system), temperature sensors, vibrations sensors, magnetic switches, and radiation sensors as well as sensors that are sensitive to chemical, electrical, magnetic, motion, etc. changes associated with the transport container or with the environment within the interior of the container.
- It offers communication by satellite, mobile telephony, and radio frequency identification (RFID), if utilized.
- It provides a deactivation code to identify the authorized individual and place accountability on that person to confirm the contents of the transport container at an intermediate point within the route and at the final destination of the shipping container.

CONSEQUENCES AND POTENTIAL BENEFITS OF USE

Shipper Benefits

- Confirmation and electronic certification of proper cargo and quantity leaving the origin facility
- Control of access and entry into the container
- Worldwide tracking and location of container for security and asset management
- Identification and placement into the supply chain of the identity of the company employee who certifies the contents of the container at sealing at origin and opening at destination (end-to-end visibility)
- Lower insurance costs

- Knowledge of departure from foreign port to destination port
- Knowledge of carrier's sail or over-the-road or rail transport time
- Expedited entry of cargo by CBP and faster through-port time
- Database intelligence identifying weak points/delays/security-risk areas in the supply chain
- Verification of compliance with Incoterms 2010 and the UN Convention of Contracts for the International Sale of Goods (CISG), specifically articles verifying cargo and quantities shipped

Consignee Benefits

- Verification of cargo and quantity and electronic certification at stuffing
- Knowledge of departure time
- Location of container throughout the supply chain
- Knowledge of opening or surreptitious access into container
- Third-party verification of all supply chain data elements and reports
- Knowledge of arrival
- Lower insurance costs
- Verifications of compliance with CISG importer provisions
- Increased or enhanced knowledge needed for Customs Importer Security Filings
- Enhanced knowledge of shipper and carrier

Carrier Benefits

- Access control into container and knowledge of container location
- Protection against claims by shippers that unauthorized contents were the result of carrier action
- Certification and verification of identity of shipper and contents
- Marketing and sales tool to increase market share in providing secure containers to shippers
- Automatic transmission to CBP of container data, for instance in the CF-1302 or data used in electronic filings such as data required by the Automated Commercial Environment (ACE) system.
- Database intelligence identifying weak points/delays/security-risk areas in supply chain
- Compliance with and protection within the new Rotterdam Rules impacting vessel carriers

CBP Benefits

- Knowledge of which containers need no inspection, improving management efficiency

- Identification of suspect container based on real-time or close to real-time electronic reports of authorized access or presence of WMD or other dangerous or illegal cargo inserted or present in the container signaled by a break in the chain
- Faster transmission of electronic data into CBP and ACE system
- Elimination of third-party reporting of trade data (i.e., motor carriers and border Customs brokers)
- Enhancement of 10+2 Importer Security Filings
- Enhanced knowledge of actual container contents from an identified supervisory employee who certifies shipment contents and quantity at stuffing
- Evidentiary data for potential legal action[6]

AN EXAMPLE OF HOW CSD USE CAN PROVIDE BENEFITS

Given these benefits, there seems to be a direct correlation with the problem the United States has with counterfeit products. Take, for example, this statement from John Morton, director of Immigration and Customs Enforcement:[7]

> We need to convince people that counterfeiting spells trouble for America, pure and simple, all right. We all know it robs Americans of jobs. It robs Americans of innovation and creativity. We need to make the point that it fuels organized crime, not in the abstract—it's not the corner of Fourth and Main—it is organized crime, and that's where the money goes; and our focus here today is that it creates a serious risk of harm to consumers. And we've got to make sure that that latter point, that counterfeiting threatens the health and safety of Americans, is not just taken as an abstract concern. It's an immediate problem.

We often see headlines like this: "ICE seizes more than $350,000 worth of counterfeit merchandise, cosmetics at area swap meets" (December 14, 2010)[8] or "ICE arrests 13 on document fraud, conspiracy, identity theft charges" (December 16, 2010).[9] However, we do *not* see headlines like these: "ICE intercepts and prevents the entry into U.S. commerce of a container of counterfeit Viagra" or "ICE, in cooperation with Mexican Customs, intercepts container with a weapon of mass destruction (WMD) added to banana shipment from Guatemala through Mexico to Port of Long Beach." We don't because the Department of Homeland Security does not use electronic traceability and container security solutions to control the entry of unlawful or dangerous cargo. In fact, DHS and CBP still require paper documentation, as indicated by CBP itself. In its statement "Overview of Textiles: A Priority Trade Issue (PTI),"[10] CBP said: "Some importers circumvent quotas by transshipment—changing the country of origin of their goods. Still others use false documents or labels or provide incorrect descriptions of the merchandise." Although CBP is doing significantly more in electronic data collection, it stills depends in some areas, like textiles, on the validity of the documents furnished.

There are also concerns about food safety. For instance, in a recent article in *American Shipper*, butter seemed to be contaminated by the use of certain plastic pallets carrying the fire retardant decabromodiphenyl ether (decaBDE). The National Wooden Pallet and Container Association suggested close examination of these pallets.[11] Today, this retardant and chemical preservatives can be detected in containers before they reach the United States.[12] Of course, some food products imported from China have also been shown to be contaminated. A recent example reflects the seriousness of the issue. An investigation by U.S. ICE Homeland Security Investigations (HSI) revealed that Chung Po Liu, 70, of Bellevue, Washington, pled guilty to federal charges that he purchased honey in China

> from Changge Jixiang and had it shipped to the Philippines or Thailand. The honey was re-labeled there to make it appear it was a product from these countries. When the honey arrived in the United States, Liu submitted documents to U.S. Customs and Border Protection (CBP) falsely claiming that the imported honey was produced in Thailand or the Philippines, when in fact it originated in China.[13]

Unlike the United States, the European Union (EU), through EC Regulation No. 1935/2004, has required all foodstuffs to be monitored from origin to destination. Thus, the EU makes it a requirement that these products be monitored in their movement from one country to another. Why is it not a normal requirement and practice of CBP to mandate the tracing of incoming cargo, especially foodstuffs and pharmaceuticals? The answer could be that traceability necessitates the use of container security solutions about which DHS seems to know very little.

CSDs are able to monitor movement of containers internationally and domestically from origin to destination. However, there is much more that CSDs can do than just report location. The smartest containers are smart because they can carry on a conversation. The user or their international control center ("platforms") can communicate with them, depending on the programming, sensors, and technology used, in real time or close to real time. Tracking and tracing functions, traits of a mentally challenged smart container, merely monitor location by RFID fixed antennas or by satellite or cellular communication, depending on the level of communication latency the user is willing to accept. However, the very smart containers also electronically tell the contents of the container, who supervised loading the cargo and who is accountable for the accuracy of the contents at origin, the time the container was sealed, when it left origin, its route, its internal environment, its progress, whether it deviated from its course, its arrival at port of embarkation, when it was loaded aboard the vessel, whether it was breached, when it arrived at the destination port, and who opened it and verified the cargo.

And there are companies out there that can provide smart containers now. Just a few of these companies are GlobalTrak, European Datacomm, Lojack, Secur-Track, and GateKeeper. And there are more. There are also multiple satellite service providers like Iridium, ORBCOMM, Inmarsat, Europe's Galileo, and the Chinese entry into satellite communication, Compass, that can provide position detection at relatively low cost. There also others in the telecommunications and satellite service arena such as Telenor-Traxion (Norway/Sweden), Vodafone (UK), Sing Tel (Singapore), Thuraya (UAE), and Telefonica (Spain).

Smart containers and satellite service providers are logical, functional, and available today, and they could serve as a weapon against smugglers, counterfeiters, and terrorists. With respect to the global supply chain, and perhaps in other ways, why does DHS react in an undeniably reactive fashion, waiting for something to happen before putting assets against it? Actually, there is also a case for mandating the use of traceability solutions because these solutions are beneficial to the user's bottom line.

CONCLUSION

The application of a chain-of-custody system is more than compelling. It would assist law enforcement, solve transshipment problems, impair drug cartel use of commercial traffic into the United States, reduce counterfeiting, eliminate the in-bond problem of unauthorized container access, control hazmat movement and movement of other dangerous cargo, and even provide for automatic hazmat emergency response guidelines to first responders in the event of an accident and resultant spill. Finally, these off-the-shelf systems will actually improve bottom-line revenue generation for the firms using them. The inescapable conclusion then becomes a question: Why aren't they being used?

NOTES

1. Jean Serra, "Connection, Image Segmentation, and Filtering," p. 1, http://cmm .ensmp.fr/~serra/communications_pdf/C-75.pdf.
2. "Chain of Custody," Lexis Nexis Applied Discovery, http://legal-dictionary.the freedictionary.com/chain+of+custody.
3. WCO SAFE Framework of Standards, pp. 12–46, http://www.gumruk.gov.tr/tr -TR/emevzuat/Uluslararas%20Szlemeler/SAFE%20Framework_EN_2007_for_publica-tion.pdf.
4. http://www.americanshipper.com/NewWeb/news_page_SNW2.asp?news=143570.
5. "C-TPAT Highway Carrier Security Criteria," CBP, March 13, 2006, http:// www.cbp.gov/xp/cgov/trade/cargo_security/ctpat/security_criteria/hwy_carrier_criteria/ hwy_carrier_criteria.xml.

6. CBP was queried about other potential benefits offered by this analysis with the request that they advise if they see other benefits. After two inquiries to them, they have not responded, which is perhaps an indicator of government–private sector cooperation.

7. John Morton, director of Immigration and Customs Enforcement, White House Forum on Health and Safety Impact of Intellectual Property Theft, December 14, 2010.

8. "ICE Seizes More Than $350,000 Worth of Counterfeit Merchandise, Cosmetics at Area Swap Meets," U.S. Immigrations and Customs Enforcement, December 14, 2010, Las Vegas, http://www.ice.gov/news/releases/1012/101214lasvegas.htm.

9. "ICE Arrests 13 on Document Fraud, Conspiracy, Identity Theft Charges," U.S. Immigrations and Customs Enforcement, December 16, 2010, San Juan, http://www.ice.gov/news/releases/1012/101216sanjuan.htm.

10. "Overview of Textiles: A Priority Trade Issue (PTI)," http://www.cbp.gov/xp/cgov/trade/priority_trade/textiles/textiles_pti.xml.

11. Chris Gillis, "Plastic Pallet Fire Retardant in Butter?" http://www.americanshipper.com/NewWeb/news_page_SNW2.asp?news=177657.

12. Joe Harden, Consearch, December 21, 2010, e-mail explaining the detection capability.

13. "Seattle Businessman Who Imported Tainted Chinese Honey Sentenced," December 20, 2010, Seattle, http://www.ice.gov/news/releases/1012/101220seattle.htm.

A mobile X-ray unit in operation at a major American seaport. Photo by Department of Homeland Security.

CBP officers checking cargo being X-rayed. Photo by Department of Homeland Security.

Cargo being unloaded by CBP officers for checking. Photo by Department of Homeland Security.

The massive Los Angeles–Long Beach seaport and storage complex. Photo by Department of Homeland Security.

A remote border crossing in northern Montana. Photo by Department of Homeland Security.

The latest X-ray machines that can monitor high-speed trains without slowing traffic. Photo by Department of Homeland Security.

A CBP officer inspecting a truck for radioactive materials. Photo by Department of Homeland Security.

The major land port of entry at Hidalgo. Photo by Department of Homeland Security.

A major port of entry on the Mexican border, which can handle thousands of vehicles a day. Photo by Department of Homeland Security.

CBP officers removing drugs discovered at a checkpoint. Photo by Department of Homeland Security.

A CBP officer checking for hazardous materials. Photo by Department of Homeland Security.

A CBP canine officer and dog checking for explosive materials. Photo by Department of Homeland Security.

Coast Guard apprehending drug smugglers. Photo by Department of Homeland Security.

CBP agricultural specialists checking incoming produce. Photo by Department of Homeland Security.

A wedge bracket to prevent tampering. Photo by Department of Homeland Security.

...creasingly sophisticated container security devices that ...n be tracked globally. Photo by European Datacomm.

The European Datacomm tracking control center. Photo by European Datacomm.

A Cakeboxx being inspected at a major seaport. Photo by Department of Homeland Security.

Specialist X-ray equipment. Photo by Department of Homeland Security.

Chapter Seven

The U.S. Department of Homeland Security and Its Programs

The U.S. Department of Homeland Security (DHS) demonstrates a lack of focus, balance, and consistency in its anti-terrorism efforts. Focusing on government gropes or embarrassing X-rays of airline passengers and not addressing outbound containers or trailers demonstrates its folly. Which is a greater threat—airline passengers or containers and trailers? Are they equal? Are they proportional? It appears that DHS is not quite sure because if it were, it would spend as much time and effort on outbound containers as it does on outbound airline passengers—especially when air travelers are merely moving from one domestic location to another. Does a successful terrorist event have to occur before threats merit DHS attention? The greatest potential threat of death, injury, and destruction is not by air but rather by sea, truck, or rail. While no single death as a result of terrorism is tolerable, there is a fundamental and significant difference between the tragedy created by downing an aircraft and the tragedy of taking out a U.S. port that can occur from container or trailer movement into and out of ports. Taking out one major port can also lead to the destruction of our economy and, ultimately, injury to all of us.

CONTAINERS AND TRAILERS
AT SEAPORTS AND LAND PORTS

There is no question that 9/11 was carried out by terrorists departing U.S. airports. By using carry-on box cutters, they were able to use the full force of a passenger plane with fuel as the explosive to kill thousands of people and to destroy significant landmarks. That horrific act caused all air traffic to be grounded until it was safe to fly again. What would result if one container with thousands of pounds of military-grade explosives and radioactive materials, a weapon of mass destruction (WMD), exploded in one of our major seaports? Because of consequential "sympathy explosions,"[1] the container blast would not only kill and injure port personnel, but also people and infrastructure for miles beyond the port. Land ports and their surrounding populations are also clearly at risk. In Laredo, Texas, the largest commercial land port of entry on the southern border, a bomb of the type described would not only take out the Customs and port facilities, but also would close down the city. As a result of either of these scenarios, all U.S. seaports and commercial land ports of entry would close, but for much longer than the shutdown of air travel that followed 9/11. All inbound and outbound vessel movements would be affected. Vessels inbound to U.S. ports could not alter their port destination to Mexico or Canada for subsequent land transport into the United States by motor or rail carriers since these U.S. land ports would also be closed for inspection of all containers and trailers within the port. U.S. trade would stop![2]

Chapter 2 treats in detail the economic impact of closing our port system even for a short time. These scenarios would mean a major shutdown of the U.S. economy with resulting consequences for our trading partners—essentially, a worldwide catastrophe. In the degree of damage and suffering, there is no comparison between the consequences of bombs in suitcases, printer cartridges, or underwear and container explosions at our seaports and land ports.

DHS FOCUS AND CONSISTENCY

On April 2, 2008, Jayson P. Ahern, deputy commissioner of Customs and Border Protection (CBP), made a statement before the Committee on Appropriations, Subcommittee on Homeland Security, U.S. House of Representatives. One of the topics included in his statement was an explanation of the layers of security used by CBP to protect the nation against potential terrorism connected to commerce through U.S. ports. "CBP uses a multi-layered approach to ensure the integrity of the supply chain from the point of stuffing through arrival at a U.S. port of entry."[3] According to Ahern, there are five layers:

1. The 24-hour manifest
2. Screening through the automated targeting system (ATS) and National Targeting Center (NTC)
3. Partnerships with industry and the private sector, like the Customs-Trade Partnership Against Terrorism (C-TPAT)
4. Partnerships with foreign governments, like the Container Security Initiative (CSI) and the Security Freight Initiative (SFI)
5. The nonintrusive inspection (NII) program

The goal of this layered approach is to combine these layers while limiting their combined effect on "hindering the movement of commerce through our ports."[4] Some of those in the trade community might take issue with this statement, believing that the layered approach has already hindered commerce. Others might take issue with the value of the layered approach in preventing a terrorist attack on a port of entry or interior target within the United States. I think that looking at each layer is important in appreciating this approach to security. Understanding the basics of each layer will indicate the knowledge CBP will likely have of the actual contents of containers reaching the United States.[5]

Layer 1: CSI's 24-Hour Manifest

In general, a cargo manifest is a document that indicates the identity and description of the cargo contained in a shipment. There is certainly no problem using data from the manifest to determine contents. However, the manifest is made by vessel carriers—shipping lines that have no idea of actual contents. Therefore, any problem will always be linked to the person or firm that completes the manifest and their real knowledge of the contents of a container. CSI's 24-hour rule places the responsibility of sending the manifest to CBP with the shipping line, specifically the liner that ladens (loads) the cargo into the vessel at the foreign port, carries it to the United States, and dischargies the cargo in the United States. "Carriers and/or automated NVOCCs [non-vessel operating common carriers] will be required to submit a cargo declaration 24 hours before cargo is laden aboard the vessel at a foreign port for any vessel beginning the voyage on or after December 2, 2002."[6] Originally, there were 14 types of data placed on the manifest; today there are 21.[7]

1. Carrier standard carrier alpha code (SCAC)
2. Last foreign port
3. Vessel name
4. Voyage number
5. International Maritime Organization (IMO) vessel ID number
6. Date of departure from port
7. Container number
8. Commodity description
9. Commodity weight
10. Bill of lading number
11. Shipper name and address
12. Consignee name and address
13. Hazmat code
14. Seal number
15. Numbers and quantity
16. Foreign port of lading
17. First foreign place of receipt
18. Vessel country

19. Date of arrival at first U.S. port
20. Port of unlading
21. Time of departure from port

Regardless of how many elements are in the manifest today, the fundamental reality is that all elements represent what the shipper, not an individual, says to be true. In effect, the manifest states what is *alleged* to be in the container. But the purpose of the 24-hour rule is to enable U.S. Customs to analyze container content information before a container is loaded and thereby decide on its "load/do not load" status in advance.[8] In reality, an NVOCC can be a motor carrier leasing space on liners. For instance, the Yellow Roadway trucking company is an NVOCC. Therefore, it accepts cargo from a shipper and provides the shipper a bill of lading to destination, including ocean travel, but Yellow Roadway does not own or operate an oceangoing vessel. Yet it is still the carrier to its shipper and then it's the shipper to the vessel carrier. But only those NVOCCs who are authorized to communicate with CBP through an approved electronic portal can file a manifest as the liner can.

There is a flaw in this layer. How does a carrier know what's in the container? The carrier does not open the container to inspect it. The carrier simply takes the word of the shipper. Who is the shipper? Does the carrier really know? Even if the carrier really knows, the carrier is still relying on the shipper's word for the contents of the container. What if we have a perfectly honorable and well-recognized shipper? Does that mean that between the stuffing of the container at origin and its arrival at the port of export, no surreptitious entry was made into that container and no WMD was placed in the container before it arrived at the port of export? Since the carrier does not know what is really in the container that arrived at the port, how would CBP know what was really in the container if CBP relied only on the carrier's manifest? Assuming the shipper has historically been honest and trustworthy, the likelihood of CBP's suspecting foul play is remote or nonexistent under this layered approach. Thus, any positive or special treatment given this container can be deadly to either the recipients of the container, the United States, or to the exporting port where the explosive could be meant to detonate.

Layer 2: Automated Targeting System (ATS) and National Targeting Center (NTC)

CBP says that ATS is one of the most advanced targeting systems in the world. "CBP uses ATS to improve the collection, use, analysis, and dissemination of information that is gathered for the primary purpose of targeting, identifying, and preventing potential terrorists and terrorist weapons from entering the United States. Additionally, ATS is utilized by CBP to identify other violations of U.S. laws that are enforced by CBP."[9] Basically, CBP, through ATS, collects various data from itself through CBP's own systems (except for one, the Treasury Enforcement Communications System). These systems as they relate to cargo are:[10]

- the Automated Commercial System (ACS)
- the Automated Manifest System (AMS)
- the Automated Export System (AES)
- the Automated Commercial Environment (ACE)
- the Treasury Enforcement Communications System (TECS)

The data obtained include the following:[11]

> electronically filed bills, entries, and entry summaries for cargo imports; ship-pers' export declarations and transportation bookings and bills for cargo exports; manifests for arriving and departing passengers; land-border crossing and referral records for vehicles crossing the border; airline reservation data; nonimmigrant entry records; and records from secondary referrals, incident logs, suspect and violator indices, and seizures.

Although AMS and ACE are CBP-based, AES is not. "The Automated Export System (AES) is a joint venture between CBP, the Foreign Trade Division of the Bureau of the Census (Commerce), the Bureau of Industry and Security (Commerce), the Directorate of Defense Trade Controls (State), other Federal agencies, and the export trade community."[12] It's a central point through which exporters and/or their agents identify the products they are selling abroad. It serves primarily for export compliance and export data used by the Bureau of the Census. However, ATS does draw more data from one source that is not its own: TECS. TECS has access to the National Crime Information Center (NCIC) database which allows further access to the National Law Enforcement Tele-communications System (NLETS). TECS also includes names of individuals on terrorist watch lists.[13] The next obvious question is who analyzes the data. CBP uses the National Targeting Center (NTC).

The NTC was established in 2001 and provides target-specific information to CBP field offices. With more than 100 employees, the Center works around the clock. According to CBP, "The NTC has given CBP the ability to identify pre-viously unknown, as well as known, persons involved in terrorism."[14] Analysts (or targeters, as they are called by CBP) are CBP personnel. These targeters also do data mining to develop potential targets. CBP says that the NTC looks at any resource that could support a terrorist effort, ranging from individuals to raw materials that could be used in constructing nuclear and chemical weaponry.

However, like most of the layered approach, the Center does not have active "boots on the ground" collecting intelligence. Instead, it analyzes the same and similar data obtained from the 24-hour manifest and from its numerous other Customs forms. If the paper is wrong or incomplete, targeting can also be wrong or incomplete. In other words, while this NTC is very important, it still is a data center relying on data and not knowing what is really in any container coming to the United States.

Layer 3: Customs-Trade Partnership Against Terrorism (C-TPAT)

In this layer, electronic data and paper data are also essential elements of CBP's security. However, the C-TPAT layer is different. C-TPAT, as announced in 2001,[15]

> is an import-oriented program that provides incentives to shippers, such as reduced cargo exams and first-in-line priority for inspections, in exchange for adopting tight internal shipment processes for themselves and overseas business partners to prevent terrorists or criminals from slipping contraband or weapons into a container. CBP checks that companies follow approved security plans that meet minimum guidelines by visiting a company's headquarters and conducting sample audits of some foreign suppliers and transport providers.

C-TPAT was and is a voluntary program for industry, initially focused on large U.S. importers and exporters, ports/terminal operators, and carriers. Other participants have since been added, and today it has 12 different categories of participants. It began with only seven major importers. In 2010, it had over eight thousand certified members in the following categories:[16]

- Importers (3,822)
- Carriers (2,270), including U.S./Canada highway carriers, U.S./Mexico highway carriers, rail carriers, sea carriers, and air carriers
- Service providers (1,400), including U.S. Marine Port Authority and terminal operators
- Foreign manufacturers (674)

With C-TPAT, CBP accepts as true the data furnished by its participating entity unless it learns or knows otherwise. Like the ATS/NTC layer, and to some degree the CSI/SFI layer, information provided is only as good as the providers' knowledge or integrity. With C-TPAT, there are clear and mandated physical requirements for the C-TPAT participants that, if followed, can and do contribute to the security of this nation. Additionally, in C-TPAT, there are auditors who review actual participant procedures at real locations around the world. With C-TPAT there are "boots-on-the-ground" actions, not only data acceptance.

Layer 4: Container Security Initiative (CSI)
the Security Freight Initiative (SFI)

CSI addresses the threat to border security and global trade posed by the potential for terrorist use of a maritime container to deliver a weapon. CSI proposes a security regime to ensure that all containers that pose a potential risk for terrorism are identified and inspected at foreign ports before they are placed on vessels destined for the United States. Its core elements are:

Identify high-risk containers. CBP uses automated targeting tools to identify containers that pose a potential risk for terrorism, based on advance information and strategic intelligence.

Prescreen and evaluate containers before they are shipped. Containers are screened as early in the supply chain as possible, generally at the port of departure.

Use technology to prescreen high-risk containers to ensure that screening can be done rapidly without slowing down the movement of trade.

Through CSI, CBP officers work with host customs administrations to establish security criteria for identifying high-risk containers. Those administrations use nonintrusive inspection and radiation detection technology to screen high-risk containers before they are shipped to U.S. ports. CSI, as a reciprocal program, also offers its participant countries the opportunity to send their customs officers to major U.S. ports to target oceangoing, containerized cargo to be exported to their countries. Likewise, CBP shares information on a bilateral basis with its CSI partners. Japan and Canada currently station their customs personnel in some U.S. ports as part of the CSI program.[17] However, the CSI program is anchored in the 24-hour manifest rule. CBP officers are only allowed to physically inspect containers in the participating foreign country ports when authorized to do so by that nation's customs authorities. The CSI program is more dependent on data acquisition and analysis.

There is a link between CSI and SFI, but not an extensive one. First, SFI is a scanning project composed of radiation portal monitors to detect radiation through nonintrusive inspection (NII) imaging systems. NII is really intended for small-package imaging and border-crossing functions. SFI is active at only three ports at full capacity (Puerto Cortes, Honduras; Port Qasim, Pakistan; and Southampton, United Kingdom), as opposed to the 58 foreign ports participating in CSI. It was active in a limited capacity at Busan, Korea; Singapore; Port of Salalah, Oman; and Hong Kong.[18] However, because there are significant problems with the SFI project, further deployment of machines is being reviewed due to recent lessons learned, as revealed by CBP's deputy commissioner, Jayson P. Ahern, in his April 2, 2008, statement before the Committee on Appropriations, Subcommittee on Homeland Security. Ahern specifically cited 13 problem areas with SFI.

Essentially, CSI, like other layers, is really anchored in data flow. Its validity is only as good as the accuracy of the data submitted. SFI is similar but slightly different; it's only as good its operators and the sophistication of its technology. According to the trade community, it is inefficient, and according to scientists, SFI is 100% *ineffective* for detecting highly enriched, shielded uranium.[19] The technology is still being developed. The project is limited in scope, and there is serious discussion about its acceptance and application around the world. In June 2008, the World Customs Organization (WCO) called for the repeal of a U.S. law requiring all inbound maritime cargo containers to be scanned at foreign ports by July 1, 2012.[20] And on June 11 in a report to Congress, DHS released all of the lessons learned from the SFI operational ports. In light of what the report revealed, it is doubtful if SFI will continue, given the level of sophistication of its development and technology and the objections of the other trading nations.

Layer 5: Nonintrusive inspection (NII)

NII is mobile gamma-ray imaging technology. It is deployed at seaports and at land ports of entry, permitting officers to detect and interdict contraband (such as narcotics, weapons, and currency) hidden within conveyances and/or cargo while simultaneously facilitating the flow of legitimate trade and travel. The mobile gamma-ray imaging system employs a gamma-ray source that permits officers to quickly see inside tankers, commercial trucks, cargo containers, and other conveyances without having to physically open the conveyance and/or container. NII machines can scan vehicles up to 125 feet in length in one pass. One version of the system is mounted on a truck chassis and is operated by a three-man crew. NII operates by slowly driving past a parked vehicle with a boom extended over the target vehicle.[21]

As a layer, NII is almost equivalent to "boots on the ground." It detects something it sees. It is not data-centered. While often the densities it reads may not turn out to be guns, drugs, or currency, but only something resembling them, NII does have very clear security usage. In fact, NII has been used at the Super Bowl in 2008 and at NASCAR events, in addition to its port security duties.

As explained in chapter 2, for DHS, the focus is not on outbound containers but, instead, on the Transportation Security Administration's (TSA) patdowns or X-rays for adult travelers, and CBP, which is responsible for container traffic, focuses only on inbound traffic—imports. DHS and CBP seem oblivious to security vulnerability to our ports posed by cargo *leaving* the United States. Each of CBP's four major container security programs—the Container Security Initiative (CSI), Customs Trade Partnership Against Terrorism (C-TPAT), the Secure Freight Initiative (SFI), and nonintrusive inspection (NII)—has one focus: inbound cargo. Other nations, however, recognize the security importance of outbound containers. These shipments are so important to the European Union (EU) that the EU's Authorized Economic Operator (AEO) security program, a counterpart to C-TPAT, acknowledges the outbound risk as equal to inbound, requiring documentation and information about EU exporters of products through its ports.

Clearly, if 100% of adult airline travelers *are* a security risk and each has to be examined for what each can attach to his or her body, then what is the risk of exported containers, which are apparently not considered a security risk and are 100% excluded from a security inspection, unless for cause? DHS's current practice of inspecting all adult airline travelers is about as distorted as deciding to inspect all domestic trailers moving from one city to another city because a trailer could explode en route to or at its destination city.

A SOURCE OF CBP ADVICE

One has to wonder where DHS and CBP are getting their advice. Does the private sector have any input? The answer is yes—perhaps unfortunately, yes. The main source of input and advice from the private sector comes from a special committee called COAC (Advisory Committee on Commercial Operations of Customs and Border Protection). Many have questioned more than once the value of COAC, especially about its membership's self-interests.[22] But now there is serious question about its role in the security of this nation's borders and ports. COAC's obvious weaknesses are first, its latest charter, and second, the self-interest of COAC's nongovernment membership, which places protecting and promoting company and industry values over the greater security of U.S. trade infrastructure essential to our nation's economic base. It has value to DHS, which needs to claim it understands both trade and security for the political agenda of the administration.

COAC's Charter or Purpose

In 2004, the COAC charter was changed to reflect the added need to be concerned about homeland security within the new Department of Homeland Security's structure and mission. Specifically, the charter stated:[23]

> The Committee shall advise the Secretaries of the Department of the Treasury and the Department of Homeland Security on the commercial operations of Customs and Border Protection (CBP) and related DHS and Treasury functions. It is expected that, during its eleventh two-year term, the Committee will consider such issues as: enhanced border and cargo supply chain security . . . and the CBP mission, and import safety.

Note: "The Committee shall advise . . . on commercial operations. It is expected that . . . the Committee will consider . . . enhanced border and cargo supply chain security."[24] In fact, the word *security* can be found only seven times, six of which are its use in the title Department of Homeland *Security*. Words such as *container, explosives, WMD, chemical, narcotic, drug, counterfeit,* or *air* are not found. However, the word *trade* appears three times: twice in titles (Deputy Assistant Secretary for Tax, *Trade* and Tariff Policy and Office of *Trade* Relations): and once as it directly relates to the qualifications of the membership:[25]

> Members are selected from representatives of the trade or transportation community served by CBP or others who are directly affected by CBP commercial operations and related functions. The members shall represent the interests of either importers (and their agents) or those associated with the carriage of international freight. . . . Members shall represent the interest of either importers (and their agents) or those associated with carriage of international freight and are not Special Government Employees as defined in section 202 (a) of Title 18, United States Code.

The charter allows for subcommittees to be established, presumably to ensure that DHS and CBP obtain information from supply chain security experts. There is a subcommittee called the Global Supply Chain Security Subcommittee.[26]

> COAC may establish subcommittees for any purpose consistent with this charter subject to the approval of the co-chairs. Such subcommittees may not work independently of the chartered committee and must report their recommendations and advice to the COAC for full deliberation and discussion.

Subcommittee Expertise in Security and Focus

In 2010, the committee had 19 members. The members represented typical areas of industry involving trade: import/export facilitators, manufacturers, trade specialists and facilitators, legal firms involved in trade compliance, insurance-related firms, customs brokers and forwarders, transportation firms, the air transport association, and one lone seaport expert. A review of numerous minutes from this subcommittee, which was designed to address supply chain security, reveals the committee's lack of experienced supply chain security experts, security technology experts, and transportation security experts. Most obvious is the absence of supply chain security technology experts. The committee is not totally without expertise in security. Testimony on port security by one member disclosed a breadth and depth of knowledge regarding containers and seaport security and the vital role they play in sustaining our economy. However, as expected, the membership's first objective seems to be to prevent the government from mandating unnecessary requirements that increase costs to the trade community.

Besides weak qualifications in security, the committee focus is also a detriment to our security. It appears that this membership is virtually consumed with the concept of cost and not the concept of supply chain security—which when used, decreases costs and increases revenue and profit. It's clear that these industry representatives do not understand how certain costs result in profit and position the firm to improve its business posture and competitive advantage.

The challenge for the committee, however, is to comprehend the value of national security connected to supply chain efficiency and security—and to set expectations accordingly. More important, the committee's paramount and overriding duty is to secure our ports and border, not to lobby for fewer CBP controls and mandates.

Subcommittee Solutions

First, the mandate of the subcommittee must be changed from "[it] is expected that it will consider" to "it shall advise on supply chain security." Second, it is important that the mix of membership and backgrounds include the following type of executives or specialists: port security experts, border security experts, trade and intellectual property rights experts, security corporate executives, and, most important of all, supply chain security experts similar to those who belong to the newly formed national Cargo Intelligence Security and Logistics Association (CISLA), which represents a cross-section of security technology experts devoted to securing and improving the value and efficiency of the supply chain as it links to our economy, and who place security first.

Third, the role of the membership should include the advice and counsel needed for DHS and CBP to be more engaging and cooperate with other nations in international efforts to secure the supply chain. In its *Bottom-Up Review Report*, DHS has acknowledged this to a certain degree:[27]

- Enhance partner capability and capacity . . . important aspects of core homeland security mission activities
- Deepen international engagement . . . We must work with key international partners to improve the critical partnerships and activities that affect the homeland security mission
- Strengthen and expand DHS-related security assistance internationally (e.g., border integrity and customs enforcement security assistance) consistent with U.S. government security and foreign assistance objectives in consultation and coordination

Fourth, it should learn more about the bottom-line benefits of supply chain security and security technology. A study on the value of smart container usage from Stanford University pointed to quantifiable benefits such as a 50% increase in access to supply chain data, a 38% drop in theft and similar losses, a 14% cut in excess inventory, and 29% reductions in overall transit times. The consulting firm BearingPoint has calculated returns of up to $700 per container per move.

An A. T. Kearney report showed a savings of $1,150 per container per move, while the U.S. Congressional Budget Office stated savings of 0.8% of the value of a smart container's contents.

Finally, it is time for committee members to take positions for and not against the value of technology's role in the securing of the supply chain—a position about which they appear to be uniformed. Not knowing about the value of supply chain security technology is no excuse for dismissing it, as a recent statement of the committee suggests. As quoted in a feature on supply chain security in *World Trade 100*, Earl Agron, of the wholly owned subsidiary of Singapore-based Neptune Orient Lines, a global transportation and logistics company engaged in shipping and related businesses, said: "Today, ocean carriers, within hours of a container status change, record location data in their proprietary systems and make that data available to their customers. The supply chain security benefit of real-time container visibility is negligible."[28]

The bottom-line question is whose interests are represented on COAC's Global Supply Chain Security Subcommittee? For instance, in its meeting on October 7, 2010, Co-chair Earl Agron, in his opening remarks informed the committee that there will be only "twenty minutes allocated to Global Supply Chain Security at the November 9th COAC meeting." Again, whose interests matter? The Global Supply Chain Security Subcommittee is just that: a security committee. Now it only needs to act like one. It's time to fix it—before it's too late to fix it—and fixing it must start with a change in its leadership.

SOME HOPE

In February 2012, COAC announced that it will have a public meeting to hear from the following subcommittees on the topics listed and will then review, deliberate, and formulate recommendations on how to proceed.[29]

- Global Supply Chain Security Air Cargo Subcommittee: air cargo advance screening (ACAS) strategic plan for public release
- One U.S. Government at the Border Subcommittee: 2012 subcommittee work plan
- Intellectual Property Rights Enforcement Subcommittee: intellectual property rights distribution chain management concept

COAC will also receive an update on and discuss the following initiatives and subcommittee topics that were raised at its December 7, 2011, meeting:

- National Supply Chain Security Strategy
- C-TPAT and the Beyond the Border initiative
- Automation of ocean and rail manifest, cargo release, and other ACE automation pilots

- Centralization of single transaction bonds and coordination of bond issues that apply to other subcommittees
- Evaluation plan regarding the centers of expertise and simplified entry pilots
- Feedback on previously submitted recommendations on trade remedies and the role of customs brokers

Perhaps COAC got the message from last year's editorial treatment in more than one publication. Regardless, this is a good sign.

ONE LAST LITTLE PROBLEM

Twenty-five years ago with the help of some colleagues—one a reserve officer in the Air Force Office of Special Investigations (AFOSI), one from the University of Alabama, and one from Troy State University—I wrote a book eventually published by the U.S. Department of Defense. The book, titled *The Training of Special IMAs Assigned to the Air Force Office of Special Investigations: An Empirical Analysis* examined the training of AFOSI special agents in the counterintelligence area. After extensive research and statistical evaluation of a scientifically sound and robust sample of input, I concluded, with statistical data to support our findings, that the counterintelligence training was poor and needed to be improved. As a result, the evaluation made the AFOSI hierarchy angry and my punishment was that they would not support me for a promotion to General. They also changed my Reserve assignment to the position of Reserve Commandant of the AFOSI Academy at Bolling Air Force Base.

To end the Air Force story, the curriculum was eventually changed to reflect a greater concentration in those operations that OSI special agents actually performed, especially in the counterintelligence field. I eventually worked in the field and even wrote one of the first "collection requirements" for a certain area of the world where we had Air Force assets and special agents. Finally, after not being included for years on the list of those to be considered for General, the Air Force Personnel Center called me one day to ask why I didn't want to be considered for General Officer. I explained the situation. Within a couple of hours I received a call from AFOSI Headquarters informing me that OSI would now support my promotion. That same day I returned my badge and credentials and resigned. I am again looking at the issue of training, but this time without colleagues or empirical evidence, and not as Air Force training, but rather the basic training provided to our CBP officers at the Federal Law Enforcement Training Center (FLETC), and without the risk of retaliation.

To appreciate the CBP training issue, one needs to understand the fundamental reason for CBP's existence and their new mission. After declaring U.S. independence in 1776 and almost being bankrupt with an immediate need for revenue, the First Congress passed the Tariff Act of July 4, 1789,[30] which was signed by President Washington on July 31, 1789, creating the Customs Administration and the nation's ports of entry. This first agency of the federal government became an organization of collectors "to regulate the Collection of the Duties imposed by law on the tonnage of ships or vessels, and on goods, wares, and merchandises imported into the United States."[31] For nearly 125 years, Customs funded virtually the entire government and paid for the nation's early growth and infrastructure. The legislation provided for presidential appointment of 59 collectors, 10 naval officers, and 33 surveyors. These collectors, under the direct authority of the Secretary of the Treasury, supervised the construction of over three hundred lighthouses, became the first Coast Guard, the first Veteran's Administration by assisting the nation's war veterans, the first Public Health Service by providing for the well-being of merchant seamen, the first Bureau of Standards by standardizing the nation's weights and measures, the first Immigration and Naturalization Service responding to immigrants seeking refuge in the United States, and even drug interdictors by having Customs mounted inspectors apprehending liquor smugglers during Prohibition. As all but its collection duties were assumed by separate agencies of government, Customs was left with its original mission, the collection of revenue and the proper function of our ports systems in supporting that function.

However, today Customs has a new mission: "And now, as we join the Department of Homeland Security, we face what may be our greatest challenge to date . . . protecting our nation and its people from acts of terrorism within our own borders."[32] Clearly the mission of Customs has become, under DHS, one of antiterrorism. Because of this gigantic mission change from its historical, important, if not critical role of tax collection to antiterrorism, there is now a question as to how well the new Customs or CBP is performing its traditional and historical role. There have been serious complaints of ineptitude in dealing with imports and exports, in-bonds, transshipments, and transcarriage issues primarily involving the importation of goods into the United States.

In light of this background, the natural question is what type of basic training is now provided to our CBP officers at FLETC? As an outsider, the only way I could examine CBP's training is by obtaining a copy of the training syllabus to see what educational areas of study and practice are covered in the program, how many hours are devoted to those areas, and what percentage of the total training hours are devoted to certain areas in which one would expect a Customs official to have expertise.

Access to and Contents of the Training Syllabus

The only syllabus available to the public was a 2003 edition that one can find online. Therefore, I had to go to insiders or former insiders in an attempt to obtain a current syllabus. Eventually, I was given the 2005 syllabus, which I was told is the one used today. I do not know if that is true. I was also told by insiders that the training as reflected in this syllabus is totally different from previous training Customs officials had in trade matters, such as the Harmonized Tariff Schedule of the United States (HTSUS), vessel and container inspection techniques, and historical Customs matters like duties and tariffs that need to be properly applied to products imported into the United States. I am also told that today the focus is not on these areas but instead on people, including air passengers, luggage, border crossers, crewmembers, and so on.

My primary insider, a retired CBP supervisor, made it very clear to me that many other retired and current CBP officers are also concerned about the shift of training away from ports and trade-related matters. Their concern is based on the natural link between historical Customs training connected to the collection of tariffs and duties, the control and knowledge of actual contents of in-bond shipments, and the knowledge and control of cargo manipulation within trans-shipment and transcarriage shipments and antiterrorism, since shipping containers are perfect hosts for WMD. One of the first difficulties of examining any government training is the use of unique acronyms used throughout the training syllabus. While I found the meaning of many, there were some I could not translate. These are some of the examples of the ones I tried to identify accurately.

AIS	automatic identification service
APIS	Advance Passenger Information Service
CFAS	Community First Aid and Safety (a guess)
TECS	Treasury Enforcement Communications System
NSEERS	National Security Entry Exit Registration System
BMI	body mass index
APHIS	Animal and Plant Health Inspection Service
PRD	personal radiation detector
PTD	Physical Techniques Division
PE	practical exercise or physical exercise
RMP/RIID	Radiation Monitoring Portals/Radiation Isotope Identification Device (?)
IACD	Inter-American Agency for Cooperation and Development
OC	oleoresin capsicum spray
PC	probable cause

Training Areas

Acronyms aside, the training program in the 2005 syllabus for CBP officers is fourteen 40-hour weeks long, or a total of 560 hours. However, there are eight examinations and some administrative time for welcome and orientation, uniform measuring, hepatitis shots, photos, and so on. Thus, actual training time appears to be 526 hours of instruction in classroom subjects, lab work, physical training, and hands-on applications of CBP functions like immigration matters, legal matters, inspection techniques, and many more areas. I examined the amount of training in the following subjects in relation to the total hours of training:

- Personal defensive (firearms, arrest techniques, self-defense, and the use of the baton)
- People-focused (questioning, observing, passenger processing, fingerprinting, nonimmigrant classification, immigrant classifications, etc.)
- Terrorism
- Trade
- Merchandise classification
- Cargo inspection

I was specifically looking for Customs trade and cargo training as a percentage of total training. I did not attempt to evaluate the law enforcement training typically devoted to legal matters, personnel matters, physical education training, hazmat, and agriculture, and training involving electronic sources of information such as the automatic identification service (AIS), the Treasury Enforcement Communications System (TECS); and the National Security Entry Exit Registrations System (NSEERS) which alone consumed many hours of training. There were also practical exercises involving equipment such as scanning techniques, report writing, seizure processing, and more.

However, what is important is the major thrust or focus of training—that is, what stands out with respect to the hours devoted to it, assuming that the intensity of instruction is relatively equal in quality. In other words, all one can do without doing empirical research into the program is to make generalized statements about the training content and hours of coverage in broad classifications without going into quality of instruction, class size, and equipment employed.

Hours of Training

I took the 526 hours of class time and divided it into people-focused, trade, terrorism, cargo-related, and merchandise classification instruction. People-focused instruction included the treatment of immigrants and nonimmigrants, crewmembers, passengers, and the questioning, observing, and fingerprinting of people as opposed to looking for or examining cargo. I did include the instructional hours devoted to physical defense training given to the CBP students in the people-focused criterion.

- People, 98 hours of instruction or about 19% of the instructional hours
- Self-defense (firearms, 36 hours; defensive tactics, 18 hours; baton, 8 hours; and defensive tactics, 18 hours), a total of 80 instructional hours or about 15%

- Trade, 23 hours or about 5%
- Cargo inspection, including passenger luggage, 20 hours or about 4%
- Merchandise classification, 4 hours or about .007%
- Sea container training, 2 hours or about .003%
- Processing land conveyances, 2 hours or about .003%
- Processing air conveyances, 2 hours or about .003%

There is a clear focus of instructional hours (98 hours) on legal and illegal entry of people and how CBP should treat these people, and on the areas of firearms use and safety, and self-defense techniques (80 hours). Combined, these two segments constitute 178 hours of the total 526 hours of training, or 34% of the total instruction given to new CBP trainees.

It also seems clear that the former concepts of trade, containers, tariffs, and duties are no long important enough for a trainee's professional preparation. Even CBP's new mission of antiterrorism accounts for only 10 hours, or about 2% of the total hours of training they receive. And how is it possible that 4 hours of merchandise classification are sufficient? It is clear that the current focus on immigration-related issues as opposed to trade issues is a distortion of proper Customs officers' basic training, including their new role of securing the United States against terrorism. How can DHS acknowledge the fact that 90% of all cargo moving into and out of the United States is by vessel and the containers they carry, and subsequently provide only 2 hours of instruction on sea containers out of a 526-hour program? Yet FLETC training for CBP does just that. How can a cadre of immigrations-handlers do the work of trade specialists? Trade specialists also provide for our security in a unique and truly distinct manner. They ensure the collection of appropriate taxes on imported products, inhibit the export of prohibited products, and at the same time provide a deterrent to the tremendous security vulnerabilities that vessel, truck, and rail traffic pose at our seaports and land ports of entry. The historical role of Customs has disappeared within DHS, along with the security inherent in historic Customs duties of supply chain and port security functions it used to provide to this nation.

CONCLUSION

While I have often criticized DHS and CBP for many of their decisions, policies, and management decisions, the layered system is fundamentally sound even though CBP's basic training may not be. The layered system is sound in spite of the lack of active intelligence gathering, the lack of container security technological applications that are currently available, and the lack of security advice and guidance from COAC. However, its weaknesses, while few, are significant. In fact, the tremendous reliance on basing security decisions on submitted information is a weakness that needs to be addressed. While C-TPAT is good, a recent Government Accountability Office (GAO) report in May 2008 pointed out numerous areas of concern. There are also GAO reports on the effectiveness of scanning at border ports of entry.

It seems that the layered security concept needs two more layers. The first is an actual intelligence/counterintelligence layer. That will be a problem. My personal experience with intelligence competency within CBP in the early to mid-1990s clearly revealed their lack of training and functioning in the intelligence area. Again, from personal experience with Customs on cross-border drug movements, I found that CBP had little or no expertise in developing intelligence. Since it was not their job to do so, one can expect it would not be done. In fact, there has always been a stigma attached to CBP's law enforcement history and status. For many in law enforcement, and for some outside of law enforcement, CBP had the image of armed government tax collectors and border guards. However, as of July 6, 2008, CBP officers have law enforcement retirement coverage, indicating a significant change in the perception that many had of them. CBP now has federal law enforcement status.[33] Under DHS, CBP clearly has enforcement status and all that should go with it, including an intelligence function.

Today there should also be greater cooperation between and among counterintelligence and law enforcement areas, unlike when I was an FBI agent. Yet it seems that it may still be a problem. What cooperation does CBP receive from those agencies that could help CBP in preventing terrorist acts? CBP's National Targeting Center should be fed more than CBP's own data. There should be, and hopefully there is, the sharing of intelligence collected by other federal law enforcement and intelligence agencies. Thus, the first new layer, the counterintelligence layer, could be attained not by CBP's own operations, but through the cooperation of those agencies that currently conduct counterintelligence operations.

The second new layer, and probably the easier to accomplish, is a layer of security provided by smart containers. The international call centers or control centers that interact with smart container messages also serve as third-party verifiers of the container's integrity and global movement. Smart boxes are essential to improving supply chain security. They must be included in CBP's layered approach. They already exist.

Finally, the proper training of CBP officers is essential in treating the global supply chain and protecting our nation from its use as a means to attack us. I think there should be a reexamination of the training focus for these CBP officers to again include trade issues and cargo movement as main factors in Customs training, not as what appear to be afterthoughts in their preparation.

All security systems are penetrable with enough time, money, knowledge, or inside help. Good security systems limit that possibility. The layered approach is good. It just needs to be better. And it can be better with three additions: "boots on the ground" counterintelligence, the use of smart containers, and a more trade-focused basic training, as the term *U.S. Customs* suggests.

NOTES

1. "Sympathy explosion" is a term often used by law enforcement bomb squads when flammable or explosive cargos are ignited by an explosive blast large enough to set off a chain reaction of explosions in a commonly shared area, as in a seaport or customs facilities at land ports of entry.

2. For an expanded treatment of this subject, see James Giermanski, "Is There an Explanation?" *Homeland Defense Journal*, February 2007, p. 49.

3. Jayson P. Ahern, deputy commissioner of CBP, Statement to the Hearing before the Committee on Appropriations, Subcommittee on Homeland Security, U.S. House of Representatives, April 2, 2008, p. 2.

4. Ahern, Statement, p. 2.

5. For an expanded treatment of this subject, see Jim Giermanski, "DHS Decision-Making: Competence or Character?" CSO Online, January 14, 2008, http://www2.cso online.com/exclusives/column.html.

6. "Frequently Asked Questions: 24-Hour Advance Vessel Manifest Rule," http:// supplychainsecurity.biz/documents/24hour_faq.pdf.

7. Pamela M. Zaresk, area port director, U.S. CBP, Charleston, presentation at the Annual South Carolina International Trade Conference, May 2007.

8. http://www.maersklogistics.com/sw18204.asp.

9. Private Impact Assessment for the Automated Targeting System (ATS), Office of Information Technology, Customs and Border Protection, November 22, 2006, p. 2.

10. Private Impact Assessment for the ATS, p. 2.

11. Private Impact Assessment for the ATS, p. 2.

12. http://www.customs.gov/xp/cgov/trade/automated/aes/about.xml.

13. Private Impact Assessment for Advance Passenger Information System (APIS), U.S. CBP, March 21, 2005, p. 6.

14. Charles Bartoldus, executive director, National Targeting and Security, Customs and Border Protection, http://www.cbp.gov/xp/CustomsToday/2005/nov_dec/targeting .xml.

15. Bradd Skinner, director of the C-TPAT, statement to American Association of Exporters and Importers, June 2008, as reported in *American Shipper—East Coast Connection*, June 5, 2008.

16. Center for Survey Research and Weldon Cooper Center for Public Service, University of Virginia, C-TPAT 2010 Survey, U.S. CBP, June 2010, p. 12.

17. "CSI in Brief," CBP, http://www.cbp.gov/xp/cgov/trade/cargo_security/csi/csi_ in_brief.xml.

18. Report to Congress on Integrated Scanning System Pilots (Security Accountability for Every Port Act of 2006, Section 231), U.S. CBP, June 11, 2008, p. 33.

19. Devabhaktuni Srikrishna, A. Narasimha Chari, and Thomas Tisch, "Nuclear Detection: Portals, Fixed Detectors, and NEST Teams Won't Work for Shielded HEU on a National Scale, So What Next?" May 16, 2005, http://iis-db.stanford.edu/evnts/4249/ disarm.pdf.

20. http://www.strtrade.com/wti/wti.asp?pub=0&story=31072&date=6%2F12%2F2 008&company=.

21. http://www.cbp.gov/xp/cgov/newsroom/news_releases/05292008.xml.

22. Richard McCormack, "Chinese Government Shipping Company Representative Sits on Customs and Border Protection's Industry Advisory Council," *Manufacturing & Technology News*, August 29, 2008, p. 1.

23. Advisory Committee on Commercial Operations of Customs and Border Protection, under the authority of the Omnibus Budget Reconciliation Act of 1987, Public Law No. 101–103, § 9503(c), 101 Stat. 1330, 1330–1381 (1987) (codified at 19 U.S.C. § 2071 note) established the COAC. This committee is established in accordance with and operates under the provisions of the Federal Advisory Committee Act (FACA), 5 U.S.C. App.

24. Advisory Committee on Commercial Operations of CBP, para. 3.

25. Advisory Committee on Commercial Operations of CBP, para. 11, p. 3.

26. Advisory Committee on Commercial Operations of CBP, para. 12, p. 3.

27. DHS, *Bottom-Up Review Report*, July 2010, pp. vii–xi.

28. Jim Giermanski, "COAC Is a Security Risk for the U.S." *The Maritime Executive*, March 7, 2011, http://www.maritime-executive.com/article/coac-security-risk-us/.

29. "Today's International Trade and Customs News," *Sandler, Travis, and Rosenberg Trade Report*, February 3, 2012, http://strtradenews.com/rv/ff0002ad61101a b9e315f6c39e4a9aa205ecc352/p=3741603.

30. "U.S. Customs Service: More Than 200 Years of History," CBP, http://www.cbp .gov/xp/cgov/about/history/legacy/history2.xml.

31. Anne Saba, "The U.S. Customs Service: Always There . . . Ready to Serve," *US Customs Today*, February 2003, http://www.cbp.gov/xp/CustomsToday/2003/February/ always.xml.

32. Saba, "U.S. Customs Service."

33. "CBP Officers Begin to Earn Greater Retirement Benefits," 1500 AM Federal News Radio, http://www.federalnewsradio.com/?nid=741&sid=2461442.

Chapter Eight

The Global Supply Chain and Its Commercial and Security Elements

Supply chain security is no longer only in the hands of governments. It has now become part of international contracting for goods, separate from export controls and other government-related practices and programs. Additionally, international contracting and cargo movement is not for those uninformed of global commercial guidelines and rules. Having been in the import-export business for many years, I learned very quickly that it is a complicated and sometimes dangerous business. It takes not only sound business knowledge but a knowledge of the global market and its players. It also involves the need to know how to protect your assets from the time of purchase and movement from a foreign origin to a domestic destination, as well as the export sale of your product and its movement to its foreign destination. The complications are the interconnectivity of government, federal laws, international business practices and procedures, modal issues of carrier choice and its legal impact—and today the security of one's nation, given the potential use of the global supply chain as an instrument of significant destruction.

Specifically, there are a number of private-sector commercial guidelines and rules directly impacting the global supply chain and, ultimately, its security. The business rules reflected in the United Nations Convention on Contracts for the International Sale of Goods (CISG), Incoterms® 2010, and the UN Convention on Contracts for the International Carriage of Goods Wholly or Partly by Sea (Rotterdam Rules).

UN CONVENTION ON CONTRACTS FOR THE INTERNATIONAL SALE OF GOODS (CISG)

To demonstrate the unique role of the CISG, let's assume that an international sale was consummated between a U.S. buyer (a dentist) and a foreign seller (dental equipment distribution company). In case of a dispute, no indication was made in the sales contract as to the legal jurisdiction the sale fell within. Now, let's assume that the U.S. dentist (the importer) bought a $5,000 dental chair from the German distributor (the exporter) over the telephone during a conference call. There is no paper document of the sale. The first time the dentist used the chair, it short-circuited and burst into flame, burning the dentist's arm seriously and virtually destroying two of the dental treatment rooms before the fire could be extinguished by the fire department. The dentist was out of work for three weeks. An inspection confirmed the chair was incorrectly wired. Can the U.S. dentist sue? If he can sue, where would it be: in the United States or Germany, in federal court or state court? Can he sue for the physical injury caused by the faulty dental chair? Can he sue to recover the costs of repairing his two lost treatment rooms? Can he sue for punitive damages?

The answers. Unless stipulated otherwise in the international contract for sale, both the exporter and importer are automatically legally bound by rules contained in the UN Convention for the International Sale of Goods. Thus, both are automatically subject to any potential legal remedy through litigation in the Federal court systems (Articles 1, 4, and 6). It is a legal sale because the CISG permits oral contracts without regard to the cost of the product (Article 11). The dentist cannot sue for any physical injury because the CISG does not permit it (Article 5) but can sue for damage caused by the faulty product (Article 5). Finally the importer cannot sue for punitive damages, only for the sum of the loss, including lost profit, if any (Article 74).

Given the size of the sales market in the United States and this country's history of domestic sales within that market, many businesses and businessmen assume that selling is the same in the international market. It is not the same. Contract law involving business-to-business sales in the United States falls within the Uniform Commercial Code (UCC). For instance, the UCC specifies that if you are selling something for $500 or more, the sale must be in writing or linked to a written document. Contrast that to the case of the U.S. dentist above. Under the CISG, even a sale of $5 million can be oral and just as legally binding.

The CISG is the uniform international sales law of countries that account for two-thirds of all world trade. "The United Nations Convention on Contracts for the International Sale of Goods is an overlay; it sits on top of the national sales code or sales law of each country that has adopted it. In most cases, this is a domestic regime that is either civil law or common law—cultures that have at times approached sales law challenges somewhat differently."[1] The CISG is a treaty and as such is the law of the land. Since the United States is a signatory, the CISG automatically provides the rules and procedures involved in an international sales contract.

Components

There are four main parts of the Convention: Part I, rules on its application and a number of general provisions; Part II, the formation of the contract; Part III, the actual "sales law" of the Convention; and Part IV, the final provisions dealing with the specifics of ratification and any possible reservations against certain parts or provisions of the Convention and when the Convention becomes law in a given country.

Part I, Sphere of Application and General Provisions (Articles 1–13)

Part I of the Convention begins by showing its application to those countries who are signatories to it. All business-to-business commercial goods qualify. There are only six categories of goods to which CISG is not applicable. It makes it perfectly clear that if the exporter's or importer's nation is a signatory to it, all commercial sales must follow its rules. Because it is a treaty and therefore U.S. federal law, a U.S. importer of qualifying products cannot avoid CISG. The only way the U.S. exporter or importer can opt out of it is by expressly invoking Article 6 in writing. Unfortunately, U.S. businessmen often assume that having a written international sales contract says that, should a dispute arise out of that contract, any litigation will fall within U.S. federal court and would free them from CISG. However, having that stated in the contract actually compels the use of the CISG.

Part II, Formation of the Contract (Articles 14–24)

Part II covers the essence of the sales contract by defining an offer to sell or to purchase. It treats its required contents; what constitutes an acceptance, rejection, and withdrawal of offer or acceptance; and revocation. It even defines when the offer becomes effective. Offers to sell can become a counteroffer to purchase if the buyer responds by changing any material terms of the original offer.

Part III, Sale of Goods (Articles 25–88)

Part III covers the seller's principal obligations like delivery and handing over proper documentation, often a requirement of the importer's customs administration or document stipulations of a letter of credit. Other seller's obligations are connected to the conformity of goods to the international sales contract; delivery specifics as to time, place, and method; examination of goods; and even issues of third-party rights with respect to intellectual property. There are special obligations to sellers when they know there might be a lack of conformity of the goods to the agreed-upon contract, e.g., early deliveries or excess quantities. Part III brings in Incoterm rules that impact the stakeholders' rights and obligations, along with issues of risk when the contract involves carriage. Where delivery takes place is spelled out for the buyer and seller even if they omit its treatment in the contract for sale. For instance, if the seller is not specifically required or bound to deliver goods at a particular place, the risk is automatically passed to the buyer when the goods are given to the first carrier (Article 67). This obligation is equivalent to using a term of sale known as free carrier (FCA, Incoterms 2010). Incoterms are specifically treated in CISG and therefore, because the new Incoterms 2010 directly and clearly now reference supply chain "security" as an obligation, the legal issue of security now impacts exporters, importers, and carriers. This security question is new and part of Incoterms 2010.

Part IV, Final Provisions (Articles 89–101)

Part IV is the administrative section of the Convention and covers the Convention's relevance to other international agreements entered into by signatory nations. It includes the application of CISG to contracting states (nations), and the rights of states to determine exceptions or exemptions. Finally, this section covers when the CISG enters into force and what mechanism a state must use to extricate itself from CISG should the state be compelled to do so.

CISG's Practical Application

CISG offers a very commonsense approach to leveling the international playing field. But it all depends on one's perspective. The parties to the CISG contract might not be happy with the aspect of what is really meant by the contract's terms. Throughout the document, there is the constant reminder that the language of the contract will be interpreted by what is reasonable in the industry involved and by the past practices of the businesses connected to the contract.

The CISG is both good and bad. It is both tight and loose, clear and cloudy. All contracts can be oral regardless of value. Contracts can be written on napkins in a restaurant and be valid since there is no required form for them. Delivery will be automatically determined if the parties fail to use Incoterms. What's written may not be as important as the statements and behavior of the parties. Because of these and a multitude of other reasons unique to or absent from the UCC, many U.S. businesses and their lawyers do not necessarily like CISG. Regardless, it is the law of the land in the United States and supersedes the UCC. Disputes arising from it, if litigated, will end up in U.S. federal court. Whether one likes it or not, the international buyers and sellers are bound under federal law to its rules, which overtly bring into any international contract the rules set forth in Incoterms, now Incoterms 2010, that make supply chain security a legal issue with respect to compliance.

THE PRIVATE SECTOR AND SECURITY: INCOTERMS 2010

As I have said, today it is not just government that has a responsibility to make the global supply chain more secure. This obligation also falls on the private sector, which is compelled by CISG in its mandate to use international commercial sales terms that clearly differentiate the obligations of the buyer, seller, and carrier within an international contract involving the sale of goods. These terms are embodied in Incoterms 2010.

The New Mortar of Global Business and Its Security Elements

Because of the complexities of international sales contracts, there is something called Incoterms, rules that link and support the smooth execution of these disparate contracts. In effect, Incoterms serve as the mortar or glue holding them together to function smoothly. Incoterms have always dealt with the international contract of sale, carriage, and payment, and provided the guidelines that distinguish duties and responsibilities of the buyer and seller. Although first published in 1936, they are updated about every 10 years. The new Incoterms 2010, a publication of the International Chamber of Commerce, went into effect in January 2011.

As the playbook of international rules for global trade, Incoterms need to be understood by all the players involved in the contract for sale (exporter and importer), the contract for carriage (carrier, freight forwarder, and customs broker), and the contract for payment (banks, insurance companies, and other financial intermediaries). Because of the rules' importance, the United States has now recognized them as also essential for domestic business practices. Incoterms have been approved as the replacement of all domestic trade terms currently used in the United States. In September 2004, the United States Council for International Business (USCIB) announced the removal of the current U.S. domestic terms:[2]

> With little fanfare, the shipping and delivery terms (former sections 2-319 through 2-324) are being written out of the Uniform Commercial Code because they are inconsistent with modern usage. The final draft revision, minus these sections, was completed by the American Law Institute (ALI) and the National Conference of Commissioners on Uniform State Laws (NCCUSL) on February 19, 2004, and awaits approval by each state legislature.

Then in July 2005, the USCIB announced: "Nearly all businesses in the United States will be affected by upcoming changes to the shipment and delivery terms commonly used in domestic B2B (business-to-business) transactions."[3] The announcement further stated that the revision of Article Two of the Uniform

Commercial Code is incorporated into the laws of the United States except Louisiana, and that state legislatures can be expected to adopt the revisions, which are the "industry-defined standard trade definitions, used in international contracts, that also provide a clearly defined alternative to the deleted UCC shipment and delivery terms."[4]

However, in addition to their international prominence in trade negotiations and seller/buyer obligations, the new Incoterms 2010 has an additional focus on global supply chain security, not present in previous editions. Within the nine main features of the Incoterms 2010 rules, feature 7 is dedicated to security.[5]

> There is heightened concern nowadays about security in the movement of goods, requiring verification that the goods do not pose a threat to life or property for reasons other than their inherent nature. Therefore, the Incoterms 2010 rules have allocated obligations between the buyer and seller to obtain or to render assistance in obtaining security-related clearances, such as *chain-of-custody information*, in articles A2/B2 and A10/B10 of various Incoterms rules. (emphasis added)

Global supply chain security has now become a mandated area of business concern, responsibility, and liability when complying with Incoterms 2010.

The Liability Issue for Buyer and Seller

In the new Incoterms 2010, as in past Incoterms, "A" articles in the text refer to seller obligations, and "B" articles refer to buyer obligations. Four new articles, Articles A/2 and A/10 and B/2 and B/10, are new and indicative of the worldwide concern for supply chain security, clearly absent from previous editions of Incoterms. While each of the 11 Incoterms is unique, in essence, the buyer and seller are obligated to ensure that customs and security formalities are met so that shipping containers can be considered safe and be transported through any country prior to delivery. Specifically, depending on the Incoterm used, the seller and buyer have obligations to provide "chain-of-custody," "security-related information" needed for the cargo's transport to destination.

Chain of Custody in the Supply Chain

Since chapter 6 is devoted to the chain-of-custody concept as it applies to the global supply chain, I will only say here that it refers to the integrity of evidence and requires a documented process showing the seizure, custody, control, transfer, analysis, and disposition of physical and electronic evidence. Documentation should include the conditions under which the evidence is gathered, the identity of all evidence handlers, duration of evidence custody, security conditions while handling or storing the evidence, and the manner in which evidence is transferred to subsequent custodians each time such a transfer occurs.[6]

The question is whether this chain-of-custody concept *can* be applied and used in the world of global container security, trailer security, and railcar security. It can, in part because of some new changes to the Federal Rules of Civil Procedure that support the electronic communication procedures and protocols referenced in the new Incoterm rules.

In 2006, the U.S. Supreme Court approved amendments to several rules. In short, the changes allow electronically stored information (ESI) to be requested during discovery for admission in trials in U.S. courts—assuming, of course, that it meets the legal thresholds for the admission of evidence. ESI evidence includes virtually all electronic records and communications, including e-mails, and may be obtained through subpoena in criminal cases and by pretrial discovery in civil cases. Thus, information contained in electronic systems used in the global supply chain now have the potential for use as evidence in civil litigation.

The most common and fundamental problem in transport today comes from the very conveyance of goods in the global supply chain. If one sent goods in an open conveyance, like coal in a rail car, it would be difficult to prove that all the pieces of coal that started the journey at origin ended the journey at destination. However, with common shipping containers, there is no problem in ensuring the sender and receiver that the all the goods "stuffed" into the container at origin are, in fact, the same goods in the same quantity that arrived at destination and that nothing has been added into the container nor taken out of the container.

Modern logistics chain-of-custody processes and capabilities are already available to sellers, buyers, and carriers through the use of container security devices (CSDs). Distinct and apart from Incoterms 2010, one version of the chain-of-custody supply chain process is officially recognized in 33 countries, with pending recognition in other countries. These chain-of-custody capabilities can offer the following benefits and are consistent with and supportive of the new Incoterm rules.

1. CSDs can provide the electronic verification of contents and its quantity. Their use can also identify the authorized and accountable person verifying the cargo's accuracy, and any logistical data agreed upon can automatically be transmitted from the container by satellite or cellular communications to appropriate entities with the need to know.

2. Depending on the robust nature of the CSD, it not only can track movement but also can allow seller, buyer, or others so permitted to query the container while it is in transit. Some CSDs also allow the container itself to independently report any movement off its intended journey. Satellite- and/or cellular-monitored and tracked smart containers automatically offer, through the use of worldwide call centers, a third-party record of any break in the chain of custody.

3. Finally, a CSD utilizing a chain-of-custody process can provide an electronic receipt of delivery and the identification of the individual authorized to

open the container through a specialized electronic communication or biometric reading needed to access the container at destination.

The only real difference with the chain of custody described in other legal circles is that the CSDs can do all of this electronically. CSDs can not only meet the challenges of providing a good control similar to that of a registered and certified letter in the postal system, but can also provide the electronic management not available in documentary chains.

Compliance with Government Programs

There are also important benefits from the use of a chain-of-custody system: support for national security programs such as the Customs-Trade Partnership Against Terrorism (C-TPAT) and the Container Security Initiative (CSI). With respect to C-TPAT, a chain-of-custody process can certify C-TPAT firms' compliance with certain components of C-TPAT, like control of stuffing at origin. With respect to CSI, container contents will be verified by an identified person at stuffing, which is not required by the government programs. Also, the chain-of-custody data stored in third-party control center servers and in the servers of shippers and consignees can be used legally to defend against negative Customs and Border Patrol (CBP) audits, legal claims regarding damage or loss by others within the supply chain, or noncompliance with cargo verifications connected to some legal requirements of the UN Convention on Contracts for the International Sale of Goods (CISG). In effect, chain-of-custody systems exceed the requirements of current CBP programs.

Finally, the U.S. decision to become a signatory to the UN Convention on Contracts for the International Carriage of Goods Wholly or Partly by Sea[7] signified a clear move to emphasize the importance of knowing what's in the container and who is liable for knowing. Instead of the current carrier liability from the time the goods are laden into the vessel until the time they are discharged from the vessel, these Rotterdam Rules will now make vessel carriers responsible for the cargo they carry from origin to destination. In effect, shippers, consignees, and vessel carriers will all have to be concerned with a door-to-door chain of custody with respect to carriage of goods by sea.

Without a doubt, Incoterms 2010 recognizes the value of global supply chain security utilizing a demonstrable and verifiable chain of custody, which can provide the following benefits:

- Make money for their users through expedited customs treatment
- Serve to prove C-TPAT compliance with stuffing at origin
- Verify the loading of proper cargo and quantity at origin
- Affirm the appropriate container environment and location during carriage
- Verify the proper cargo and quantity at destination
- Protect against the unauthorized placement of contraband or counterfeit products while en route to destination

- Provide to parties of contracts for the international sale of goods a level of confidence in the expectation of accuracy in sending and receiving that which was purchased

With respect to securing the global supply chain, the international private sector has done what national governments so far have not been willing to do. Incoterms 2010 embodies that accomplishment. The private sector will be doing even more to secure the supply chain. This will occur when the new Rotterdam Rules begin to go into effect.

THE ROTTERDAM RULES

In September 2009, the United States became a signatory to the UN Convention on Contracts for the International Carriage of Goods Wholly or Partly by Sea (Rotterdam Rules).[8] When signed by the U.S. president with the "advice and consent" of the Senate, there could soon be a new day for shippers, consignees, and vessel carriers with respect to carriage of goods by sea. In the United States, the 1936 Carriage of Goods by Sea Act (COGSA) will be replaced by the Rotterdam Rules. Also, the Rules "will supersede the Hague, Hague-Visby, and Hamburg Rules."[9] The COGSA's "tackle-to-tackle" mode (where the period between the time the goods are laden into and the time they are discharged from the vessel are the responsibility of the vessel carrier) disappears under the Rotterdam Rules. According to the UN General Assembly, the Rotterdam Rules is a "uniform and modern global legal regime governing the rights and obligations of stakeholders in the maritime transport industry under a single contract for door-to-door carriage."[10] The UN General Assembly adopted the Rotterdam Rules on December 11, 2008. On September 23, 2009, the Rules were ratified by sixteen original signatories (Congo, Denmark, France, Gabon, Ghana, Greece, Guinea, the Netherlands, Nigeria, Norway, Poland, Senegal, Spain, Switzerland, Togo, and the United States) in a formal ceremony in Rotterdam. Today, a total of twenty countries have signed the Rules.[11]

The new door-to-door liability instead of the tackle-to-tackle liability places the carrier directly in a virtual chain-of-custody regime. Now, instead of the vessel carrier filing the 24-hour rule based on what other supporting carriers said is in the container, the vessel carrier will be automatically and actually responsible to know what is in the container. The vessel carrier will have to use vetted motor carriers for direct shipper-carrier business and vetted forwarders and third-party logistics providers for indirect relationships between shipper and vessel carriers.

While a new world with respect to liability, it's also a new world for the requirement of electronic commerce. The heart of communication within the new Rules is electronic data flow and the value of electronically stored information. The Rotterdam Rules allow and promote that all the data involved in the door-to-door movement be transmitted electronically. Chapter 3 of the Rules, "Electronic Transport Records," contains Articles 8, 9, and 10. Article 8 specifically deals with the "use and effect of electronic transport records."[12]

> (a) Anything that is to be in or on a transport document under this Convention may be recorded in an electronic transport record, provided the issuance and subsequent use of an electronic transport record is with the consent of the carrier and shipper; and
>
> (b) The issuance, exclusive control, or transfer of an electronic transport record has the same effect as the issuance, possession, or transfer of a transport document.

Article 9 sets forth procedures for the use of negotiable electronic transport records, and Article 10 treats the replacement of negotiable transport documents or negotiable electronic transport records. Article 10 further covers when the negotiable electronic document should be surrendered or replaced. This use of electronic data transmission is consistent with guidelines from the World Customs Organization (WCO) Standards, the Kyoto Convention Information and Communication Technology (ICT) Guidelines to facilitate cross-border trade,[13] and the UN "Single Window" adopted by the United States and exemplified in CBP's e-Manifest and ACE (Automated Commercial Environment) usage. It also fits nicely with some changes to the Federal Rules of Civil Procedure that took effect on December 1, 2006. Rule 16, Rule 26, Rule 33, Rule 34, Rule 37, and Rule 45 were modified, resulting in the principle that electronically stored information is a class of evidence and equal to paper or any other type of physical evidence. Each rule is distinct but related. Rule 16 allows pre-trial meetings to discuss discovery issues regarding electronically stored information (ESI). Rule 26 clarifies the need to disclose information about holders of ESI and its description before a discovery request, and allows the safeguarding of privileged information to be withheld or returned. Rule 33 makes it clear that ESI includes business records. Rule 34 defines computer-based and other digitally stored data as ESI and its format as a separate category and subject to production and discovery. Rule 37 addresses the destruction of ESI and when it can or cannot be destroyed. The strongest rule alteration is probably in Rule 45. It recognizes ESI as a distinct category of discoverable information, allowing for subpoena of it in the same way as with paper documents. Subpoenas may also be executed on individuals or companies not directly involved in the litigation. ESI clearly includes electronic transport documents and records.

Impact of the Rules on Supply Chain Security in the Future

The change from port-to-port liability to origin-to-destination liability will make all vessel carriers review their liability exposure and begin to focus on security issues connected to it. Specifically, the new Rules should cause the following:

- First, responsibility begins at the shipper's place of business, not at the port.
- Second, truck or rail bills of lading from the shipper's place of business to the port of debarkation will have to be validated as true. Therefore, the vessel carrier may finally know what's in the container, making the vessel carrier's submission of CSI's 24-hour manifest more accurate by reflecting known data about contents for which the ocean carrier is responsible.
- Third, the ESI transmitted is subject to discovery and is usable for not only criminal, as it has been, but now also for civil matters. Accuracy is then paramount, and records of the international movement must be maintained.
- Finally, the Rotterdam Rules should encourage vessel carriers to use some form of container security device (CSD) or suggest to their shipper-customers to use CSDs that will provide the identify of an accountable agent at stuffing who verifies cargo and quantity, potentially limiting or mitigating the vessel carrier's legal responsibility and providing an increased degree of security to comply with government needs and mandates.

Even though the United States is a signatory to the Rotterdam Rules, the Rules cannot take effect until they are ratified by the consent of the U.S. Senate and the signature of the president. In this case, the only potential objectors are likely to be the vessel carriers themselves. However, given that all of the major vessel carriers are foreign and in light of other nations agreeing with the Rules, it seems that the adoption of them in the United States is not only appropriate but also compelling and hopefully inevitable. Moreover, these Rules should have a positive impact on this nation's security by enhancing our existing supply chain security programs and by encouraging the use of container security systems that augment the Rules by verifying the cargo, tracking the container's movement, detecting and reporting unauthorized access, and reporting any violation of the cargo movement's integrity. Therefore, for the sake of our security, and in contrast to other contentious actions within the Senate, a positive vote for the Rotterdam Rules should be a welcome event for the nation. That vote should be expedited.

CONCLUSION

Never has security of the global supply chain been so important and accepted as necessary. This is now clearly shown to be important in the application of commercial practices involving the international sale of goods and their carriage. It will only be a matter of time for imports, exporters, and carriers to recognize the need to address security conditions because of the serious legal liability to which they will expose themselves should they disregard them.

Finally, these commercial obligations will enhance U.S. government programs by contributing to the standards set forth in C-TPAT, CSI, and even CBP's 10+2 Program.

NOTES

1. "CISG Database," Pace Law School, http://www.cisg.law.pace.edu/cisg/text/cisgint.html.

2. "Latest UCC Revision Drives Universal Use of Incoterms 2000," *USCIB in the News*, p. 1, http://www.uscib.org/index.asp?documentID=2954.

3. "A Handy Replacement for Obsolete UCC Trade Terms," p. 1, http://www.uscib.org/index.asp?documentID=3345.

4. "A Handy Replacement," p. 1.

5. *Incoterms 2010*, International Chamber of Commerce, Paris, France, 2010, p. 9.

6. Prachee Ratnaparkhi, "Safe Handling, Preservation of Orginal Media and Its Cahin of Custody," http://www.scribd.com/doc/98801921/Chain-of-Custody-PPT.

7. General Assembly Resolution 63/122, Annex, UN Doc. A/RES/63/122 (December 11, 2008).

8. General Assembly Resolution 63/122, Annex, UN Doc. A/RES/63/122 (December 11, 2008). For a comprehensive treatment of the Rotterdam Rules, see Jim Giermanski, "New Rules for Vessel Carriage: Is the U.S. Ready?" *Maritime Executive Newsletter*, June 24, 2010.

9. Michael F. Sturley, "The UN Convention on Contracts for the International Carriage of Goods Wholly or Partly by Sea: The Top Ten Ways that the Rotterdam Rules Will Change U.S. Law," October 1, 2009, p. 2, http://www.utcle.org/eLibrary/preview.php?asset_file_id=22387.

10. http://www.americanshipper.com/NewWeb/news_page_SNW2.asp?news=143570.

11. http://www.americanshipper.com/NewWeb/news_page_SNW2.asp?news=143570.

12. "Convention on Contracts for the International Carriage of Goods Wholly or Partly by the Sea," http://www.fog.it/convenzioni/inglese/rotterdam-2009.htm.

13. "ICT Solutions to Facilitate Trade at Border Crossings and in Ports," United Nations Conference on Trade and Development, October 2006.

Chapter Nine

Radio Frequency Identification (RFID) and Container Security

It seems that RFID (the acronym for radio frequency identification) has become the current buzz word among some of the largest retailers and importers in the country. Wal-Mart and Target are just two of the giants discussed in the literature. Recently, an A. T. Kearney report titled *Smart Boxes*[1] lauded the potential and actual use of RFID for certain supply-chain applications. However, the application of RFID to container security and port security is less laudable, less effective, more costly, and certainly questionable as a primary means of international transportation security for containers. RFID applications, whether active or passive,[2] have very clear weaknesses and impediments to usage in a worldwide context. The impediments are the absence of agreement on RFID worldwide standards, RFID's land-based character, and the rights to acquisition, cost, and control of required RFID infrastructure.

WORLDWIDE PROTOCOLS AND STANDARDS

RFID applications require the carriage and transmission of data through a wireless system. Data can be loaded into a device called a transponder and can then be transmitted via radio waves when the transponder is triggered by a corresponding device called a transceiver or reader. The transponder is a slave RFID unit that reacts to a triggering radio frequency message from the master transceiver. The transceiver, through its antenna, sends the triggering frequency, which produces a return transmission of the data preloaded into the transponder (like manifest or shipping data) or information acquired by the RFID device (like the opening of the container door). Since the transmission of these data is by electromagnetic waves, the successful transmission is subject to the use of the proper frequencies or waves and the absence of distortion like noise or same-frequency emissions from competing antennas whose direction (footprint) unintentionally or intentionally obstructs or interferes with the intended RFID transmissions of the intended transponder.

In order for the transponder and reader to talk to each other, they need to speak in the same way. In other words, they must follow a protocol or a set of instructions. While no analogy is perfect, assume it is something like one person speaking Spanish and the other English and at different speeds, with different volumes and both talking at the same time. In this analogy, protocols tell each person (in the real world, the container and the reader) when to start and stop, what language to use, how fast to talk, and so on. Unless the instructions are clear to each, communication may not take place.[3] There are no global protocols or standards, however. Imagine the lack of standardized instructions for a container and its transponder on a global voyage: different regions will have different standards. There are national standards like ANSI (American National Standards Institute), international standards like ISO (International Organization for Standardization), and industrial standards like EPC (EPCglobal, which alone is in about 100 countries). ISO has many standards related to RFID.

Frequencies also have different bands, like low, intermediate, and high. Each band is appropriate for unique usage. For instance, low-frequency RFID is used for short to medium distances, low speed, and somewhat simple applications such as access controls. Intermediate-frequency bands can also be used for access control also but offer a little faster read speed. High-frequency RFID is used for fast read speeds, and if the specific standard allows high-wattage output, longer range can be obtained.

The major problem is the frequency approved for use by different governments. Like protocols, RFID-approved frequencies differ globally. Thus, RFID on which the data ride in the United States will not work in another part of the world. The foreign transceiver cannot trigger the data transmission because the United States may use a different frequency. For example, the United States Federal Communications Commission (FCC) issued a final rule, effective on June 23, 2004, that only 433 MHz RFID systems may be used for commercial shipping containers. Likewise, other countries in other RFID frequency regions have approved different frequencies for different uses. Therefore, RFID for container security is applicable only to those areas of the world that have agreed on the same frequency for the same usage, precluding a standardized global use of RFID for shipping containers.

LAND-BASED CHARACTER

In addition to the frequency problem exemplified by a lack of worldwide standardization, an equally troublesome area for RFID usage in container security is the overland movement of containers and the corresponding creation of a land-based infrastructure of antennas and readers. Unlike the RFID tags used in products and pallets that are read in controlled distribution systems, active RFID devices in containers that move around the world through uncontrolled environments require the construction of antennas at chokepoints (those points along the journey of the container that cannot be circumvented by the carrier). Constructing a globally controlled distribution path is really impossible. The A.T. Kearney report defines chokepoint location this way: "Chokepoints where readers might be positioned include the spot where a truck is loaded or unloaded, on a crane that transfers containers, a weigh station, the port of loading, or at the port of discharge."[4] A land-based system is a reasonable option only for these obvious chokepoints at origin and destination. In areas along the route of the container's movement, a land-based system is often complex.

RFID generally requires line-of-sight transmissions. In the case of container security, each RFID transponder connected to a container would have to "see" the transceiver that triggers the transmission of data from the container. The approved 433 MHz frequency requires line of sight. How close the reader is to the container is also a troublesome issue. Geography and topography are consequently a potential issue in constructing antenna systems close enough to the container but far enough away to see the antenna of the transponder connected to the container.

ACQUISITION AND COST OF RFID INFRASTRUCTURE

Although the land-locked constraint can likely be overcome by proper use of topography and construction techniques, there is another problem related to a land-based system of security, particularly container security. The issue for the user of RFID technology on containers is that the user will not likely own the land on which readers (transceivers) would have to be installed as fixed sites, nor have rights to install the antenna system along the routes the container and chassis travel. Unlike railroads, which are perfect candidates for RFID usage because they have rights-of-way and own their own track infrastructure, motor carriers using public roads are not good candidates. However, there is some concern about whether 433 MHz (the low end of the high-frequency band) is good enough for reading rail-carried containers and railcars at the speed they pass a fixed transceiver or antenna. Another good candidate for RFID container security usage is the U.S. Department of Defense (DOD). However, DOD, like rail, can often, although not always, control its chokepoints in a manner superior to that of a commercial motor carrier.

To construct fixed-position readers, one needs access rights to the land or the equipment on which one installs the reader. Take, for example, a seaport. Who owns the port? Is it the property of the city in which it is located? Is it managed by a port authority? Who owns the gantry cranes on which a user of RFID technology wants to place the transceiver? The same scenario is applicable to U.S. land ports of entry. In the case of Laredo, Texas, on the U.S.-Mexico border, the city owns the bridges. Therefore the city would have to give or lease the right to erect an antenna or fixed-position reader on its bridge for a single shipper or carrier. Since private or government real property will be on each end of the bridges between Mexico and the United States, will the governments or landowners provide proprietary usage to individual shippers or carriers?

INTERFERENCE FACTOR

How does one control the footprint problems at busy ports with multiple transceivers, transponder-fixed containers, and antenna footprints? As mentioned previously, the protocol or instructions for the container and transceiver to communicate have to be clear. Who talks first and what bandwidth is used are critical. The combination of finding the corresponding talkers (transceivers outside and transponders inside containers), instructions on which talks first, the speed of talking, and the volume of data transmitted make for increased distortion and interference, especially at congested ports and land-based chokepoints. In the mid-1990s, the NATAP (North American Trade Automation Prototype) tests, of which I was a part, were conducted at a few selected land ports of entry along the Mexican and Canadian border using RFID. These tests encountered these exact problems.

At major modern seaports like Rotterdam, everything is moved by RFID applications. There are no drivers in the tractors that pull the containers. There are multiple gantry cranes seemingly working on their own in coordination with moving trucks and chassis. Superimpose on this RFID-layered seaport RFID frequency and protocol differences between the United States and the Netherlands, for example, and one will see immediately that RFID applications to container security would be quite difficult if not impossible.

Associated with the access and cost of RFID infrastructure is the cost of container modification. An inexpensive passive RFID tag can be hung on the outside of the doors and respond to a transceiver as to whether the doors have been opened in the normal manner. A more expensive active RFID device can also be hung on the outside of the doors and send a signal on its own at a chokepoint indicating whether the doors have been opened (assuming the doors can be read at the chokepoint). However, an active RFID device placed inside the container that can sense access to the container through means other than the doors is an expensive proposition compared to the inexpensive passive tag. Not only does the active device itself cost more, but also the container has to be structurally modified to accommodate the internal RFID transponder and its antenna. Since the RFID frequency approved for containers does not emit through steel, the RFID device internal to the container must have access through the steel to the outside in order to function—which requires modification to the container. Permanently modifying a container for only RFID may be unacceptable to the owners.

VULNERABILITY AS AN IMPROVISED EXPLOSIVE DEVICE (IED) TRIGGER

The following illustrates a serious vulnerability at U.S. seaports and land ports of entry because of the use of RFID mandated for use with shipping containers. DHS is fully aware of the vulnerability but has done nothing to change the current port situation. To empirically demonstrate the seriousness of this vulnerability, an international transportation security company, established in North Carolina in 2002 and focused on developing a container security system, proved the vulnerability. Initially, this company believed that RFID approved by the FCC for use with shipping containers should be considered for incorporation into the firm's satellite-based system. However, problematic issues surfaced. Multiple global frequencies, protocols, government set-asides, infrastructure access and costs, maintenance, and the historical nature of the data transmitted at land-based networks of chokepoints needed by RFID transceivers to interrogate RFID tags and devices, all caused doubt and concern about the value and viability of RFID use in global container management and security.

Recently, however, another more ominous concern about RFID usage in seaports and land ports has developed. Engineers of this firm believed that RFID usage, as approved in the United States, was a serious vulnerability because of the ease of detecting these RFID emissions. RFID emissions can serve as the trigger mechanism for detonating an explosive device within the container. Because an explosive device can easily be wired to detonate with the proper RFID frequency signal at any of our nation's seaports and land ports, all our nation's ports that employ the approved RFID frequency for shipping containers become more vulnerable to terrorist attack.

A review of the literature seemed to confirm what was suspected. There were conflicting claims, and the process of selecting a frequency for container security was contentious. Ultimately, a decision was made by the FCC to set aside a frequency of 433.5 to 434.5 MHz spectrum band, and their rule would allow these RFID systems to transmit for 60 seconds rather than only for 1 second. The American Radio Relay League (ARRL), also known as the National Association for Amateur Radio, took issue with the decision, mostly because of predicted interference problems. On February 13, 2002, the ARRL said that the FCC "cannot legally proceed with the rules proposed for unlicensed RFID tags at 433 MHz," and it asked the FCC to not adopt them. The league filed comments on February 12, 2002, as part of its continued opposition to what it called an ill-conceived proposal, citing its own studies of interference generated by unsuitable power levels and duty cycles approved for this frequency.[5] Above objections, the spectrum and transmission time were approved for use with shipping containers and in commercial and industrial areas.

Over and above the interference issues cited by the ARRL, the fact that the U.S. government reserves, restricts, requires, and publishes the specific frequency for RFID use with shipping containers is questionable on security grounds alone. Furthermore, the fact that only approved and published RFID signals are required to be transmitted on a given frequency at U.S. ports by both the private and public sectors, in effect, makes government policy usable as an instrument of terrorist tactics. The need for surreptitious port penetrations, elaborate electronics, intricate timing, or other specialized terrorist tradecraft or operations in the United States is diminished if not eliminated. The U.S. private sector and government agencies like CBP and DOD can themselves, through routine and normal procedures, detonate explosive devices carried in containers entering our ports.

DECISION TO TEST

To test the validity of its concerns, this firm constructed controller boards to serve as relays or detonators using off-the-shelf, over-the-counter products. Using these detonators, it simulated multiple explosions at varying distances using the frequency required by the U.S. government. Each simulation was successful. Additional simulations were made at a container yard with the detonator placed in a closed container. In each case, and without fail, 433 MHz signals penetrated the enclosed container from varying distances and from behind multiple rows of stacked containers and triggered a simulated bomb. Further work on this vulnerability revealed that signals emitted to detonate explosive devices could be made at significant distances from locations even outside the port facilities with the use of high-gain antennas. However, the company had not used an actual RFID tag to verify its concerns nor actually detonated explosives in this manner.

Because of these findings, the transportation security firm approached experts in the area of improvised explosive device (IED) defense, municipal bomb squads, and engineers with blast contracts with the U.S. DOD, DHS, and CBP to examine these concerns. At first, only the municipal bomb squad and engineers from a local firm with blast contracts with DOD responded; they concurred that RFID usage as approved for container usage in U.S. ports appeared to be dangerous. The international transportation firm also contacted the U.S. House of Representatives Homeland Security Committee to inform them of our concerns and to be on record of having done so.

BLAST DEMONSTRATION

To demonstrate this vulnerability in an irrefutable fashion and transparent format, the following firms and organizations joined to support the demonstration on November 13, 2007: Powers International and Raytheon Homeland Security Division, Raytheon Co. with the cooperation of Zapata Engineering, the University of North Carolina at Charlotte College of Engineering, the City of Gastonia Bomb Squad, and the 321 Equipment Co. The demonstration used an actual RFID tag that sent a signal to a receiving circuit (detonator) prepared from over-the-counter components. The detonator was made by an undergraduate college student for approximately $20. The RFID signal detonated a very small amount of live explosives in a container by means of a simple emission of a radio signal traveling on the approved RFID frequency. The demo was "brand agnostic." At no time during the demonstration was any port, political subdivision, manufacturer, distributor, or user of RFID for container security promoted or criticized for its use.

GOVERNMENT INTEREST AND SUPPORT

Because of the serious and potentially controversial nature of this demo, many government officials and personnel of the administration were invited, including the Department of Defense. Due to its interest in and extensive use of RFID, DOD sent two persons, the chief engineer and his supervisor, the product manager of a joint DOD-RFID unit: the Automatic Identification Technology. Therefore, on November 13, 2007, representatives from the U.S. Army were among the attendees who observed the preparation and demonstration of an RF-detection and triggering device utilized to detonate explosives in a shipping container at the City of Gastonia Ordinance Range. Subsequently, the U.S. Army confirmed in writing (in DOD's own words), that "U.S. Army representatives examined the device and wiring and confirm that a commercial RFID interrogator was use to 'wake up' a commercial RFID tag. When the RFID tag responded on the 433 MHz frequency, the relay closed and the blasting cap set off the explosive charge." Thus, DOD representatives recognized and confirmed the validity of the IED concern over the routine RFID use, its vulnerable nature, and the accuracy and relevance of the demonstration to homeland security. Other witnesses were invited to attend and verify the process used and the results obtained from the demonstration. The demonstration was filmed, and the film and presentations given at the demonstration are available for review by government entities and interested parties. So far, the results of the demo have been covered by the *San Antonio Express News* and two local TV affiliates (CBS and NBC) in South Carolina. CNN also taped an interview with me for national coverage, but for reasons known only to them, the demo and taping were never aired.

The demonstration was 100% successful and it empirically showed the vulnerability of RFID transmissions as approved for use with containers passing through our international ports of entry.

GOVERNMENTAL AGENCIES' PROBLEMS AND RESPONSES

Unfortunately, the blast supporters met resistance from both DHS and CBP, who refused to attend or to indicate any recognition of the demonstration's value, even though both had local offices and personnel within 20 minutes of the demonstration site. CBP actually attempted to put obstacles in the path of the demo by not allowing its transceiver or activators to be used at the demonstration, even by their own personnel. Pro bono support from a major law firm was given to the international transportation firm to help make the proper contacts at the appropriate levels in CBP in an attempt to elicit CBP's support. Attempts at both the national and local levels failed to encourage CBP's help or attendance.

Additionally, while the U.S. Coast Guard initially supported the idea of this demonstration with enthusiasm, it ultimately refused to attend and did not respond to communications. The General Accountability Office was invited but did not respond to the invitation nor attend. The following ports and port authorities were also invited to attend:

- Alabama State Port Authority
- American Association of Port Authorities
- Georgia Port Authority
- Jacksonville Port
- Maryland Ports
- North Carolina Ports
- Port Authority of New York/New Jersey
- Port of Charleston
- Port of Hampton Roads (Virginia Maritime Association)
- Port of Portland
- Port of Virginia

None of these entities responded or attended. A total of approximately 50 invitations were sent with marginal results. Finally, invitations were made to some members of Congress in those states having seaports. Only one staff member of one U.S. congressional representative attended. There were, however, follow-up calls made by a southern-border congressman, personally indicating an interest in and an acknowledgment of the importance of the demonstration.

CONCLUSION AND RECOMMENDATION

First, this demonstration proved beyond doubt that RFID usage can become a trigger of container IEDs in our ports. Second, this demonstration produced agreement among those present that because this vulnerability is real, it must be recognized by those government entities whose mission is to protect the United States. Third, although this demonstration was intended to examine the vulnerability of RFID use in our seaports, it exposed more than that. During the course of preparation, many other methods of detonating containers in our ports were discovered and successfully tested. These other methods are directly linked to the 433 MHz signal. Pointing out the vulnerability was relatively easy. Fixing it may be more difficult. In light of the potential impact on the U.S. economy of closing one or more U.S. seaports or land ports of entry and the cost of human life at and around those ports, it seems imperative that cooperative steps be taken by both the public and private sector to remove or minimize this recognized, demonstrable vulnerability and potential threat to the United States.

POSTSCRIPT

In January 2008, two months after the demonstration, DHS made an official statement regarding it. It is self-explanatory and represents the thinking and management posture of DHS:

> DHS recognizes and benefits from the use of RFID technology to ensure the smooth and secure movement of both people and cargo into the United States. It is accurate that RFID systems are in use at U.S. ports of entry (air, sea and land) and have been adopted by a number of private-sector companies for supply chain management, asset and shipment tracking and inventory purposes. While RFID systems used in maritime ports rely upon a variety of transmission frequencies for port and terminals operations, there is currently no one common RFID frequency in use throughout the global supply chain. . . .
>
> While it is technically feasible that the detection of RFID emissions could be used to trigger an explosive device within a container, DHS does not agree with the report's assessment that ports that employ RFID technology become more vulnerable to terrorist attack.

Its meaning should not be disguised. DHS admits in writing that RFID use at U.S. ports of entry is, in fact, unique and mandated with respect to frequency, amplitude, and length of transmission. Additionally, DHS admits that using this frequency to trigger an explosive device is technically feasible (capable of being carried out). The logic is indicative of the leadership. It seems that DHS is saying: "Let's wait until it happens." Like the lessons of Hurricane Katrina, let's wait and learn from the death and destruction that follows the event. Then we can act. While shameful, that would be more honest and representative of DHS's leadership. It is clear that RFID alone is certainly not the "silver bullet" or even an ideal method, nor necessarily the least expensive method of container security. So far, the literature on this subject has focused not on a solution to the problem of security but on a communication device that is one part of the solution. The security solution requires a complete system of end-to-end coverage, a solution from origin to destination, one without the disparate protocols and frequencies and the problems of access to and cost of land-based infrastructure.

The future of container security is a satellite solution, which by its nature avoids the limitations and infrastructure costs of RFID configurations. The global movement of containers requires a global solution not encumbered by the constraints inherent in current RFID applications and lack of standards. The apparent rush to RFID applications for container security in a global market is premature and limited as a land-based system.

NOTES

1. A. T. Kearney, *Smart Boxes*, 2006.
2. Passive RFID devices respond only when activated by an outside signal emitted from a transceiver. A passive device has no independent power supply. An active RFID device has its own power and can emit a signal on its own without having to be triggered by a transceiver.
3. For a more complete explanation of protocols, see "The Interference Issue in RFID Protocols: Reader-talks-first versus Tag-talks-first," *Transponder News*, http://transponder news.com/ttfrtf.html.
4. Kearney, *Smart Boxes*, p. 7.
5. "ARRL Asks FCC to Drop RFID Rules Proposed for 425–435 MHz," www.arrl .org/news/stories/2002/02/13/2/.

Chapter Ten

Transshipments and the In-Bond Vulnerabilities

We need to convince people that counterfeiting spells trouble for America, pure and simple, all right. We all know it robs Americans of jobs. It robs Americans of innovation and creativity. We need to make the point that it fuels organized crime, not in the abstract—it's not the corner of Fourth and Main—it is organized crime, and that's where the money goes; and our focus here today is that it creates a serious risk of harm to consumers. And we've got to make sure that that latter point, that counterfeiting threatens the health and safety of Americans, is not just taken as an abstract concern. It's an immediate problem.[1]

Among many of its problems, there are two serious port-related vulnerabilities for the United States: transshipments and in-bonds. These two issues are also important for commercial reasons, as indicated in Immigration and Customs Enforcement (ICE) Director John Morton's statement, and for the role of the U.S. International Trade Commission (USITC) in protecting intellectual property rights. These are not new, and there are multiple ways to address and correct them. What is more disturbing is that it is well known that these agencies are aware of these vulnerabilities but have not addressed them. The fact that the Department of Homeland Security (DHS) focuses on air, as recently demonstrated by the Transportation Security Administration's (TSA) recent patdown situation, seems to suggest that because terrorists used aircraft, its attention should be on air travelers. Clearly, the more obvious mode of transport in causing the greatest degree of injury is motor and rail carriage. It could be that DHS is primarily a reactive agency, and it is waiting for a container- or port-related attack to address these obvious container and port issues.

This analysis will provide a summary view of each of these vulnerabilities and provide solutions to address them with existing technology and processes available in private-sector markets today. The solutions will also identify different firms with different offerings that have no financial dealings together or joint operational or joint corporate activities. These potential solutions are out there to be reviewed and used as appropriate.

TRANSSHIPMENT VULNERABILITY

A few years ago, I wrote a short treatment that was published in *Textile World* of the problem with the China memorandum of understanding (MOU) and the requirements of Customs and Border Protection (CBP).[2] Essentially, China and the United States agreed to cooperate in enforcing certain levels of textile trade. Specifically, the United States had concerns about the "transshipment" issue, which would circumvent the levels and avoid appropriated taxes and hurt the U.S. producer of certain textile products. The MOU required, in addition to paper documentation, electronic transmissions of data directly to CBP to describe the shipment, country of origin, descriptions, quantities, and so on, all normal information required for a legal entry into the Customs territory of the United States. Then in 2009, I wrote in *The Maritime Executive*[3] a treatment of the Container Security Initiative (CSI) and how it doesn't work. Specifically, even if the electronic data transmitted 24 hours before the goods are laden into the vessel in a foreign port were true, we would still have a transshipment problem that has yet to be addressed by CBP. Therefore, we have waited many years for a fix that apparently nobody in the Department of Commerce (DOC) or DHS has heard about or knows about or has seen. However, based on my direct knowledge, the rest of the trading world is considering or is in the process now of evaluating existing systems that can provide the solution to transshipments, specifically the European Union (EU), China, South Africa, South Korea, Pakistan, Malaysia, and Mexico. Therefore, one must necessarily ask why it is that the United States is not evaluating solutions to the transshipment problem.

CBP considers transshipment as sending an exported product through an intermediate country before routing it to the country intended as its final destination. Specifically, transshipment means that the cargo does not arrive on the vessel it was laden into. So how does this arrival and discharging of cargo in the United States from a vessel different than the one that debarked from a foreign port impact U.S. security? Under CSI, high-risk containers receive security inspections, including X-ray scanning and radiation scanning, before being loaded on board vessels destined for the United States. Once high-risk containers are scanned at CSI ports, they are not scanned again until arrival at the U.S. seaport. Worldwide, there are 16 major transshipment ports:[4]

- Singapore
- Hong Kong
- Shanghai

- Kaohsiung (Taiwan)
- Busan (Korea)
- Tanjung Pelepas and Klang (Malaysia)
- Rotterdam
- Dubai
- Gioia Tauro (Italy)
- Algeciras (Spain)
- Hamburg
- Salalah (Oman)
- Klang (Malaysia)
- Colombo (Sri Lanka)
- Port Authority of Jamaica
- Antwerp

While not classified as major, there are many more in the Caribbean and South Atlantic that are of special interest to the United States:[5]

- Colon and Manzanillo (Panama)
- Cartagena and Barranquilla (Colombia)
- Kingston (Jamaica)
- Havana
- Cristóbal and Balboa (Panama)
- Rio Haina (Dominican Republic)
- Bridgetown (Barbados)
- Pointe-à-Pietre (Guadeloupe)
- Vieux Fort (St. Lucia)
- Point Lisas (Trinidad)

So what happens when a container is scanned in Japan but goes to Panama, where it is discharged and placed in the port until it can once again be laden onto another smaller container vessel for entry into the United States? It is not rescanned, since many of these smaller transshipment ports do not have scanning equipment. Additionally, while there are CBP authorities at CSI-operational ports that are also transshipment ports, they are subject to the law of the country in which they were placed and may not personally check or inspect these containers—even with intelligence that they contain drugs, counterfeit materials, or explosives.

DHS admits that transshipments are a serious problem. DHS's failure to solve this problem is confirmed in this official statement: "There is currently no proven technology which can address transshipped containers." This incredible admission was contained in the official testimony on container security of then Acting CBP Commissioner Jayson P. Ahern before the House Appropriations Committee, Subcommittee on Homeland Security, released on April 1, 2009.

Although the quotation from Ahern represents just one issue of this country's treatment of container security, it is based on the standards against which Ahern and others in DHS form their conclusions. It is not only the issue of standards that influences their decisions; laws and policies are equally important. In the case of container security, Ahern's statement demonstrates the lack of knowledge of container and cargo security technology and practice that relates directly back to standards established by DHS. If one looks seriously at the claimed standards of technology and/or practices of Congress, DHS, and CBP in the global container and cargo security arena, it becomes obvious that the standards and practices to which they adhere are either scientifically or practically unsupportable, or, at best, weak in light of the standards in the rest of the world.

In fairness, Ahern's use of proven technology may extricate him from an otherwise seemingly false statement. Therefore, we have waited many years for a fix that apparently nobody in DOC or DHS has heard about or knows about or has seen. However, based on my direct knowledge, the rest of the trading world is considering or is in the process now of evaluating existing systems that can provide the solution to transshipments, specifically the EU, China, South Africa, South Korea, Pakistan, Malaysia, and Mexico.

IN-BOND VULNERABILITY

In-bond shipments to and within the United States are shipments not intended to enter the commerce of the United States and therefore do not bear the requirement of payment of the appropriate import duties and taxes required under the law. To ensure that the United States collects its duties in case an in-bond shipment does enter the commerce of the United States, CBP requires the posting of an import bond as security to guarantee payment. Bonded cargo is carried in sealed containers or trailers. Ordinarily, these conveyances, with their cargo, have a final destination outside the United States, but they can transit through the United States to a border port of export or to a U.S. seaport for export. In-bonds also could have a temporary destination in the United States but not technically in the Customs territory of the United States—destinations like foreign trade zones or bonded warehouses.

For merchandise eventually entered into the commerce of the United States, an importer may have a single transaction bond (STB) for a single customs transaction, or a continuous bond for successive transactions used for bonded refining warehouses like smelting warehouses. In-bonds classified as transportation and exportation bonds (T&E bonds) are bonded goods that must transit from a port of entry to a port of export. In-transit bonds can be used for the movement of bonded cargo to internal ports of entry such as Dallas, St. Louis, or Charlotte, where they are cleared and any obligated duties and fees are paid. Even the container's transport and handling must be done by a bonded carrier. All these bonds are surety or indemnity bonds that ensure Customs the payment of the scheduled duty listed in the Harmonized Tariff Schedule (HTS) should the goods be lost or misdirected, fail to arrive at the port of export, bonded warehouse, or foreign trade zone, or be illegally entered into U.S. commerce.

Given the nature of in-bond shipments transiting the United State, there is no government monitoring of their movement or accessibility to the cargo. In 2008, I wrote about the vulnerability of this practice[6] and the lack of oversight by CBP and the resulting security and fraud risks of this system. Yet, now four years later, nothing has been done to address the security risks or the potential fraud issues that have now become more blatant and potentially dangerous.

In its report GAO-07-561 of May 17, 2007, the Government Accountability Office (GAO) found that CBP frequently does not follow up on shipments processed through the in-bond system. GAO stated:

> The limited information available on in-bond cargo also impedes CBP efforts to manage security risks and ensure proper targeting of inspections. In-bond goods transit the United States with a security score based on manifest information and do not use more accurate and detailed entry type information to re-score until and unless the cargo enters U.S. commerce. As a result, some higher risk cargo may not be identified for inspection, and scarce inspection resources may be used for some lower risk cargo.

Not only has CBP failed to address the security problem, it now has also failed to address the import tax issue, which costs the United States hundreds of millions of dollars in revenue; it raises the likelihood that contraband could move on to other U.S. destinations to illegally enter the commerce of the United States, thereby avoiding import taxation, or duties. This possibility is evidenced by CBP's March 3, 2008, announcement of seizing more than $67 million worth of clothing illegally brought to the United States via the in-bond system. The shipment was supposed to transit through the U.S. Southwest to a Mexican destination. Clearly, introducing contraband into the U.S. commercial system is a recognized problem. In fact, DHS has established the National Intellectual Property Rights Coordination Center (IPR Center) to meet the counterfeit problem, which, according to Erik Barnett, assistant deputy director of U.S. Immigration and Customs Enforcement, "is to address the theft of innovation that threatens U.S. economic stability and national security, undermines the competitiveness of U.S. industry in world markets, and places the public's health and safety at risk."[7]

The IPR Center has the following partners working together for this purpose:[8]

- U.S. Customs and Border Protection (CBP)
- Food and Drug Administration Office of Criminal Investigations (FDA OCI)

- Federal Bureau of Investigation (FBI)
- U.S. Postal Inspection Service (USPIS)
- Department of Commerce International Trade Administration
- U.S. Patent and Trademark Office
- Defense Criminal Investigative Service
- Naval Criminal Investigative Service
- Army Criminal Investigative Command Major Procurement Fraud Unit
- U.S. Consumer Product Safety Commission
- Inspector General's Office from the General Services Administration (GSA)
- Defense Logistics Agency Office of Inspector General
- U.S. Department of State
- U.S. Air Force Office of Special Investigations
- Royal Canadian Mounted Police

Along with these partners, DHS has Immigration and Customs Enforcement (ICE), with its Homeland Security Investigations International Affairs (HSI-IA), representing the largest investigative law enforcement presence abroad for DHS. However, one hardly finds the word "in-bond" within the lexicon of DHS. In fact, in Assistant Deputy Director Erik Barnett's recent 5,000-word testimony before the Senate, the word "in-bond" did not appear.

Perhaps more disturbing is the recent nearly 3,000-word testimony of Assistant Commissioner Allen Gina of CBP on the fight to prevent counterfeit products from entering the United States. In the "Deterrence" section of his testimony, he stated:[9]

> In conjunction with our IPR enforcement efforts directed at goods entering and exiting the United States, CBP is working proactively to deter future violations. Such initiatives include strengthening the deterrent effect of fines and penalties by appropriately levying them and increasing collections; expanding and increasing the effectiveness of IPR audits to deprive counterfeiters and pirates of their illicit profits; and promoting criminal enforcement against counterfeiting and piracy by collaborating with ICE and supporting the IPR Center.

But, just as in the testimony of Erik Barnett, the word "in-bond" is *conspicuously absent* from Commissioner Allen Gina's testimony. Unfortunately, there may be a real and honest basis for this omission. As I was told by a retired CBP law enforcement supervisor, the problem with in-bonds and CBP is that today, CBP's focus is on interdicting illegal aliens and there are only a few CBP personnel left with the training, experience, and knowledge of the in-bond process and its concomitant risks and vulnerabilities. But we know in-bond shipments are, without doubt, a major source of counterfeit products. One merely has to look at one U.S. port of entry on the U.S.-Mexico border to see the vulnerability.

In support of this contention, in cities like Laredo, Texas, there are now allegations that CBP may be willfully avoiding its responsibility to ensure proper duty and even tax collection. In Laredo, the largest land port on the southern border, CBP, instead of enforcing and supervising the legal in-bond process, is accused by many of looking the other way. As a result of CBP's avoidance of action, reputable businessmen in Laredo have now stepped up to contest CBP's lack of enforcement.

SOLUTIONS TO THESE VULNERABILITIES

It isn't a question of whether there are solutions. The question is really how much is the price for these solutions? There is both a monetary and political price. The monetary questions rest in what a firm is willing to pay to make its supply chain more visible, efficient, and financially beneficial. The political question is to what degree DHS will move to fix a vulnerability in the face of objections by the industry, since any mandated solution will likely be opposed on both political and financial grounds. Therefore, the solutions that follow will be limited to restricting government-mandated solutions to just the three areas of vulnerabilities discussed in this analysis: in-bond shipments, shipments going through transshipment ports, and all outbound containers.

There are basically three ways of correcting these weaknesses. The first is the use of newly designed, ISO-compliant (International Organization for Standardization-compliant) containers that were designed here in the United States and serve as critical security and efficiency improvements over existing shipping containers. Second is the use of human inspectors from legitimate global firms whose primary service is the certification of the contents of the container prior to shipment. Third is a container security device (CSD), the use of which can identify the person verifying the contents, monitor the container's movement, detect and report breaches and the presence of explosives, radiation, temperature, and so on, and certify that an authorized person opened the container at destination. Each performs a slightly different but essential purpose. Combined, they would be, without question, the *complete* solution to all the vulnerabilities.

A New Container

In October 2010, the World Customs Organization (WCO) announced the existence of containers without doors. It went on to say:[10]

In terms of structure this "no doors" container is said to be stronger and greatly reduces the risk of collapse during shipment as it does away with the door frame which is inherently weaker than the rest of the box, thus weakening the entire structure. From a security perspective the advantages are manifold. Customs and law enforcement authorities in particular benefit from increased security and easier inspection, both of which impact positively on international efforts to secure and facilitate global trade.

These new containers have been developed and marketed by CakeBoxx in Aurora, Oregon.[11] While these containers eliminate "casual theft," as the company asserts, they also provide ease of access for government inspections, making any inspection more efficient and faster. Lifting off the top allows a view of cargo without having to remove all the cargo from the container, which is the practice of CBP. Having no doors, they are even easier to load and unload, speeding up the shipment. But probably most important is that they cannot be entered during their conveyance, even when unlocked, without special equipment, and any forced entry will be obvious. All the dimensions of the standard CakeBoxx meet the same standards required of ISO containers. However, because of their construction and their core-frame design and construction, CakeBoxxes are actually stronger and unlike ordinary containers.

Most of all, their security features are perfectly fit for the vulnerabilities cited. According to CakeBoxx, the containers:

- Don't allow access by unauthorized persons
- Are easy to open and inspect
- Have greater and faster return on investment
- Dramatically heighten cross-border security
- Streamline customs inspections
- Reduce security-related dwell times in port
- Thwart cargo theft
- Allow faster loading and unloading than with standard containers
- Can be opened, loaded, and unloaded by forklifts

What must be recognized is that DHS knows about this container, and while the WCO thought it significant and important enough to announce to its member nations and readership of its magazine, DHS's only comment was in words to this effect: "What a great concept, if only it had a couple of doors." It appears that no more needs to be said.

Private Sector Inspection and Certification

There are major global firms that can provide preshipping inspections that can verify the contents of containers: SGS, Cotecna, and Intertek. It is best I use the words of each in describing its service. It is quite clear that the use of any of these firms provides a neutral, detached agent to physically confirm a container's contents at stuffing.

SGS. "SGS is a global service provider for technical verification, inspection, and testing, and has the necessary experience, expertise, and accreditations to provide preshipment inspection. SGS experts perform a detailed inspection for exporters/importers of the industrial sector, covering important criteria such as quality, quantity, marking, packing, and loading. Our preshipment inspection offers our customers the certainty that goods arriving to their place of destination are in compliance with the agreements specified in the contract. [We offer] visual inspection, dimensional inspection, witness test, documentation review, packing, and marking."[12]

Cotecna. "Cotecna's PSI [preshipment inspection] services cover: detailed physical inspection (quality and quantity) of goods; container integrity checking and sealing of FCL [full container load] containers; documentary check and investigation services; tariff codes classification of goods; price verification; duties and taxes calculation; valuation of goods and up-to-date price database for customs; regular reporting on operations and statistics; training and capacity building."[13]

Intertek. "A physical inspection of goods before they are shipped, in the country of export, establishes the exact nature of the goods. The invoice and other documents are then scrutinised, and an accurate valuation, and customs tariff code, are assigned. These are used, in conjunction with the client country's published duty rates, to calculate the correct duties and taxes payable. An Intertek certificate is issued to the importer. This is used to substantiate the payment of full duty, prior to clearing the goods. The actual duty collected is compared with the Intertek certificates, and any shortages can be investigated and corrected."[14]

One can readily see that if one of these companies had an authorized person who verifies the cargo at the time the container is sealed, the movement would be more secure, in addition to the business benefit brought about by a more efficient and transparent supply chain since the use of firms like this is consistent with the United Nations Convention on Contracts for the International Sale of Goods, U.S. Federal Law. Imagine the effect the combination of these inspection services would have simply on liability issues involved in international contracts and cargo damage and loss.

The Use of Container Security Devices (CSDs)

Unfortunately, not much has been written about particular CSDs that are now being used in the private sector. There is a quantity of current literature on smart containers and the use of CSDs that make the container smart. It appears that the focus of DHS has been on the development of technical hardware like frequencies, sensors, and communications rather than on solutions to the problem of security. This is evidenced by DHS grants to universities that have good scientists but are not noted for their security expertise. In practice, a truly effective security solution requires a complete system of end-to-end coverage—from a container's origin to its destination. The importance of beginning control at stuffing (loading) cannot be overemphasized. It is required by the World Customs Organization, the Customs-Trade Partnership Against Terrorism (C-TPAT) and the authorized economic operator (AEO) program. Also, the U.S. SAFE Port Act of 2006 defines global supply chain as beginning at a container's origin and ending at its destination.

Obviously, the security process must acknowledge the human element—a vital component that is often eclipsed by preoccupations with technology. At origin, CSDs should include the identification of a party responsible for final inspection of the cargo prior to its dispatch and subsequent international movement. Someone must take responsibility for confirming the accurate accounting of cargo listed on the bill of lading or booking sheet, for activating the smart container system, and for sealing the container. This responsible person must be vetted for his or her integrity and competence. A CSD is the sine qua non hardware required to do this.

Logistics information typical of what is contained on a booking order or bill of lading, along with the unique identifier of the authorized person who verifies the contents, can be entered into the CSD by a secure electronic key, RFID card, or cellphone program. Equally important, there must be a counterpart at the destination, and both parties must be electronically associated with the CSD by unique identifiers in order to complete the system. When the key or equivalent is used to activate the CSD attached on the container at origin, the data contained in the container device's memory can be read at almost any time during the voyage through satellite or cellular communication. The activation also allows a CSD-equipped container to notify appropriate parties of an unauthorized breach or to report the condition of the container. CSDs can also detect the presence of shielded highly enriched uranium that portal scanning machines cannot. Besides the reporting of integrity and environment, CSDs can also provide off-course alerts all the way from origin to destination.

In effect, the process becomes the equivalent of a chain of custody. As I have said many times, it treats the container as if it were a certified and registered letter. Finally, CSDs provide data to serve as a third-party record of the origin-to-destination movement and events, recorded automatically by a worldwide call center. It offers an electronic receipt of delivery, accomplished by the opening of the container by an approved and authorized person at the destination. The process exceeds the security of registered mail by offering breach detection not just through the doors, but through any part of the container. A smart container system, then, is much more than just a locked door. It is a complete system that must[15]

- Electronically identify the authorized personnel stuffing and securing the container, and accept and report information such as container/trailer number and booking data;

- Detect a breach in any part of the container;
- Report the breach in real time (or close to real time);
- Track the container through the supply chain;
- Identify the authorized personnel unsealing the container; and
- Be software-friendly to accommodate disparate logistics programs in communicating critical data.

Current CSDs provide monitoring, detection of access, and the sensing and reporting of multiple contents within the container. While DHS has spent millions trying to reinvent the CSD wheel, which it has failed many times to do, companies like European Datacomm, GlobalTrak, LoJack, and others already provide these CSDs. And those firms producing CSDs licensed to offer chain-of-custody technology will be able to electronically identify and maintain the integrity of the container from stuffing to opening at destination.

CONCLUSION AND RECOMMENDATION

It doesn't require a gigantic intellectual leap to see that the vulnerabilities addressed in this analysis can be solved by these solutions. In the example of the in-bond problem, a container without doors could not be surreptitiously entered without leaving clear indications of entry. If entry indications are present, it would be an obvious signal to CBP or other customs administrations to take a look. If that in-bond was preinspected to verify the cargo, Customs would have evidence of the cargo entered versus the cargo found when opened. Now add to that a CSD, and we solve the in-bond problem.

Each problem will require specific solutions or an amalgam of all these technologies to solve the vulnerability. But DHS cannot now testify that no known technology exists to solve the transshipment problem, let alone the in-bonds and the outbound problem. Imagine a combination of all three. All it would take is the courage to mandate the adoption of these systems and technologies. Its use would pay for itself and even improve the bottom line of those firms using those systems, and at the same time would provide greater security for all of us. These solutions are valuable to both the government and the private sector, especially with respect to protecting multiple products such as pharmaceuticals, fashions, and other intellectual property from counterfeiting. If DHS and the USITC were really serious, they could solve some of their major problem and vulnerabilities. My recommendation is simple: require all in-bonds, outbound containers, and inbound containers moving through transshipment ports to use these technologies. Who knows? Their use may even cut unnecessary government paperwork, employees, and managers. Of course, that might be the real problem.

NOTES

1. John Morton, director of Immigration and Customs Enforcement, White House Forum on Health and Safety Impact of Intellectual Property Theft, December 14, 2010.

2. James Giermanski, "The China/US Textile Agreement and Verifications," *Textile World*, October 17, 2006.

3. Jim Giermanski, "So You Think CSI Works? Gummy Bears or Cocaine," *Maritime Executive*, March–April 2009.

4. For a list of the world's busiest transshipment ports ranked by total containerized transshipment cargo handled, see http://en.wikipedia.org/wiki/List_of_world%27s_busi est_transshipment_ports.

5. Ernst G. Frankel, "The Challenge of Container Transshipment in the Caribbean," http://www.cepal.org.

6. James Giermanski, "Analysis: In-Bond Shipments, the Trojan Horse," *Journal of Commerce Online*, Wednesday, March 19, 2008.

7. Testimony of Assistant Deputy Director Erik Barnett, U.S. Immigration and Customs Enforcement, before the Senate Committee on the Judiciary, "Oversight of Intellectual Property Law Enforcement Efforts," release date June 22, 2011.

8. Barnett, Testimony.

9. Testimony of Office of International Trade Assistant Commissioner Allen Gina, U.S. Customs and Border Protection, before the Senate Committee on the Judiciary, "Oversight of Intellectual Property Law Enforcement Efforts," release date June 22, 2011.

10. "Future Containers May Have No Doors," *WCO News*, October 2010, p. 9.

11. The referencing of companies is done without any compensation from them or with any intention of recommending one over another, and to my knowledge, those cited do not have corporate or company financial relations with each other. They were selected because they have products to solve supply chain security problems. In addition to these companies selected for this analysis, there are others with solutions readily available. I recommend that the reader review those listed as members of the national organization the Cargo Intelligence, Security, and Logistics Association (CISLA) (http://cargointelligence .org/) for other firms that can provide security solutions.

12. "Industrial Manufacturing," SGS, http://www.sgs.com/pre-shipment_inspection ?serviceId=16291&lobId=5550.

13. "Pre-Shipment Inspection Services," Cotecna, http://www.cotecna.com/com/en/ psi.aspx.

14. "Pre-Shipment Inspection (PSI)," Intertek, http://www.intertek.com/government/ pre-shipment-inspection/.

15. Robert W. Kelly, *Containing the Threat: Protecting the Global Supply Chain through Enhanced Cargo Container Security*, Reform Institute, October 3, 2007, pp. 8–9.

Chapter Eleven

Hazardous Materials Movement Security

Our nation sees more than 1 million shipments of hazardous materials every single day, and it is critical that we be on the cutting edge of research to ensure the safety and security of these shipments. Likewise, we must ensure that our first responders are adequately equipped with the information and research necessary to effectively and efficiently react to any accidents or incidents involving hazmats.

—Representative Elijah E. Cummings[1]

Given the volume of cargo, both international and domestic, that moves throughout this nation, tracking and control are paramount, and tracking sensitive materials carried by truck and rail is supposed to be subject to federal law. But is it? What follows is the scope of the issue, what has been done to address it, and the importance for supply chain stakeholders to understanding the solutions.

SCOPE OF THE RISK

Representative Cummings went on to say that nearly one-fifth of our nation's cargo contains hazardous materials. The American Association of Railroads (AAR) stated in 2006 that 1.8 million carloads of hazardous materials are transported by rail throughout the United States each year. Hazardous materials (hazmat) of all types account for 5% of total rail carloads. AAR estimates that about 68% of rail hazmat moves by tank cars, 28% on intermodal flat cars, and the rest in covered hoppers, gondolas, and other car types.[2] Hazardous cargo like liquefied chlorine gas and anhydrous ammonia rail shipments, a high concern to Department of Homeland Security (DHS) officials, alone total nearly 100,000 railcars per year in the United States.[3]

The stakes are high. During hearings the District of Columbia held in 2005, for instance, representatives of the U.S. Naval Research Laboratory testified that in a crowded urban event, a worst-case release of a chlorine gas cloud from just one pressurized 90-ton railcar could cause 100,000 deaths and injuries. The Chlorine Institute's venerable "Pamphlet 74" has for decades estimated the worst-case release from one chlorine railcar as being 4 miles wide and traveling 15 miles downwind, a fact cited in the railroads' (unresolved) federal court case aimed at deterring protective local rerouting.[4]

Although major accidents involving toxic-gas release are rare, one need only recall the 1984 disaster in Bhopal, India, when a Union Carbide gas cloud there killed an estimated 8,000 people overnight and seriously injured 100,000. The combination of rail and truck hazardous cargo amounts to 20% or more cargo moving throughout the United States. Therefore, federal and state law must ensure that first responders are adequately equipped with the information and research necessary to effectively and efficiently react to any accidents or incidents involving hazmat. They are not adequately equipped, however. It seems that only placarding and the use of material safety data sheets (MSDS) are the primary focus of the motor carrier industry. Title 49 of the United States Code of Federal Regulations (49CFR), also known as the Federal Motor Carriers Safety Regulations (FMCSR), requires the use of hazardous materials placards when shipping hazmat cargo and dangerous goods in the United States, Canada, and Mexico. MSDS documents travel with sensitive or hazardous materials, describing how to handle the material, health effects, storage, disposal, and incident procedures. These are of particular use if a spill or other accident occurs. However, trying to find examples of motor carrier compliance with federal guidelines with respect to tracking, tracing, reporting incidents, and so on is difficult and concerning, since the law now requires the tracking and monitoring of sensitive materials by the trucking industry. What's even more troubling is the apparent disregard of hazardous materials serving as weapons of mass destruction (WMD) and the vulnerability they pose, especially while in transit. The following analysis will demonstrate the lack of security enhancement in trucking these materials and the need for more work by the Transportation Security Administration (TSA) in complying with the law and developing, through demonstrations and pilots, systems and programs that will reduce the level of vulnerability this nation now faces. This analysis will include, in a minor fashion, the role of the American Trucking Associations (ATA), if any, in the trucking of hazardous materials.

ADDRESSING THE RISK

In September 2002, well before the Implementing Recommendations of the 9/11 Commission Act of 2007 (IRCA) was passed and signed into law, an operational field test was conducted by Battelle, an international science and technology enterprise that develops and commercializes technology through contract research and development. Its team included Qualcomm, the American Transportation

Research Institute (ATRI), the Commercial Vehicle Safety Alliance (CVSA), Saflink, Savi Technology, Spill Center, and Total Security Services International (TSSI). The Battelle team conducted the Hazmat Safety and Security Field Operational Test (FOT) test for the U.S. Department of Transportation's (DOT) Federal Motor Carrier Safety Administration (FMCSA). The test was conducted over a period of two years, culminating in a six-month field test of multiple technologies.

The purpose of the test was to quantify the security costs and benefits of an operational concept that applies technology and enforcement procedures to the transportation of hazardous materials. Specifically, it addressed:[5]

- Driver verification
- Off-route vehicle alerts
- Stolen conveyances (tractors and trailers)
- Unauthorized drivers
- Cargo tampering
- Suspicious cargo deliveries

While the research project found many problems, one seemed to stand out. Nobody knew who verified the hazmat cargo and drove the vehicle transporting it. The report said that there was no off-the-shelf supply chain management software at the time of the project to validate the driver's identification nor link the movement to the public sector, presumably first responders, nor the person or entity responsible for tracking the hazmat cargo. There simply was nothing to integrate the shipper, consignee, carrier, driver, and public sector. In the most fundamental fashion, the research project demonstrated what was needed for controlling hazmat movement. The technologies used were electronic seals for the trailers that would determine a breach, and geofencing, which was limited to predetermined areas where the hazmat could not enter—for instance, the White House area. The technologies included wireless voice and data communications, satellite-tracking technology, and alerts to authorities through a 24/7 control center. The results were real-time alerts based on monitoring of hazmat shipment information to increase load security and to enhance law enforcement actions and incident response in the selected test areas.

Three years later, Congress passed the Implementing Recommendations of the 9/11 Commission Act of 2007 (IRCA). In Section 1554, Motor Carrier Security-Sensitive Material Tracking, it was mandated that the secretary of transportation, through the administrator of the Transportation Security Administration,

shall develop a program to facilitate tracking of motor carrier shipments of security-sensitive materials and to equip vehicles used in such shipments with technology that provides—

(A) frequent or continuous communications;

(B) vehicle position location and tracking capabilities; and

(C) a feature that allows a driver of such vehicles to broadcast an emergency distress signal. (p. 549)

Additionally, the act called for "any new information related to the costs and benefits of deploying, equipping, and utilizing tracking technology, including portable tracking technology, for motor carriers transporting security-sensitive materials not included in the hazardous material safety and security operational field test report released by the Federal Motor Carrier Safety Administration on November 11, 2004" (p. 550). Appropriated funding was $7 million for each fiscal year in 2008, 2009, and 2010. In each year $3 million may be used for equipment.

The IRCA made it clear that hazardous materials generation, storage, control, and transportation are serious components of any hazmat vulnerability in the United States. However, nothing was done to comply with the new law. Two years later, in 2009, Congress again attempted to legislate new hazmat controls through H.R.1013, the Hazardous Materials Cooperative Research Act of 2009, which was introduced by Representative Cummings. Section Two, "Findings and Purposes," of the proposed legislation revealed to what extent hazardous material can pose a threat to this nation. This analysis is limited to only one aspect of the vulnerability, the movement or transport of sensitive materials over our highways. Section Two of H.R.1013 states the following with respect to the size of the risk and the motor carriers' role.

Congress finds the following:

(1) There are more than 1,000,000 shipments per day in the United States of materials identified as hazardous by the Department of Transportation. These shipments are estimated to total 2,100,000,000 tons of hazardous cargo per year and to comprise more than 18 percent of the total freight tonnage moved in the United States annually.

(2) . . . It is estimated that there are currently 400,000 large trucks . . . dedicated to the shipment of hazardous materials.

(3) More than a dozen Federal agencies have regulatory, enforcement, and operational responsibilities for ensuring the safety and security of hazardous materials shipments. In addition, a variety of State and local agencies have responsibility for developing and enforcing State-level regulations and for responding to incidents involving hazardous materials.

(4) Decisions regarding the packaging and routing of hazardous materials shipments, the development and implementation of procedures to ensure both the safety and security of such shipments, and the regulation of hazardous materials shipments are made by industry groups and government entities at a variety of levels and in all modal administrations of the Department of Transportation on a daily basis.

(5) . . . Much of this research is program- or mode-specific and as such is focused on addressing only the regulatory, inspection, enforcement, or operational needs of the group undertaking the research.

(6) There is a documented need for the establishment of a cooperative research program that will engage all modes and actors, both public and private, involved in the transportation of hazardous materials in conducting cross-cutting assessments of hazardous materials transportation issues that are national and multi-modal in scope and application.

Unfortunately, this bill was never passed. Given this situation, what is the federal government doing to mitigate the vulnerability, and what is the role of the American Trucking Associations in the research, pilot program development, or support of programs to minimize the potential risk? In reviewing the remarks of Robert Petrancosta, who testified on behalf of the ATA on May 14, 2009, one finds only six issues discussed. None related to the new federal requirement to track and monitor hazardous materials carried by truck. In fact, his testimony was more historical in nature, complaining about unnecessary obligations and costs placed on the trucking industry by state and federal governments. No references were made to any laws or regulations in the years of 2001, 2003, 2006, 2007, and 2008. Petrancosta made eight references to issues in the years of 2002, 2004, 2005, and 2009 unrelated to the carriage and monitoring of hazardous materials by motor carriers. However, the federal government has been quite busy in this regard.

In effect, nobody seemed to take seriously the incredibly serious threat of hazmat carriage being used as a WMD. On May 27, 2008, the TSA released its report, complying with the IRCA's mandate to issue a report. The report, titled "HAZMAT Truck Security Pilot" (HTSP), was produced by the TSA Office of Transportation Sector Network Management Highway and Motor Carrier Division. The report described a project "to demonstrate the feasibility of an eventual national truck-tracking center (TTC) capable of interfacing with carriers' tracking systems through a non-proprietary, universal interface." TSA made two contract awards, one to the Science Applications International Corporation (SAIC) that provided the analysis, and one to General Dynamics Advanced Information Systems (GDAIS) that addressed the design and implementation of the truck-tracking system. The results of the HTSP "demonstrated a platform for the development of a program" that would satisfy mandated requirements.

This pilot demonstrates the inability of TSA, in particular, and DOT, in general, to even understand first, the fundamentals of supply chain tracking and security, and second, what technology is currently available in the market—precluding any need for development of a program. It is clear by virtue of the report's recommendations that the pilot was limited, questionably crafted, and fundamentally flawed. In addition, the Congress has shown, again, its lack of commitment in addressing the hazmat vulnerability of trucking sensitive materials. Finally, there was the conspicuous absence of the ATA in any of the activities. Reading the HTSP report makes one wonder if DOT ever read the Battelle Report of 2004. TSA seemed ignorant of any of the research preceding the Battelle Report that demonstrated a need to have a chain-of-custody process beginning with the identity of the driver (although it should begin with the person loading the hazardous materials) and control of the entire movement. It also listed the projected tactics of terrorists who wish to use hazardous materials as their weapon.

THE SUPPLY CHAIN

Not only is there a domestic concern for hazmat carriage vulnerabilities, there is also an international issue. According to both IRCA and the SAFE Port Act of 2006, "the term 'international supply chain' means the end-to-end process for shipping goods to or from the United States, beginning at the point of origin (including manufacturer, supplier or vendor) through a point of distribution to destination" (pp. 491–92 of IRCA). One assumes that although the HTSP was domestic in character, the supply chain would continue to be defined from the shipper at origin to the consignee at destination. Unfortunately, the data flow revealed in the HTSP report never included a consignee at destination. In other words, while sensitive hazmat materials could manage their way through the chain, there was no conclusion to it. In a real supply chain one must know and be accountable for the proper contents that are loaded at origin and equally accountable in verifying the same cargo and quantity at destination. The logistics data must be complete and flow between shipper and consignee and to appropriate regulatory agencies until a safe arrival and verification at destination.

The data path begins with the identification of content. Usually, the shipper will have a prewritten bill of lading for the motor carrier to sign and accept. However, one cannot depend on the accuracy of the contents as listed on the bill of lading unless the driver actually watched the loading. If the conveyance or transport container were sealed at origin, before the motor carrier arrived, how does the motor carrier accurately know the contents? The carrier must accept the word of the shipper—but whose word, that of a vetted and accountable person who verified the contents or the person at the shipper's loading dock who may not know what is in the conveyance? The carrier cannot even placard the contents with surety unless one can verify the contents. Therefore, data flows must begin at origin, continue throughout the container's movement, and end at destination with the identity of the person at each end verifying the contents and quantity, the minimum for proper placarding of the conveyance for its movement.

General Dynamics, one of the vendors, admits that there was a "challenge of obtaining cargo data" and recommended three options:

1. Entering cargo data directly into the tracking system data stream
2. Manually entering cargo data into a web application
3. Interfacing with carrier dispatch systems to extract cargo data

All of these options can be satisfied today with current off-the-shelf technology. How could TSA be unaware of the technology's existence?

LIMITATIONS OF THE PILOT

One can often find the limitations of a project or demonstration by examining its objectives, findings, and recommendations. Actually, the HTSP was quite limited and bore little resemblance to reality given the absence of real supply chain functions. Its focus appeared to be on communications, while it claimed to "establish best practices and identify security enhancements in the trucking industry." In fact, security enhancement in the trucking industry was not included in the objectives of the pilot. The pilot did little, if anything, to enhance security in the trucking of hazardous materials. HTSP objectives were to

- Develop and demonstrate a centralized truck-tracking center (TTC)
- Develop and demonstrate a nonproprietary universal interface system or set of protocols that will allow alerts and tracking information to be transmitted from all commercially available tracking systems to a prototype TTC
- Evaluate the feasibility of utilizing the developed universal set of protocols or interface system to pass truck-tracking information between a TTC and a 24-hour government intelligence operations center
- Provide an independent analysis of the recommendations and validate the results of the above objectives

It is clear by the choice of vendors that communication was the objective. Unfortunately, communication is only one part of any security in moving hazardous materials. Even so, the recommendations of the report did little to support the communication objective.

RECOMMENDATIONS OF THE REPORT

The HTSP listed eleven categories of recommendations. These categories again revealed what appeared to be a lack of awareness of off-the-shelf technology. In fact, the private sector is far ahead of what the HTSP demonstrated. This is borne out in the report's own words: "Motor carriers who participated in the HTSP Staged Event testing had mixed feelings overall about the usefulness of the HTSP system. Most were very satisfied with their current security equipment and technology use in performing operations." The private sector already has access to smart conveyances or transport containers that can do more than the HTSP has demonstrated.

In fact, the use of smart containers precludes the need for a driver's participation in the communication process; smart containers can communicate on their own. Additionally, the user or the third-party international control center ("platforms") can communicate with the container, depending on the programming, sensors, and communications technology, in real time or close to real time. The very smart containers not only electronically tell one the contents of the container but also who supervised loading the cargo and who is accountable for the accuracy of the contents at origin; the time the container was sealed; when it left origin; its route; its internal environment; its progress; whether it deviated from its course; its arrival at destination; and who opened it and verified the cargo.

Each recommendation in the report indicated positive steps that needed to be taken to improve the HTSP results and revealed the level of sophistication at which TSA worked. Recommendations covered:

- The need for interface of communications
- The need for redesign of system architecture
- The need to develop a reliable geofencing capability
- The need to solve the problem of inconsistent alert signals, which was directly linked to the role of the driver
- The need to solve the flaw in vehicle-based communications as opposed to stand-alone, untethered transport container/trailer/tanker conveyances
- The need to incorporate HTSP system's fit with other technologies and protocols
- The need for cooperation on the regional level
- The need to align technological applications to national incident management frameworks
- The need to leverage the value of tracking and control to the lowering of insurance premiums
- The need for tax incentives because of the extra security it would provide to our government
- The need to optimize the supply chain and information on loads, threats, and sequencing of response information

In every case of recommendations contained in the report, existing technology would accommodate and fulfill the recommendations. In fact, the pilot appeared to be so rudimentary that it simply failed to show what can be done.

THE OBVIOUS: A NEED FOR A REALISTIC PILOT

When one looks at the mandates from the IRCA, one would expect that given the money authorized for this project and the potential vulnerability of moving sensitive materials, more comprehensive pilots using up-to-date technologies should follow. To the contrary, a TSA insider stated that the money referenced in the IRCA was immediately "re-programmed" away from hazmat tracking. So where is the money? What other projects or pilots are scheduled to meet the requirements of the law?

There is a need for a real-world pilot to evaluate a security response to a motor carrier hazmat incident involving a genuine supply chain. Around 2009, there was a tentative agreement from a major U.S. motor carrier affiliated with the American Chemical Council (ACC) to participate in a realistic hazmat supply chain project. There was also an agreement from a container/trailer security service provider to provide technology available today and recommended in the HTSP report. The technology would include the chain-of-custody process from origin to destination. All communications would be real-time or close to real-time and automatically generated by a system contained in the "untethered" container/trailer/tanker, not from the tractor or by the driver. While any hazmat cargo could be used in the pilot, it seems prudent to choose one of the 42 chemicals contained in Attachment C of the American Chemical Council Facility Security Prioritization Process. These chemicals are contained in the FBI's listing of the "potential for misuse in weapons of mass destruction"[6] and are most likely to be targeted for theft, diversion, and use in WMD. Additionally, a new pilot would allow all communications to be coordinated by TSA and link all designated, appropriate local, state, regional, and national entities having a need to be cognizant of the movement and any incident that may occur from shipper to consignee. All communication monitoring and reporting movement throughout the supply chain would be via satellite, Internet, telephone, or cellular communication.

Finally, all alert information of unauthorized breaches into the transport container and spills would be automatically and initially transmitted by satellite communications that can inform appropriate local, state, regional, and national centers of the description of the cargo, its origin and destination, its placard identification, its decontamination instructions, and its safe area parameters as contained in the North American Emergency Guide Response Guidelines. This is especially important if the driver is incapacitated or the conveyance is hijacked. However, that proposed pilot never took place.

CONCLUSION

Today, the off-the-shelf (OTS) technology developed by the private sector in the form of container security devices is robust and inexpensive. Existing OTS chain-of-custody technology can be applied and used in the world of hazmat movements with smart containers, trailers, and railcars with respect to controlling the integrity of a hazmat shipment.

1. Smart containers provide the electronic equivalent of a receipt, showing evidence of contents and evidence of shipping. The evidence is provided by a specialized electronic data key or comparable electronic device usable only by an authorized individual at the point of origin. Similar to a law enforcement officer collecting evidence, that person is identified as the authorized person supervising the stuffing of the container and verifying its contents. At the time the electronic data key or biometric information is inserted into the smart container system, there is a data transfer of logistics and booking information agreed upon by the shipper and consignee, to include information for government agencies as necessary, into the smart container's hardware. Within seconds of the insertion, the activation of the system takes place. The identity of the authorized and accountable person verifying the cargo's accuracy and any logistical data agreed upon will automatically be transferred from the container by satellite or cellular communications.

2. Depending on the robust nature of the hardware, the smart container provides a unique identifier for tracking and communication, which allows the consignee or consignor to query the container while it is in transit and also allows the container itself to independently report any movement off its intended journey. Satellite and/or cellular-monitored and tracked smart containers automatically offer, through the use of worldwide call centers, a third-party record of any break in the chain of custody.

3. A smart container employing the chain-of-custody process can provide an electronic receipt of delivery, generated by the opening of the container at destination by a person approved and authorized to open the container or trailer. Its opening is accomplished by another specialized electronic data key or biometric reading directly linked to an authorized individual at the point of destination.

The only real difference with the chain of custody described in other legal circles is that the smart containers can do all of this electronically. Smart containers not only meet the challenges of providing a good control similar to that of a registered and certified letter in the postal system, but also provide the electronic management not available in documentary chains, thus exceeding the demands of jurisprudence.

These smart container security devices (CSDs) are able to monitor movement of containers internationally and domestically from origin to destination. However, there is much more that CSDs can do than just report location. The smartest containers are smart because they can carry on a conversation. The user or their international control center ("platforms") can communicate with them, depending on the programming, sensors, and technology used, in real time or close to real time. Tracking and tracing function traits of a mentally challenged smart container merely monitor location by RFID fixed antennas or by satellite or cellular communication, depending on the level of communication latency the user is willing to accept. However, the very smart containers electronically tell one the contents of the container, who supervised loading the cargo and who is accountable for the accuracy of the contents at origin, the time the container was sealed, when it left origin, its route, its internal environment, its progress, whether it deviated from its course, its arrival at port of embarkation, when it was loaded aboard the vessel, whether it was breached, when it arrived at the destination port, and who opened it and verified the cargo.

And there are companies out there that can provide smart containers now. Just a few examples of these companies are European Datacomm, LoJack, and GlobalTrak. There are also multiple satellite service providers like Iridium, ORBCOMM, Inmarsat, Europe's Galileo, and the Chinese entry into satellite communication, Compass, which can provide position detection at relatively low costs. It will provide a chain-of-custody system starting with a trusted agent who supervises the loading of the hazardous materials and secures the cargo. It then detects any intrusion into the conveyance carrying the cargo, reports the intrusion into the conveyance or any accident or spill of the cargo without the initiation or participation of the driver, reports any off-course deviation from the planned route of the cargo's movement, and when programmed to do so, will automatically inform the closest first responders of the identity of the hazardous materials and all action necessary for them to take to safeguard the public.

All admit that the transport of hazardous materials is a genuine vulnerability. Its apparent shelving is a greater vulnerability. The claim, especially by the ATA, that nothing has happened so far (meaning no tragic hazmat event), so there is no need for action now, is fundamentally flawed and ignorant. Will it take an actual catastrophic event to occur before serious action by TSA is taken? Is there a more active role for the ATA to play? Perhaps a shift from focusing on the costs and jurisdictional obligations to the real control of the supply chain in which hazardous materials move will automatically solve the problems of jurisdictional controls and costs. It's time for both the TSA and ATA to do more, and for Congress to do its job in seeing that the law is followed!

POSTSCRIPT

Recently, representatives from the Chinese government came to the United States to discuss the development of a hazmat control process in China. China was able to find a small firm in South Carolina that can provide the chain-of-custody process. The Chinese representatives explained through volunteer interpreters from Clemson University that China has 500,000 domestic movements of hazardous materials that not only present a security threat but provide a loss of revenue for China since every level of business activity is taxed; without being able to know all the movements, the government was losing revenue in addition to risking injury and potential destruction of areas that could be contaminated by hazardous material spills for many years in the future.

The obvious question is how did China find a U.S. firm in South Carolina that used individuals from Clemson University to provide the translations for providing hazmat transportation security in the form of a chain-of-custody process, when the U.S. government has not moved to secure hazmat material movements in violation of U.S. law or even find a U.S. private sector firm to do so? Again, it seems that securing the supply chain, whether domestic or global, is an obstacle that other nations can overcome, but not something the United States can accomplish.

NOTES

1. Elijah E. Cummings, congressional representative from Maryland's 7th District, "Statement on National Security," http://cummings.house.gov/issues/national-security .shtml.

2. American Association of Railroads, "Hazmat Transport: Mandatory Routing and Pre-Notification," January 2006.

3. Resolution Number 52.52.09R, Resolution calling upon the Obama administration and the United States Congress to reconsider the new routing rule that allows the railroad companies to determine the safest and most secure routes for transporting chlorine and other hazardous materials, and to amend the rule to require railroad companies to work with state and local officials to determine the safest and most secure routes, City of Albany, May 4, 2009.

4. Fred Millar, "Terror Threats Ought to Factor into Rail Routes: We Deserve to Know the Worst-Case Scenarios for Toxic-Gas Releases," *Minneapolis Star Tribune*, June 18, 2009.

5. Battelle, *Hazmat Safety and Security Field Operational Test Final Report*, August 31, 2004, p. vi.

6. American Chemistry Council Responsible Care Program, *ACC Facility Security Prioritization Process*, March 2002, p. 8, https://docs.google.com/viewer?a=v&q=cache: ZiBsAfZhjrIJ:209.190.250.114/Security-Facility-Prioritization-Process+FBI+-+List+ Chemicals+Attachment+C+of+ACC+Facility+Security&hl=en&gl=us&pid=bl&srcid= ADGEESi0TTjjgyX3HO81iesJG8P91LTedNikEvYXXlPSDxohOp1ARHgmz6BBhIrm e7JaqnLGjdQuaYuXIu4avvftGHKxi8AsKC7a2EH352bSmKrRTSkQyJRdoVA0FLQy WKonFpmwxunE&sig=AHIEtbRYaXRwp8MkYQblcg3jj81FwSQlWg.

Chapter Twelve

Hazardous Materials:
The Cross-Border Threat

For many years, there has been increasing public awareness and concern about the large quantities of hazardous materials and wastes generated in Mexico by U.S.-owned companies and transported between Mexico and the United States. Because of the North American Free Trade Agreement (NAFTA) and other trade liberalization, the application of the laws and regulations that control the movement of hazardous substances will be changing rapidly. Regulators on both sides of the border are under pressure to provide the industry with information about the regulatory requirements to be mandated in the future.

Additionally, the tragedy of September 11, 2001, and the ensuing federal legislation like the USA Patriot Act, which amended 49 U.S.C. Chapter 51 by adding a new section (5103(a)), underscores the importance of the control of hazardous materials and the potential impact of their wrongful use.

U.S. LAWS AND REGULATIONS

Resource Conservation and Recovery Act (RCRA)

RCRA gives the U.S. Environmental Protection Agency (EPA) the authority to control hazardous waste from "cradle to grave." This includes the generation, transportation, treatment, storage, and disposal of hazardous waste. RCRA also sets forth a framework for the management of nonhazardous wastes.

Waste is considered hazardous under RCRA if it is expressly identified as hazardous in provisions of the Code of Federal Regulations (CFR) issued pursuant to RCRA or if within other designated regulatory categories. EPA codes are correlated to each listed waste. Every EPA code that applies to a waste is required for notification, recordkeeping, and reporting requirements under RCRA and the regulations. Wastes not expressly listed may still be classified as hazardous, however, if they satisfy requirements under other regulations.[1]

RCRA also requires that all hazardous waste generated in the United States be accompanied by a hazardous waste manifest. This document is the key to the "cradle-to-grave" control of RCRA. A manifest must be completed for every shipment of hazardous waste. The manifest is signed by the transporter and the disposal facility and then returned to the generator of the waste. Manifests are also required for hazardous waste generated outside of the United States.[2]

Comprehensive Environmental Response, Compensation, and Liability Act (CERCLA)

CERCLA provides a federal "superfund" to clean up uncontrolled or abandoned hazardous waste sites as well as accidents, spills, and other emergency releases of pollutants and contaminants into the environment. Through the act, EPA was given power to seek out those parties responsible for any release and ensure their cooperation in the cleanup. CERCLA classifies hazardous substances by the corresponding Chemical Abstracts Service (CAS) and RCRA waste numbers where applicable.

Toxic Substances Control Act of 1976 (TSCA)

TSCA was enacted by Congress to require testing, regulation, and screening of all chemicals produced or imported into the United States. Many thousands of chemicals and their compounds with unknown toxic or dangerous characteristics are developed each year. TSCA requires that any chemical that reaches the consumer marketplace be tested for possible toxic effects prior to commercial manufacturing. In this way, TSCA tracks all existing chemicals that pose health and environmental hazards. The EPA is required to compile, keep current, and publish a list of chemical substances manufactured or processed in the United States.

Hazardous Materials Regulations (HMR)

The transportation of hazardous materials is regulated by the Research and Special Programs Administration (RSPA) in the U.S. Department of Transportation (DOT). RSPA is charged with the responsibility to promulgate the Hazardous Materials Regulations (HMR).

The hazardous materials tables in the Hazardous Materials Regulations consist of seven elements: (1) symbols, (2) proper shipping name, (3) hazard class or division, (4) identification number, (5) packing group, (6) labels, and (7) special provisions. Identification numbers preceded by the letters "UN" are commonly referred to as the LJN/DOT number and can be used for international shipments. Some numbers are preceded by "NA." NA identification numbers are only permitted for shipments between the United States and Canada.[3]

Harmonized Tariff Schedule of the United States (HTSUS)

As a result of the 1950 Customs Cooperation Council convention, the Brussels Tariff Nomenclature (BTN) was established and is used virtually throughout the free world. The United States, however, failed to become a signatory. The BTN ultimately became simply a nomenclature to classify imports, while the Standard International Trade Classification (SITC) was used by most countries to classify their exports and production.

In 1973, the Customs Cooperation Council created a group to study the feasibility of creating a harmonized code for global applicability. A Harmonized Code Convention resulted, and with the passage of the Omnibus Trade and Competitiveness Act of 1988, the United States adopted the Harmonized Code on January 1, 1989, replacing the Tariff Schedule of the United States (TSUS). Now known as the Harmonized Tariff Schedule of the United States (HTSUS) the convention remains the primary statistical source of information on merchandise trade for all signatories.

The United States International Trade Commission (ITC) is responsible for the HTSUS and the HTSA (Harmonized Tariff Schedule of the United States Annotated). The mission of the ITC is to (1) administer U.S. trade remedy laws within its mandate in a fair and objective manner; (2) provide the president, U.S. trade representative (USTR), and Congress with independent, quality analysis, information, and support on matters of tariffs and international trade and competitiveness; and (3) maintain the HTSUS. Specifically, the ITC (Office of Tariff Affairs and Trade Agreements) is responsible for publishing the HTSA. The HTSA provides the applicable tariff rates and statistical categories for all merchandise imported into the United States; it is based on the international Harmonized System, the global classification system that is used to describe most world trade in goods. The 2012 HTSUS has a chemical appendix.[4]

This appendix enumerates those chemicals and products which the President has determined were imported into the United States before January 1, 1978, or were produced in the United States before May 1, 1978. For convenience, the listed articles are described (1) by reference to their registry number with the Chemical Abstracts Service (CAS) of the American Chemical Society, where available, or (2) by reference to their common chemical name or trade name where the CAS registry number is not available. For the purpose of the tariff schedule, any reference to a product provided for in this appendix includes such products listed herein, by whatever name known.

USA Patriot Act

The Uniting and Strengthening America by Providing Appropriate Tools Required to Intercept and Obstruct Terrorism Act (USA Patriot Act) was enacted on October 25, 2001. Section 1012 of the Act amended 49 U.S.C. Chapter 51 by adding a new section (5103(a)) titled "Limitation on Issuance of Hazmat Licenses." The Interim Final Rule makes it clear that hazardous materials control is needed and now mandated to preclude an accidental catastrophe or intentional terrorist attack utilizing hazardous materials.

Safe Explosives Act (SEA)

Congress enacted the Safe Explosives Act (SEA) on November 25, 2002. Sections 1121–1123 of the SEA amended section 842(i) of Title 18 of the U.S. Code by adding several categories to the list of persons who may not lawfully "ship or transport any explosive in or affecting interstate or foreign commerce" or "receive or possess any explosive which has been shipped or transported in or affecting interstate or foreign commerce."

Implementing Recommendations of the 9/11 Commission Act of 2007 (IRCA)

As discussed in chapter 11, IRCA became law in 2007. In Section 1554, Motor Carrier Security-Sensitive Material Tracking, it was mandated that the secretary of transportation, through the administrator of the Transportation Security Administration,

> shall develop a program to facilitate tracking of motor carrier shipments of security-sensitive materials and to equip vehicles used in such shipments with technology that provides—
>
> (A) frequent or continuous communications;
> (B) vehicle position location and tracking capabilities; and
> (C) a feature that allows a driver of such vehicles to broadcast an emergency distress signal. (p. 549)

INTERNATIONAL AGREEMENTS

La Paz Agreement

On August 14, 1983, U.S. President Ronald Reagan and Mexican President Miguel de la Madrid signed the bilateral executive Agreement between the United States of America and the United Mexican States on Cooperation for the Protection and Improvement of the Environment in the Border Area (La Paz Agreement). The La Paz Agreement established a framework to solve environmental problems affecting the two countries and designated a 100-kilometer (62.5-mile) zone of mutual interest on either side of the international boundary.

The La Paz Agreement established a national coordinator for the United States and a national coordinator for Mexico. The U.S. Coordinator in Washington, DC, is the assistant administrator of international activities for the EPA. In

Mexico, the national coordinator is the Secretaría de Medio Ambiente, Recursos Naturales y Pesca (SEMARNAP).

Annex III to the La Paz Agreement addresses the transborder movement of hazardous wastes and substances between the United States and Mexico. Annex III seeks to safeguard the quality of public health, property, and the environment from unreasonable risks by regulating exports and imports while recognizing the close trading relationship and the common border of the two countries.

Annex III provides that each nation shall ensure, "to the extent practicable, that its domestic laws and regulations are enforced with respect to transboundary shipments of hazardous waste and hazardous substances." The general obligations of this annex state that the U.S.-Mexico transboundary shipments shall be governed by the annex and the respective domestic regulations, that each party shall enforce their respective domestic laws and regulations, and that each party shall cooperate in the monitoring and spot-checking of transboundary shipments along their common border.

Three articles of Annex III deal specifically with the transboundary movement of hazardous waste. Article III states that the exporting country is to provide the importing country 45-day advance notice prior to the importation of hazardous waste. The importing country has 45 days to conditionally or unconditionally consent or object to the importation. The notification and consent process occurs between the national environmental authorities, EPA and SEMARNAP. U.S. Customs takes no part in the process of notification, consent, and objection.

Article IV provides for the readmission of exports. Shipments of hazardous materials and/or waste may be returned for any reason to the original exporting country responsible for generating the waste in the foreign nation.

Article XI governs hazardous waste generated from raw materials admitted in-bond—those materials temporarily admitted to Mexico under Mexico's maquiladora program (or PITEX, Program for Production of Articles for Exportation) for processing, finishing, and/or assembly. As an original condition of admission, the finished products must be exported back to the country of origin along with the waste produced in their processing.

According to Article XI, the United States agrees to readmit any hazardous waste resulting from the production or manufacturing of products using U.S. raw materials in Mexico. However, under this agreement to readmit waste, the United States requires that waste returned from Mexico comply with all relevant U.S. import regulations and policies.

North American Free Trade Agreement (NAFTA)— Environmental Side Agreement

The environmental side agreements to NAFTA impose trade sanctions against NAFTA signatories that fail to enforce their environmental standards. The thrust of the side agreement is to ensure that each country actively enforces its environmental laws. Any country that does not effectively enforce its laws pertaining to the importation, exportation, and disposal of hazardous wastes could ultimately be compelled to do so through mechanisms available through the environmental side agreement.

Agreement Concerning Transboundary Movement of Hazardous Waste

Formalized between the United States and Canada in 1986, Articles 5 and 7 obligate the parties to enforce their domestic laws regarding hazardous waste management and cooperate in enforcement efforts regarding waste shipments moving across the shared border.

The Basel Convention on the International Transportation of Hazardous Waste

The Basel Convention is the first attempt to deal with hazardous waste exports on a global scale. Its objective is to protect countries against the uncontrolled dumping of toxic wastes. It also promotes environmentally sound waste disposal and minimization of waste generation. The U.S. Senate has given its advice and consent to the Basel Convention, but Congress must still approve implementing legislation.

THE SUPPLY CHAIN VULNERABILITY

Although there are clear definitions and regulatory procedures for the transportation of hazardous materials and waste, there are no effective methods for identifying and monitoring the movement of hazardous materials and waste through Canada, Mexico, and the United States. Therefore, there is no information based on empirical data regarding the actual number of crossings and the identity of the hazardous substance being imported and exported. Proper identification of hazardous materials is critical to public safety and the safety of those who must handle or inspect the substances. Proper identification should provide information regarding the toxicity, flammability, corrosiveness, and requirements for decontamination and cleanup in case of an accident or spill.

The movement of hazardous materials is linked to many agencies of government, for instance, the Federal Carrier Motor Safety Administration (FMCSA). Monitoring hazmat movement and control is essential in promoting and ensuring public safety and contributes to the planning of facilities to manage the treatment, storage, and disposal of these substances. In an environment of international terrorism and in the aftermath of September 11, 2001, the control of hazardous material moving between and among countries is critical and essential for the safety of the United States.

In the United States, importing and exporting hazardous materials and waste involves five parties: (1) the exporter/shipper, (2) the importer/receiver, (3) the transporter, (4) the customs administration, and (5) the state regulatory agency. EPA approval is required for exports of hazardous materials and wastes; verification of importer consent may also be required.[5] EPA, in conjunction with Customs and Border Protection (CBP), is authorized to enforce requirements relating to hazardous materials imports.[6] EPA, however, is not involved in the daily dynamics of importing and exporting hazardous materials and waste.

Responsibilities of Parties

The Exporter/Shipper

The exporter/shipper is responsible for satisfying the requirements of the exporting country with respect to packaging, marking, labeling, and placarding. The shipper must also comply with the packaging and marking laws and regulations of the state in which the hazardous wastes will be disposed, treated, and stored. The shipper must also accommodate the unique requirements of the importer/receiver, who is the responsible party in the country of importation.

The Importer/Receiver

The importer/receiver is responsible for meeting the requirements of the country of importation and the state in which the materials are to be disposed, treated, or stored. The importer has perhaps the most important responsibility of all the parties in that he or she becomes the generator of hazardous wastes. For instance, in the United States, the generator is responsible for the treatment, storage, disposal, and transport of hazardous waste. It is the generator of hazardous waste that must provide the hazardous waste manifest.

The Transporter

The transporter is responsible for the safe movement of the hazardous materials and waste. The transporter must place specific placards on the transportation equipment identifying the substance being transported. Placards assist those involved in a cleanup because different types of hazardous materials have specific guidelines for decontamination and cleanup in the case of an accident or spill. The transporter is also responsible for ensuring that the shipment is properly documented and complies with all other requirements under federal guidelines.[7]

Customs and Border Protection (CBP)

CBP is responsible for determining if the hazardous substance is properly documented for import purposes. Under a memorandum of understanding with the EPA, CBP has agreed to the following:

- Make reasonable attempts to ensure that transporters deliver manifests to Customs in compliance with export regulations and promptly transmit these forms to EPA
- Make reasonable attempts to receive import manifests that are voluntarily supplied (this is now required) by import transporters and promptly transmit those manifests to EPA
- Instruct Customs officers regarding requirements applicable to hazardous waste imports and exports
- Provide training to Customs officials enabling them to enforce hazardous waste import and export requirements and other regulations pertaining to hazardous materials imports and exports

The State Regulatory Agency

The EPA delegated regulatory authority to the state, and the state regulatory agency is responsible to the EPA and to each state to ensure that the treatment, movement, storage, and disposal of hazardous substances are in accordance with state and federal law. Additional functions performed by the state environmental regulatory agencies include monitoring waste, assigning generator and transporter ID numbers, and issuing permits for waste facilities.

The Resource Conservation and Recovery Act (RCRA) state authorization is a rulemaking process through which EPA delegates the primary responsibility of implementing the RCRA hazardous waste program to individual states in lieu of EPA. This process ensures national consistency and minimum standards while providing flexibility to states in implementing rules. Currently, 49 states and territories have been granted authority to implement the base, or initial, program. Many are also authorized to implement additional parts of the RCRA program that EPA has since promulgated, such as Corrective Action and the Land Disposal Restrictions. State RCRA programs must always be at least as stringent as the federal requirements, but states can adopt more stringent requirements.

Importers and transporters are required to mark the inward manifest or bill of lading "Hazardous Cargo" and provide a full description of the substance. 49 C.F.R. Section 172.202(a)(5)(b) requires that the hazardous substance description, class or division, identification number, and packing group be included on a shipping document or bill of lading.

The United States International Trade Commission (ITC)

As previously stated, the ITC has responsibility for publishing the Harmonized Tariff Schedule (HTS) and HTSA, but they do not have the responsibility of enforcing compliance with it. Therefore, in actual practice, importers and carriers often fall short of the regulatory requirements of a full description. A shipper may enter "4 drums of gasoline" on the inward manifest and include the proper HTS number rather than the description required by the HMR: "Gasoline, 3, UN1203, PG II." Unfortunately, there is no means by which a customs inspector or other individual can cross-reference the HTS number with the proper description or the UN Department of Transportation (UN/DOT) number. Cross-referencing the HTS and LJN/DOT classification, however, ensures that the complete and proper information can be accessed by the authorities.

At the present time, the essential HTS number does not alert Customs or state agencies that the product being imported is hazardous because the HTS is not used as a hazardous material identifier. If an accident occurs while hazardous materials are in Customs' control, Customs inspectors must be fully trained in hazardous materials requirements, refer to other publications, and rely on the proper placarding and EPA documentation to identify the hazardous material and the decontamination and cleanup requirements. The problem is exacerbated if there is no placarding or documentation.

The HTS number is unique, however, in that U.S. Customs will not consider any shipments for entry into the United States unless the cargo is assigned an HTS number. The shipment is simply ineligible for entry into the United States unless it is assigned an HTS number. The use of the HTS in this manner also provides an additional incentive to importers to properly declare hazardous substances. If a party incorrectly classifies the shipment under the HTSUS, CBP may fine the party. If the party intentionally misclassifies the shipment, penalties can also be imposed.

Unfortunately, the HTS designation for a broad category of goods coming into the United States is "articles exported and returned." This classification allows for the return of hazardous goods under a general tariff heading (HTS 9800.00.00 and subsequent subheadings), which fails to identify the goods as hazardous by means of a specific HTS-number identification of the substance. By modifying this basket-type entry with either an additional specific HTS number to identify the hazardous substance or an electronic code attached to the 9800 HTS subheading used, it would be possible to determine the actual identity of the hazardous materials being returned.

All of the responsibilities of the environmental regulatory agencies depend upon the proper identification of the cargo and knowledge of its entry into the United States. The inability to identify hazardous shipments properly is the weak link in the system. Present regulations only require that the international UN hazardous materials numbers be used on the carrier's bill of lading or shipping documents.

Although the HTS number is required on all international shipments of goods entering or departing the United States, there is no cross-reference of the HTS number and the UN hazardous substance identification number. This means that Customs authorities and other federal agencies must rely on the documentation required by the EPA and the proper placarding of the cargo by the shipper and/or the carrier in order to carry out their regulatory responsibilities. There is no requirement for an HTS number for shipments exported from the United States if the goods being exported are valued at less than US$2,500 per HTS number.

Import shipments valued at less than US$2,500 do not require a formal entry under Customs bond; such a shipment is allowed to be entered as an "informal entry." Thus, it is possible for a truckload of highly toxic waste to be entered without any Customs-required hazardous materials protocol if it is valued honestly and correctly at less than US$2,500.

The maquiladora decree establishes an in-bond scheme for hazardous materials that, in concert with Mexican environmental law, ultimately requires importers to return waste products of the raw materials to the country from which they originated. Even while the concept of maquiladora has disappeared under NAFTA, the in-bond scheme still exists. This cross-border flow of hazardous cargo is also invoked by the La Paz Agreement, in which wastes from this in-bond scheme are required to be returned to their place of origin (Article XI of Annex III). The bonding system was created to circumvent the payment of tariffs on materials coming into Mexico. NAFTA eliminated all tariffs in the year 2008. Neither EPA nor SEMARNAP has taken the initiative to address this issue to date. Therefore, CBP must be prepared to handle even greater levels of confusion with hazardous cargo in the future.

Waste classification differences also exist between the legal schemes of the United States and Mexico. The National Law Center for Inter-American Free Trade completed a summary of these distinctions in the summer of 1996. No harmonized listing exists between the United States and Mexico or within the United States itself. A variation of HTS designation could greatly improve identification of materials moving through the ports. A more easily recognizable listing of hazardous cargo is essential to port and public safety.

A POTENTIAL SOLUTION TO THE VULNERABILITY

The current system of categorizing hazardous cargo border crossing is inadequate for the purposes of identifying, quantifying, and monitoring hazardous substances. This system could become effective if the HTS number used in all non-9800 occurrences of hazardous material entry or exit were electronically cross-referenced to the UN/DOT hazardous substance number or other classifications, and if 9800-type entries were electronically coded or modified to reflect the identity of the hazardous materials and to automatically provide the proper emergency response should an accident occur.

Smart containers can incorporate these essential identifying data into a chain-of-custody system that begins with the identity of the person verifying the cargo, the identification of the cargo at its loading into the conveyance, and the monitoring of the crossing and movement of hazardous materials and waste throughout North America, thus serving as the means of controlling hazmat movement. These smart containers can also, if incorporated into the system, automatically notify appropriate first responders of the location of an accident or spill and also provide the emergency response information for cleanup and safe distance requirements in the case of an accident. The essential element of the solution is the use of container security devices (CSDs) to control hazmat movement from origin to destination and automatically provide the necessary emergency responses to any potential accident. Additionally, smart containers will provide breach detection and automatic notice of any breach across U.S. borders and within the territory of the United States.

It is clear that the HTS is the primary instrument for obtaining and recording identifying data on merchandise entering and leaving the United States. No other instrument provides the legal mandate for shippers to comply with requirements to identify their cargo completely, and no other mechanism exists for routinely recording cargo that is crossing our borders. Furthermore, it is in the public interest, as well as in the interest of the business community, to adjust the HTS to more adequately identify and record all materials and substances, including all hazardous materials and substances that enter and exit the United States.

In addition, a change to the HTSUS could inspire changes to the HTS in Canada and Mexico. Potentially, a harmonized system to identify and record dangerous substances, which at this point are not identified through the harmonized tariff schedule of the three countries, could be created and be effective for all of North America.

RESULTS AND BENEFITS

I would propose that a project be conducted to accomplish four goals:

- Cross-reference the Harmonized Tariff Schedule of the United States (HTSUS) with all UN, DOT, CERCLA, RCRA, and Federal Emergency Management Agency (FEMA) identification numbers of hazardous substances, regardless of the value of the shipment. Cross-referencing with the UN/DOT number will benefit Mexico and Canada because they also use this dangerous-goods classification system. The result is a cross-reference that will work throughout North America to effectively monitor hazardous shipments, treatment, disposal, and storage.

• Amend the HTSUS to include a column that automatically identifies the hazardous substance and provides the emergency action guide number for the proper emergency response information.

• Develop computer software and standards that automatically alert the appropriate state agencies of the import and export of hazardous substances, their destinations, and the emergency action guide numbers necessary for proper emergency response through the use of the HTSUS.

• Demonstrate the capacity and ability to monitor location, and detect and communicate in real time unauthorized breaches into containers or trailers containing hazardous materials anywhere in the world with satellite coverage.

A variety of software systems exist that could be modified to include this new customs coding. Through the cooperation of other agencies and entities, there would be a series of discussions with community groups, regulators, and industry officials. The purpose of the meetings is to identify ways to improve hazardous cargo routing between the countries' sister cities, their port facilities, and through community neighborhoods. The final product of the project will be a set of recommendations regarding these issues, including reference to conflicts that have arisen with existing rules, and suggestions for needed changes to legal requirements. This could serve, at least in part, as a project match component and would give the CBP a public participation element to any new procedures established for hazardous cargo management.

Unfortunately, the movement of hazardous materials simply does not seem to merit the attention of DOT or DHS. While it is clear that federal law mandates its monitoring, the law is simply not followed by these two agencies of the administration. Clearly, this monitoring and control can be accomplished today with the hardware and software already available, and with a little more effort, all the software necessary to incorporate the new HTSUS and official North American emergency response guidelines can easily be added to what CSDs can do. The three-phase model in tables 12.1 through 12.3 lists the amount of time necessary to complete each phase; it can be easily accomplished if USDOT and CBP wish to do so. It seems a model of this type is only reasonable, given the risks and vulnerabilities of the movement of hazardous materials.

Table 12.1. Phase I: Needs and Feasibility Assessment

Tasks	Months						
	1	2	3	4	5	6	7
Task I-A. Establish contact and liaison with CBP service to obtain the dedicated services of an import specialist or Customs.	▓						
Task I-B. Review literature documenting hazardous materials and waste shipments crossing the U.S.-Mexico border.	▓						
Task I-C. Evaluate computer technology, techniques, and methods currently used by various agencies to document and monitor hazardous materials and waste shipments.		▓	▓	▓			
Task I-D. Evaluate the necessity of cross-referencing all of the various classifications of hazardous substances.	▓	▓					
Task I-E. Initiate cross-referencing of the HTS of the United States with those classification methods identified in Task I-D.		▓	▓	▓	▓		
Task I-F. Access computerized systems needs (software, databases, and hardware) to conduct remaining phases of project.		▓	▓	▓	▓		
Task I-G. Evaluate the feasibility of developing software and systems support needed for harmonizing hazardous materials and waste referencing systems.				▓	▓	▓	
Task I-H. Assess national and international policy implications with regard to (1) the impact of changes to the HTSUS on the ITC, Customs, and trade community and (2) the impact of change to the HTS on Mexico and Canada.	▓	▓	▓	▓			

Table 12.2. Phase II: Develop Computerized System to Integrate Modifications to HTS

Tasks	Months											
	5	6	7	8	9	10	11	12	13	14	15	16
Task II-A. Complete cross-referencing task begun in Task I-E.	▓	▓	▓	▓								
Task II-B. Develop new HTS numbers as needed.			▓	▓	▓	▓	▓					
Task II-C. Design and develop working version of software package.			▓	▓	▓	▓	▓	▓				
Task II-D. Evaluate performance of software package and identify improvements needed.								▓	▓			
Task II-E. Incorporate improvements and complete final version of software.									▓	▓		
Task II-F. Prepare manuals, other documentation, and implementation plan for use in field tests in Phase III.										▓	▓	▓
Task II-G. Complete analysis and assessment of policy implications (begun in Task I-H), and design a strategy for the evaluation of work product conducted to date.											▓	▓

Table 12.3. Phase III: Field Test of Computerized System and Evaluation

Tasks	Months								
	16	17	18	19	20	21	22	23	24
Task III-A. Evaluate potential test sites and participants.	▓								
Task III-B. Select appropriate test site and participants.		▓							
Task III-C. Select neutral evaluator to conduct evaluation.	▓								
Task III-D. Design and document appropriate testing procedures, measurements, and criteria for evaluation.		▓							
Task III-E. Utilize software package and implement satellite monitoring and breach detection and reporting system to conduct test.			▓	▓	▓	▓	▓	▓	
Task III-F. Evaluate test results and (in conjunction with evaluator) prepare final report of test.							▓	▓	▓

CONCLUSION

No one can refute the conclusion that the United States really does not know what hazardous material crosses its borders and enters the country. It relies on the placarding used by the carriers of the cargo. There is no harmonized tariff mandate to follow with respect to hazardous waste. And specifically, there is no mandate to verify hazardous cargo and its movement from its origin in Mexico to destinations in the United States. What is worse is the flagrant disregard for federal legislation that requires the tracking and monitoring of the hazardous materials movement within the United States. Why?

NOTES

1. 140 C.F.R. §§261.21–261.24.
2. 240 C.F.R. §262.20.
3. 349 C.F.R. §172.101.
4. Chemical Appendix to the Tariff Schedule, Harmonized Tariff Schedule of the United States (2012), p. 2.
5. 40 C.F.R. §§262.51–262.53.
6. 515 U.S.C. §2612 and 40 C.F.R. §707.20.
7. *1996 North American Emergency Response Guidebook*, U.S. Department of Transportation; Transport Canada; and Secretariat of Communications and Transportation, Mexico.

Chapter Thirteen

Innovations in Supply Chain Security

The main source of progress in the supply chain security realm comes not from government but from the U.S. private sector, which, in many cases, without federal funds, has already developed technology to support the security mission of the Department of Homeland Security (DHS) while also improving their business bottom-line benefits. This chapter will give short examples of new ideas and products that, if adopted, could greatly improve both our homeland defense and return on investment. It is not comprehensive in coverage but merely presents some examples of innovation in container and supply chain security about which DHS seems to know very little.[1]

CAKEBOXX

Independent of DHS, private industry has developed shipping containers without doors; composite construction containers; freezer boxes without the need of onboard refrigeration or shipboard power; hazmat containment containers; vacuum containers; and gondola containers that can carry liquids, solids, and up to 25 tons of heavy ore.

An Oregon-based shipper was experiencing costly product thefts from its Asian logistics chains to the European Union (EU) and the United States. An unusual solution to this was a container that had two front ends but no doors. Entry is gained by removing the sidewalls, endwalls and ceiling as a single unit, similar to the old cake boxes people used long ago to walk Sunday dessert to their neighbor's, serving as the basis for the name CakeBoxx. The optional composite panels are lighter in weight and both X-ray and radio transparent. This doorless design reduces thermal shock to the cargo in its FreezerBoxx configuration, and all CakeBoxxes have composite roofs that prevent moisture condensation and subsequent water damage.

The CakeBoxx easily solves the pilferage problem, and when opened, it has a flat platform for loading and unloading. Also, searching a container that doesn't require that the cargo be removed is a benefit for customs agents anywhere. They can search a CakeBoxx in minutes, right on a dock, using existing equipment to move and open them. Enabling trusted human agents to verify the nature and safety of the contents of a container reduces the need for expensive new sensors and technicians from other countries. And the search done in minutes, not the days or weeks that scheduling such thorough searches takes now. The ability to search a container so easily results in fewer security-related cargo holds and faster trips across terminal properties. The design allows an increase in the number of random searches and means safer work for the world's customs personnel, with better results.

During the design process for the "dry cargo" version of the CakeBoxx, it became clear that there should be other versions of this doorless design that could be brought to the commercial container market. Since it was side-loadable, long bundles of cargo-like pipe and structural steel that were frequently heavy could be loaded into half-height CakeBoxxes. Not hauling five or six feet of air inside taller containers saves onboard space. It also increases the load density of the ship as a whole, reducing the need for ballast water. According to CakeBoxx, on an 8,000-TEU (twenty-foot equivalent unit) ship this results in revenue capacity increases of more than $2 million *per trip*! Now, it is likely that much of the world's steel will be shipped this way, fully protected from vandals, weather, and the incidental damage exposed cargos are always susceptible to.

The FreezerBoxx is another evolutionary development. Again, since it is side-loadable, it is possible to surround a frozen cargo with insulation so sufficiently thick that it keeps the cargo frozen from Asia to the middle of North America or vice versa. Once it has arrived, it's easy to plug that same FreezerBoxx into a frigid CO_2 source. This keeps the cargo frozen indefinitely, while at the same time it can be quickly disconnected and hauled away, by any weight-qualified truck, for a three-week journey anywhere in the world.

As with many innovations, solving one problem has created unexpected benefits in several unrelated areas. In the case of the CakeBoxx, the pursuit of security has yielded better frozen food and cheaper steel. Other types and forms of CakeBoxxes include the "convertible," which converts from a standard flat-bed cargo-carrying CakeBoxx into a food-grade liquids and powders carrier. It is capable of carrying 10,000 liters of fluid. The typical cargo for convertibles would be wines, cooking oils, animal fats, and other agricultural and food-grade products in demand worldwide. It will be the least expensive method to ship these types of liquids in the intermodal environment. There is also a CakeBoxx that is 12.75 feet high. It allows shippers to send cargos of unusual size or shape with complete weather protection and security. Fully assembled equipment can be sent ready to use, with no risk of corrosion or vandalism. This over-height CakeBoxx is suitable only for direct ship-to-rail transport.

At one time CakeBoxx had the opportunity to brief DHS on its ISO-compliant (International Organization for Standardization-compliant) doorless containers and all the security they provided in addition to facilitating Customs and Border Protection (CBP) inspection procedures. As I mentioned before, I was told that DHS responded enthusiastically throughout the briefing until the very end when the final comment was essentially, "These are great, if only they had doors."

Perhaps the best explanation of CakeBoxx came from a West Coast port engineer who is not affiliated with CakeBoxx. After examining this innovative container, he released the following evaluation:

In today's threat of world terrorism and cargo theft, safety and security of cargo can't be guaranteed in a standard rear-door shipping container. Standard containers can be broken into and cargo can be stolen or damaged, whether on a terminal waiting shipment or onboard a ship in transit across oceans. Import and export cargo inside containers is impossible to inspect or verify without removing the door locking seal, opening the container doors, and physically removing (unstuffing) each piece of cargo inside the container, and, conversely, replacing each piece (stuffing) of cargo back inside the container. Inspecting selective cargo shipments in this manner can potentially cause damage, increase the risk of theft of cargo, and take hours and is costly to the shipper.

The introduction of the Cakeboxx to shippers has redefined containerization. The Cakeboxx will revolutionize worldwide shipment of cargo in containers. The Cakeboxx provides a means to guarantee that what was put in the container at the start of embarkation will arrive at the destination. Selective customs inspection of cargo that is shipped in a Cakeboxx container can proceed without having to remove the cargo and yet will have visual and physical access to all of the cargo.

The Cakeboxx in every aspect looks like and is a standard shipping container. It has the same overall size and cargo capacity of a standard container. It has the same twist-lock pocket corners for picking, hoisting, setting, and loading. What's the difference? It has four steel sides, a top and bottom, but it does not have doors. The Cakeboxx is a shipping container that consists of a modified flat rack with a perimeter latching system that receives and locks into place the other five-sided (four sides and a top) Cakeboxx. To put cargo inside the Cakeboxx, typical terminal container handling equipment like a Reachstacker, Top Pick, or Strad Carrier picks the Cakeboxx off the flat rack. Putting cargo in the container envelope on the flat rack can be accomplished from 360 degrees or all four sides. It provides the means to maximize and efficiently and expediently load a container. Verification and completion of loading is completed by reinstalling the Cakeboxx over the cargo and activating the locking latching system. If at the embarkation or discharge terminal customs inspection is necessary, typical terminal container handling equipment can lift the Cakeboxx top for 360-degree or all four-sided inspection within minutes.

The applications of the Cakeboxx are just starting to emerge. For instance, why put heavy cargo in a standard container that takes only a fraction of the volume?

The Cakeboxx also offers a half-height container top option. Now two containers by weight can fit in the same volume space of one container.

The Cakeboxx will provide added cargo safety and security that is not available in a standard container. It's such a simple concept and was in plain view of every dock worker. We'll all be waiting to view the first Cakeboxx come into a terminal and see if anyone sees the absence of doors. If they say things are safe behind locked doors, how much safer are things behind walls without doors?

CONSEARCH

Although there is much discussion about the detection of shielded highly enriched uranium (HEU) with the use of scanning technology, we know that scanning technology cannot detect shielded HEU by scanning (see chapter 2). Consearch, a small South Carolina firm, has developed a chemical and radiological detection system for determining the presence of contraband (e.g., nuclear weapons, illegal drugs, chemical weapons, explosives, concealed humans) in shipping containers, including ISO "dry box" containers, railcars, and trucks. The detection system will automatically perform radiological and chemical analyses for contraband materials "while the containers are in transit." The detection system will be interfaced with a container-tracking and breach-detection system that can report anomalies at any point along the shipping route—i.e., as containers are in transit on container ships, stored in ports, or anywhere else en route (by rail or road) for distribution to the U.S. supply chain. Since the analyses and the reports of the analyses are performed and reported during "dead time" of the container transit process, the smooth and unimpeded flow of containers through U.S. ports or across international borders is ensured. Detection of contraband or other abnormalities would be reported instantaneously at any point during the progress of the container.

The Consearch detection system is small and unobtrusive (it will fit in container headspace or wall corrugations), and it is self-powered. The complete contraband detection system will consist of the Consearch detector interfaced with a container security device (CSD) that offers a total chain-of-custody concept to verify container contents (bill of lading), uniquely track each container through its transit, and provide reports of breaching of any part of the container. Thus, reports of abnormalities (i.e., presence of contraband, breaching, unauthorized movement) can be transmitted to appropriate authorities at any point along the transportation route, from point of origin (stuffing and securing the container) to point of delivery (authorized unsealing of the container).

The premise of the method is that concealed radioactive contraband radiates from contaminated surfaces or penetrates container packaging and can be detected by placing detectors in empty spaces within the container. Chemical substances that are contraband materials or chemicals associated with contraband either evaporate from contaminated surfaces or permeate packaging into the empty spaces within the container. In both cases the contraband is detected using the in situ detection method while the container is in transit.

Nuclear Contraband Detection

Nuclear detection systems employed for container security have been criticized for their inability to distinguish gamma rays originating from nuclear sources from gamma rays originating from a large variety of benign cargo of naturally occurring radioactive materials that emit radioactivity (e.g., bananas, cat litter, granite, porcelain, stoneware). Such substances have accounted for 99% of nuisance alarms. In order to combat the nuisance alarms, the Consearch detector, operating inside the container during transit and interfaced with a chain-of-custody system, will incorporate the knowledge of container contents and, therefore, the natural radioactivity background. The Consearch detector will then search for and report levels of radioactivity that are consistently above and two or more times this known natural background.

Chemical Contraband Detection

Contraband chemical materials and chemicals associated with the contraband material evaporate from the surfaces into the container space, or these chemicals permeate the packaging materials into the container space. Exterior surface contamination is the basis for the detection of explosives and illegal drugs in airports around the world. In the case of concealed humans, the proposed method will allow for the monitoring of increasing levels of human effluvia such as ammonia, CO_2, and diamines into the container space. Organic human effluvia are readily detectable using the same detection concept as for contraband materials; inorganic gases will be analyzed using electrochemical sensors that are integral components of the Consearch contraband detector.

Feasibility of the Consearch chemical contraband detection method has been demonstrated and described in the following abstract.[2]

It is paramount in the worldwide shipping container industry that the smooth and efficient movement of containers through ports be unimpeded by contraband inspection methods. To date, this has not been realized since any inspection process requires a minimum of some minutes and possibly as long as hours. We will report on an initial demonstration of a system concept and an approach to develop a chemical detector for determination of the presence of chemical contraband (e.g., illegal drugs, chemical/biological weapons materials, explosives, and humans) in shipping containers—shipping containers include standard "dry box" containers, rail cars, and trucks. The detector will automatically perform chemical analyses for contraband materials and report results of the analyses instantaneously when interrogated as containers are being loaded or offloaded, stored in ports, or in route (by rail or road) to a U.S. border for distribution to the U.S. supply chain. Time-consuming chemical analyses are performed during "dead time" of the container transit process and reports of analyses are reported instantaneously; thus, the smooth and unimpeded flow of containers through U.S. ports or across international borders is ensured.

To test the question posed in the title of this paper, 3 kilograms of a recently confiscated sample of cocaine, loaned and protected by local enforcement agencies, was placed in a standard 40-foot shipping container along with an IMS [ion mobility spectrometry] detector. Detector response data was recorded continuously for a period of five days. Post-processing of the data indicated that with proper instrumental analysis techniques the answer is in the affirmative. The test was repeated using a simulated container which was constructed such that the ratio of the volume of the simulated container to the 3-kg sample of cocaine was representative of approximately that of 500 pounds (220 kg) in a standard 40-foot container. The contraband detection results were even more definitive.

GATEKEEPER USA

GateKeeper USA touts its container automated monitoring system (CAMS) device as one that has one of the smallest if not the smallest footprint in the industry with an extended battery life rivaling the average life of a container. CAMS can search, identify, and transmit over the strongest available frequency without the limitations of dependence on a single frequency (analog, digital, GSM [global system for mobile communications], MARSAT, Inmarsat, etc.). Transmissions are encrypted with proprietary technology that allows information to be sent securely, in real time, worldwide. Transmissions can typically contain more information than always on radio frequency identification (RFID), GSM, or cellular-based devices. CAMS can be queried while en route by shipper, receiver, governing agencies, and insurance and/or bonding companies. Bandwidth or transmission costs are calculated on actual use; as CAMS transmission needs are exceedingly small, normal operating costs can be considerably less.

CAMS are smart devices and will seek to communicate with other CAMS devices and mesh or self-network to create optimal communications; they are not line of sight (LOS)–dependent to communicate. This allows buried containers or containers located on the bottom of a stack to transmit information to other equipped containers. Installations can be either concealed (covert) or in plain sight (overt) and will supplement GPS location, independent of that network. CAMS can be given information on destination, speed, weather, and so on and can calculate location with advanced fuzzy logic and inertial guidance techniques. Sensors monitor atmospheric continuity within the container, if a door has been opened, and the contents, and they can identify narcotics, explosives, radioactive material, biological contaminates, or other unwanted or restricted substances within the container, including people and animals.

According to GateKeeper, CAMS is exceedingly accurate and needs only minute samples to determine if a substance exists within a container, and it is secured within a Hardware Firewall™ that also protects internal software. This secure case will actually cause the contents of the CAMS device to self-destruct, ensuring that no tampering or reverse engineering has been attempted or occurred. Historical data will be transmitted intact and remain intact and available for forensic uses. CAMS will transmit information if an attempt has happened or is happening, in real time, and it can be designed to collect information on the attacker or attackers. It cannot be signal-scanned in an attempt to locate the device, as it does not transmit for any discernible amount of time. Transmissions are controlled independently and internally and not sent at regular intervals.

CAMS technology is years ahead of the RFID development standard and exceeds even those most optimistic technology projections. CAMS performs in similar domains, but far outperforms RFID standards. CAMS technology transcends and overlaps other market sectors currently being serviced by RFID because, according to GateKeeper, there was no other available technology until now.

In summary, Gatekeeper presents the CAMS CSD as an affordable, multipurpose device to be affixed inside each individual shipping container, which combines various functions including intrusion detection, geolocation, detection of dangerous materials, and communication. These multiple functions provide the following uses:

- Protecting from intrusion into and tampering with the container
- Full detection capabilities for nuclear and radioactive materials, narcotic drugs, or other dangerous or unwanted materials
- Monitoring the location and security of the container throughout its voyage and transfer to land transportation modes
- Communicating a warning of any attempted theft of container goods

VISIBLE ASSETS

Visible Assets is a firm that developed a product called RuBee® (Institute of Electrical and Electronics Engineers Standards Association [IEEE] 1902.1) that provides real-time automated visibility and the highest possible security of mission critical assets (MCA). MCA are assets that simply cannot be lost or stolen, worth far more on the street or in the hands of terrorists than the cost to replace. Visible Assets provides automated MCA visibility and security using three important security layers.

Security layer 1: Real-time storage physical inventory. Assets in storage on racks or shelves in a warehouse or weapons in armory racks or other secure facilities have RuBee wireless tags embedded or attached. RuBee-enabled smart racks and smart shelves turn the steel in these racks into an antenna, and Visible Assets software applications do daily or hourly audit trails of each item and report inventory and asset status. Inventory can also be obtained manually with handheld devices or automatically with smart shelves and racks.

Security layer 2: Issuance checkout/in. When an asset is removed from inventory, one knows it has been removed from the shelf, but ownership has to be transferred from a "storekeeper" to a new owner, a soldier or guard or asset guardian. This is done using ruggedized Apple iPads known as gRaps® that have a RuBee-embedded reader. Tags are read as the asset is passed across the checkout counter.

Security layer 3: Exit/entry detection. When the asset leaves the facility, RuBee portal platforms provide identification detection and alarms using Door-Guard® and GateGuard®. Both detect RuBee-enabled assets and IDs as a person passes through a door or gate, on foot or in a vehicle. These systems have passed many objective user acceptance tests (UAT) with 100% detection of assets, even if hidden inside a steel case, reducing that human trust reliance with full process-free automation in all three layers. For example, if something is removed from inventory off the racks but does not get checked out, an alarm is issued. If an asset exits the facility but is not checked out, an alarm is issued, and so on.

RFID and barcode systems are blocked by steel and the human body. As a result, security is based on new human processes focused only on layer 2. Both become human-assisted asset tracking systems, not real-time automated security systems. Visible Assets has repeatedly proven that RuBee is the wireless technology that can provide fully integrated visibility with three-layer security automation.

RuBee also delivers a high return on investment (ROI). Independent customer studies consistently find payback of few months. Physical inventory required for most mission critical assets can take two to three people and from a few days to weeks. Visible Assets has several customers who require audited physical inventory reports each quarter, but it can take almost an entire quarter to do just one audit. RuBee, in layer 1, does unchallengeable physical audits in a few minutes many times each day.

According to Visible Assets, RFID cannot provide any more security over a barcode system. Exit-entry detection is not possible with RFID, because the radio frequency (RF) signals are blocked by people, and automatic inventory is not possible because steel racks and shelves also block RF signals. A RuBee visibility system can start very simple, at lower cost, with tags and handheld devices only. That means it can do full assisted inventory on shelf or rack, with the ability to upgrade to three-layer security automation.

To provide the three security layers, RuBee wireless is magnetic, not RF. Each tag on a RuBee network is like a mini-website with a programmable address and subnet address. Tags have static memory (500 bytes to 5 kB) with a real-time clock and a processor that has the ability to securely encrypt transmissions. RuBee tags are not blocked by steel or by humans. RuBee can actually go through steel and liquids. Unlike RF wireless systems, RuBee has the ability to control range from a few inches to more than 50 feet and therefore has no tempest, target, or eavesdropping risk. RuBee is the only wireless technology in use and permitted in secure areas in the United States. RuBee has no known intrinsic safety risks and has been shown in independent studies to be safe, with a zero safe separation distance (SSD) on high explosives. RuBee is many millions of times below Occupational Safety and Health Administration (OSHA) human safety limits, and independent studies at the Mayo Clinic have shown no untoward effects on pacemakers or implantable cardioverter defibrillators. RuBee-embedded tags can also have sensors to monitor the status of an asset.

It is clear that this technology would be instrumental in controlling inventory and container stuffing by comparing the inventory removed from the warehouse for loading into the container to the actual inventory loaded. RuBee could automatically identify the cargo stuffed into the container. RuBee, combined with CSDs using a chain-of-custody system of cargo identification data that could be communicated along with the identity of the person verifying the cargo, would remove all need for hard documentation and could provide evidence in case of forged documentation—clearly a supply chain benefit.

CARGOTRAX SINGAPORE PTE

Developed by Tampere University of Technology in Finland, mesh wireless sensor network (WSN) technology for the transmission of data from containers has been commercialized since 2009. The patent issued in the United States and Europe is owned by Traxer Ltd. Its major advantage is the logistics and security monitoring of both cold reefer containers and dry containers. The primary users of this innovative technology are cold food shippers, such as the exporters of meat to the Middle East; seafood products to the United States, the European Union, and Japan; fruit, vegetables, pharmaceuticals, and, according to CargoTrax, blood plasma exporters who consider the monitoring of temperature of prime, critical importance in human safety and quality control.

Furthermore, recently highlighted terrorist threats to attack and compromise food containers by injecting biological or chemical agents into a food reefer have increased concerns of food products exporters from several parts of the globe, especially to the United States, the EU, and the Middle East. With the global financial crisis creating further unemployment in developing countries, the opportunities to recruit terrorists among the radicals may open new dimensions in attacks against the West. Many hazmat, cobalt, and other high-value easily disposable shipments, including defense shipments, have succumbed to sudden disappearance and have never been recovered due to lack of continuous GPRS-GPS (general packet radio service-global positioning system) tracking and monitoring, which may be secured through an integrated, CargoTrax Singapore solution.

A range of optional sensors may include temperature, light, CO_2, O_2, gas, vibration, volume changes, container doors, and acceleration; CargoTrax can deliver end-to-end data in real time or near real time, 24/7, with global visibility. CargoTrax technology may be installed within minutes, delivering seamless transmissions with self-healing qualities. While the reefer containers stacked on deck may require a few gateway nodes to communicate with a laptop on the ship's bridge, the dry TEUs below deck in cells or steel compartments may require additional gateway nodes. The data accumulated on the server on the bridge may transmit the information packets at predetermined intervals via the ship's satellite to control centers on land. CargoTrax also states that aging reefers may enjoy an extension of their life span.

The CargoTrax WSN concept, with a reliable, parallel, complementary, stand-alone, nonintrusive, miniaturized mesh wireless sensor network with optional GSM-GPRS-GPS satellite-solar power, does offer a comprehensive back-office 24/7 monitoring support option. Additionally, WSN gateway nodes may be deployed in container farms and ports to deliver a continuous, seamless audit and information on the container traffic.

CargoTrax has also developed a highly dynamic system, with a patent issued in the United States, to allow containers to talk to each other without existing access points or base station infrastructure. These WSN station nodes organize autonomously and route each others' traffic in a multihoop routing fashion to a gateway or several gateways that connect the wireless network to other technologies—e.g., Internet delivery or database server. The container unit, mesh network, and system reporting container events enable a reliable end-to-end monitoring system by means of which the location of containers and other conditions related to the containers can be continuously or almost continuously monitored. The containers are equipped with such container units that are capable of cooperating with each other, which is especially needed in challenging radio environments. The cooperation of the container units is based on mesh network algorithms. Each container unit placed in a container includes a short-range radio and a cellular network radio. Thus, the container unit is able to connect to two different types of communication networks. In addition, each container unit uses a specific connection set-up logic. When a set-up attempt results in a connection, the container transmits its message through the connection. The invention comprises the container unit, a mesh network composed of container units, and a system reporting container events. The system includes message switching equipment for transmitting messages between container units placed in containers and a monitoring server. CargoTrax describes the functioning this way in its patent:

> The message switching equipment comprises at least a container unit, a gateway unit providing communication links, and a message handler which is coupled to the monitoring server. The message switching equipment is adapted to send a first message from the container unit via a cellular network to the message handler in response to an event relating to the container. In more detail, the first message is sent through a cellular network radio of the container unit. The equipment is further adapted to receive through a short-range radio of the container unit a second message originated from one of the container units and to transmit the second message from the container unit via the cellular network to the message handler. The equipment is further adapted to receive through a short-range radio of the gateway unit a third message and transmit the third message through the gateway unit to the message handler.

CONCLUSION

What is striking about examples like these is that they are the product of U.S. and foreign private sector firms. Yet DHS has a Science and Technology Directorate (S&T). One of the functions of S&T is to develop CSDs. S&T began this process in 2006. To date, they have not developed anything that is used today as a CSD, nor have they set standards on CSDs. The positive aspect of this is that given their ignorance of CSD hardware, software, sensors, and communications capacities, their setting of standards would be foolhardy. Because of what appeared to be DHS's being out of touch with the reality of container security and the private sector's advancement in this area, in September 2009, DHS was requested to respond to four questions submitted by a member of the U.S. House of Representatives. I think it's best to use the actual questions and responses from DHS to highlight the failure of S&T in developing a CSD. The questions and responses follow:

Question: How much money has DHS spent since 2003 in creating CSDs, including the evaluation and development phases?

Answer: DHS S&T began developing container security device (CSD) technology in 2006 in response to a requirement from CBP. The numbers reported below for CSD development, testing, and evaluation are approximate as work (primarily T&E [testing and evaluation]) for the CSD; the Advanced Container Security Device technologies were funded via a single contract and conducted in tandem.

(a) FY06: $3.9M
(b) FY07: $1.9M
(c) FY08: $1.9M
(d) FY09: $2.0M
Total obligated to date: $9.7M

Question: Have manufacturers received funding for the creation of CSDs?

Answer: DHS S&T is funding two vendors to develop CSDs, Georgia Tech Research Institute and Science Applications International Corporation.

Question: Have the products used been found viable from these efforts?

Answer: DHS S&T believes that at least one vendor will meet the performance requirements set forth by CBP. DHS S&T will deliver Open Performance Standards to CBP in November–December 2010 that will define the performance and operational characteristics for approved CSD technology.

Question: Have any of these products been deployed by the private sector?

Answer: Not yet.

I applaud them for their honesty. It is quite clear that they have, so far, failed, even with a $9.7 million budget for this development. And assuming that they would have succeeded, we would likely have only a sophisticated (one hopes) door lock. What is profoundly incredible is that DHS does not know that the world already has forms of CSDs that do more than the minimum that DHS expects. Industry has already developed and is using containers that detect entry through any portion of the container and report it automatically by satellite or satellite/cellular technology. The containers talk and respond to a central control center and can send alerts of all types, including radiation detection, to whoever is set up to receive those messages. These containers also provide a literal chain-of-custody feature, from stuffing at foreign origin with the identity of the person accountable for supervising and verifying the cargo sent to the authorized, identified, accountable person opening and verifying the cargo at destination.

All of this not only exists but has been demonstrated in Europe and Asia and soon in South Africa. Even the U.S.-Mexico border will soon see trials generated by the private sector, although there is the hope that DHS will carry through with its own alleged border pilot. Unfortunately, there is ignorance of not only CSD but also other technological developments and systems that can be used to improve our supply chain security. Additionally, the engineering tests of the units actually operating in Europe show that they are 100% effective and accurate. Unlike the Department of Defense (DOD), DHS has no industrial complex to develop its technology. It seems that the industry has done this for them free. Smart containers as they exist today not only provide the security DHS can't seem to develop, but also make the supply chain visible and cheaper, making money for the user. It also happens to provide security for the nations employing them, including the United States. So what did we get for the $9.7 million spent by S&T? My answer is mismanagement connected to politically driven decision making.

POSTSCRIPT

With all the private sector innovation and all the money spent by government to develop what already exists, it is not surprising that our official policy on container security is this: lock the doors! Perhaps the dumbest policy, model, or standard of all is the sealed-door standard. No scientific or empirical data are necessary to demonstrate its weakness. It was the outcome of DHS's inability to develop an alternative. For some time now, when treating conveyance security devices, both DHS and CBP have focused only on doors. First, in November 2005, in a request for information (RFI), an information-gathering and planning vehicle used by DHS in support of CBP, Johns Hopkins University's Applied Physics Laboratory, on behalf of DHS, stated, "The purpose of this request is to gather information to identify and evaluate available state-of-the-art container and trailer tracking devices suitable for in-bond shipments." The level of sophistication needed and stated in the RFI seems clear. "The container and trailer security device must be able to electronically detect closing and opening of either door of the container/trailer. Monitoring the door status must be continuous from time of arming to disarming by authorized personnel."

The former commissioner of CBP, Ralph Basham, diverged from his predecessor and said in 2007 that[3]

> any device developed to monitor the security of a shipping container must be able to detect unauthorized intrusions anywhere on the container, not just through the doors, to be part of a layered defense strategy in securing the global supply chain. . . . I'm saying that just because you have a device that secures the doors does not mean that the container is secure. It just means that the doors are secure and not the whole container. If technology is being developed it should be toward making sure the entire container is tamperproof.

But in the same year on December 18, as posted in *American Shippers NewsWire,* Basham's boss, Homeland Security Secretary Michael Chertoff, went to the other extreme by saying, "Therefore, effective October 15, 2008, we expect to have the requirement in place mandating that all containers be secured with a standard bolt seal." Or, in my words, let's just bolt the doors. And, one week before Chertoff's deadbolt-the-doors statement, CBP released an RFI on its CSD requirements.

This RFI, like the one two years before, was still focusing on "doors only" in spite of Commissioner Basham's statement on the need to secure the *whole container.* In the face of fairly clear direction contained in the SAFE Port Act of 2006, DHS and CBP failed to move at the pace specified in the law with respect to container security. They are also inconsistent with and lag behind the progress of the private sector in moving away from doors-only detection and reporting. The private sector already has affordable technology that begins at stuffing with the verification of contents and identification of the verifier, "all-sides" detection of entry, and satellite communication and control through to destination, including the identity of the authorized agent opening the container. One such system was demonstrated between Bremerhaven, Germany, and Port Everglades, Florida, in December 2006.[4] Although the Germany-U.S. pilot was for demonstration purposes, in reality, the system actually caught thieves stealing from one of the containers and it located one of the containers unintentionally lost in transit. DHS is so far behind industry in container security that its decision making in this area is anything but confidence-producing.[5]

At the time of this writing and with knowledge of private sector advancements well beyond door seals, *and* in light of videos and Immigration and Customs Enforcement's (ICE) own PowerPoint presentation, both of which I possess, CBP knows how easy it is to bypass door seals. Yet DHS continues to develop a doors-only system, to be demonstrated in 2012 in a southern-border security pilot called "APEX Secure Transit Corridor Technology (Apex-STC) Demonstration." The demonstration is to test the integrity of "doors-only" container/ trailer security. Specifically, it is a project in partnership with CBP to develop a secure transit corridor for goods shipped between Mexico, the United States, and Canada.[6] Although set forth in 2011, in June 2012, DHS has still not been able to initiate this project even though potential private sector participants have offered to cooperate by participating through the offering of their technology and processes that surpass DHS's weak "doors-only" mentality, including Consearch, which demonstrated its sensors under the authority of DHS at the DHS Container Security Test Bed facility at the Transportation Security Laboratory in Atlantic City, New Jersey, in 2011.

While DHS continues to claim that seals along with their electronic seal component constitute a layered security mechanism, they know the seals can be bypassed. What is worse is that DHS knows and has tested technology that can today provide security by detecting a breach into the container through any of its construction. DHS also knows that standard shipping-size containers exist that have no doors to breach and could also be tested! Yet it is stuck in its out-of-date, ignorant perception of container security. Its vacuous level of understanding and competence in the area of container security is breathtaking, especially in light of private sector advances and use of CSDs and processes.

Two important observations must be addressed here. First, CBP acknowledges that the doors-only concept is flawed and unworkable. Second, CBP acknowledges that it is ignorant of existing security systems that detect and report access to any part of the container, including doors! The conclusion: doors-only, although still the official standard, is fatally flawed and constitutes a vulnerability still not addressed. Innovation comes from the private sector, not government. With all the money spent, all the RFIs published, and all the statements made, DHS still has not developed or encouraged the use of technology already existing that is essential for the security of the global supply chain and, ultimately, the security of this nation.

NOTES

1. I am not financially connected to the firms cited in this chapter, nor have I been nor will I be compensated in any fashion by these firms for coverage of their products in this chapter.

2. J. C. Harden and C. S. Harden, "Detection of Contraband in Shipping Containers without Impeding the Flow of Commerce," IEEE International Conference on Technologies for Homeland Security, Waltham, Massachusetts, May 2008.

3. Calvin Biesecker, "CBP Chief Wants Total Container Security Device," *Defense Daily International*, January 3, 2007.

4. Rick Eyerdam, "Cargo Insecurity: Locals Offer a Better Mouse Trap," *Florida Shipper*, May 28, 2007.

5. For a treatment of a series of DHS decisions, see James Giermanski, "DHS Decision-Making: Competence or Character?" CSO Online, January 14, 2008, http://www2.csoonline.com/exclusives/column.html.

6. Statements of Tara O'Toole, undersecretary, Science and Technology, Department of Homeland Security, "Overcoming Hurdles in Project Management, S&T Goal 1," before Subcommittee on Technology and Innovation, Committee on Science, Space, and Technology, House of Representatives, 112th Congress, First Session, March 15, 2011.

Chapter Fourteen

Final Observations

While no analogy is perfect, I think there is one that at least makes sense, especially to those who do not have direct knowledge and experience in the global supply chain but must understand its significance to our nation's health. The health analogy seems fitting, given the nation's political postures over health care today and the role of government versus the private sector in it.

The global supply chain is for the trading world the arteries that provide the vital flow of blood to the major organs of the body. This continued uninterrupted blood flow is necessary for life. So, too, is the global supply chain necessary for continued economic health and life. The major organs of the body are the equivalent of our seaports and land ports of entry. Like the degradation or complete breakdown of a major organ, the complete breakdown or significant degradation of a port or multiple ports can signal a serious, if not fatal, health issue. Therefore, the United States has to not only take measures to maintain our health but also to treat or medicate an injury to our health and vitality as a nation. Clearly, maintenance is a better option than facing the necessity of treatment—especially treatment that was preventable with proper maintenance.

The Department of Homeland Security (DHS) has apparently been designated as the government physician. Therefore, it must first prevent an event that would disrupt the flow of needed cargo. Second, it would have to take steps to respond to an event that would disrupt this flow and be a detriment to our health as a nation. The question is whether this government physician can perform the duty alone, without the help and innovation of the private sector. One must ask, does DHS possess the requisite knowledge of the science of global supply chain security? So far, DHS demonstrates little scientific knowledge of how to treat vulnerabilities. Its decisions seem to be focused on air cargo and people movement, something like treating a virus instead of responding to a fatal incident. The following illustrates the level of scientific knowledge DHS has in its make-believe physician's role. I think it proves the need for outside assistance from those who do understand science and the security of the global supply chain. The following, if perpetuated, could be fatal flaws in DHS's treatment.

THE PROBLEM OF ERRORS IN TESTING

Errors or mistakes occur in just about any human endeavor, including in medicine, in the legal system, in scientific research, and even in those areas that concern DHS. There is no perfect system or practice that will keep us 100% safe, especially in a global supply chain that, like it or not, is indispensible for our economy's survival. Trying to make it perfectly safe based on what we know about shippers, consignees, carriers, governments, and individual people is impossible. But we can scientifically reduce the possibility of risk or worse by using fundamental scientific principles. Some years ago, Peter Lodge, a colleague of mine and a college professor in the social sciences, wrote with me a response to a very unscientific requirement of DHS that by its very nature stifles the development of technologies like container security devices (CSDs) that could have a significant, positive role in our security. An example from medicine will serve to illustrate the range and the types of errors DHS has made. Male readers over the age of 50 may well have had a prostate-specific antigen (PSA) test to screen for prostate cancer. Under normal circumstances, one assumes that a low level of antigens indicates the absence of prostate cancer and a high level alerts us to the possibility of cancer (or at the very least, the increased risk of developing cancer). Typically, a finding of high levels of PSA would lead to additional diagnostic testing. There are, however, two possible errors that can occur in such cases. One is that although the test indicates worrisome levels of antigens, further diagnostic testing finds no evidence of cancer. This is referred to as a false positive.[1] A false positive increases levels of anxiety and leads to additional (unnecessary, as it happens) costs. As irksome, worrisome, and expensive as a false positive might be, they are typically tolerated since alternative tests subsequently establish that we are cancer-free.

The other error that can occur is a false negative[2]—that is, a failure to uncover a true high level of antigens, and the failure therefore to discover what might be an actual case of prostate cancer. Concerns regarding undiagnosed disease and the accompanying consequences mean that in matters of health we would prefer to deal with the inconvenience of secondary testing so that cases of cancer are not missed. All things being equal, the lower the tolerance for a false positive, the greater the probability of a false negative occurring.[3] Said the opposite way, the more we allow mistakes in detection (false positives), e.g., "a bomb was in a container" when, in fact, it wasn't, the less likely we are to have a false negative—that is, the greater chance we'll find a bomb in a container said to be without one.

THE PROBLEM OF NEAR PERFECTION

If one understands the operational complexity of any system that accomplishes the above, one must question a current decision of DHS to require a 99% false positive fail rate. Specifically, in a request for information (RFI), an information-gathering and planning vehicle used by DHS in support of Customs and Border Protection (CBP), Johns Hopkins University's Applied Physics Laboratory (under contract with DHS) sent a letter dated November 8, 2005, to potential vendors. The letter stated in part, "The purpose of this request is to gather information to identify and evaluate available state-of-the-art container and trailer tracking devices suitable for in-bond shipments." That statement alone poses two serious questions. What does DHS believe is "state-of-the-art," and why did it take so long after 9/11 for DHS to realize that CBP had little or no knowledge of or control over in-bond containers coming into the United States and moving throughout the country with literally no control or monitoring?

State-of-the art assumes not only the latest versions of technology, but also the highest level of reliability through the use of the latest technology. Therefore, part of the evaluation process is the requirement of achieving and maintaining quality standards. In both the RFI in 2005 and in the 2006 requirements, DHS determined that a 99% false positive threshold should be the standard. The latest manifestation of this is contained in the Transportation Workers Identification Credential (TWIC) program requiring special ID cards for port workers and those who have routine access to U.S. seaports. As reported in *Washington Technology*, there is concern over the potential inoperability among cards produced by different manufacturers and the "1 percent system error rate inherent in FIPS [Federal Information Processing Standards] 201."[4] FIPS 201 serves as the guideline in developing the port workers' identification card. Some industry leaders are objecting and are concerned about card failures, which would mean costs and delays at our nation's ports. So why has DHS chosen the 99% false positive standard?

It seems that the 1% or 99% false positive rate is directly linked to the National Institute of Standards and Technology (NIST) and can be traced to Special Publication 800-76-1. When discussing the reliability of fingerprints as part of biometric data, the publication states: "Authentication performance is quantified in terms of both the false reject rate (FRR) and the false accept rate (FAR). . . . The former would quantify the proportion of legitimate cardholders incorrectly denied access; the latter would be the proportion of impostors incorrectly allowed access."[5]

Specifically in Special Publication 800-76-1, one can see, in Section 7.7, that "FRR values are less than or equal to 1% at a fixed FAR operating point." Further, with respect to the interoperability of different fingerprint templates and speed of computation, an "FRR less than or equal to 1% at a FAR of 1%" is required.[6] So it seems that this is the basis for the false positive standard.

This standard might be reasonable when dealing with biometric identification techniques, but then again, how valuable is a 99% false positive threshold to the safety of our nation's ports and to us as individuals? DHS wants a 99% false positive threshold—that is, DHS allows the device to fail once in 100 uses. This criterion may or may not be the right one. It might be that the false positive rate of 1% or less is unrealistic but that the 1% false negative standard is far too lax. If we accepted this standard for the border inspection of containers/trailers for WMD (weapons of mass destruction, nuclear, biochemical, etc.), any device used to establish the presence of WMD must have no more than a 1% rate of false positives. Inevitably such a rate would reduce the amount of time (and hence money) devoted to a secondary test (i.e., physical search) of the container. However, given the potential dire consequences of a false negative in this example, a 1% false negative is too generous—one dirty nuclear device could be (assuming a port detonation and depending on the port) a significant disruption of international commerce at that port for months or years. Which is more disruptive: tolerating a higher level of false positives or the increased possibility of a false negative? (The problem of errors here is further complicated by the kinds of technology employed to monitor incoming containers. For instance, we use portal X-ray machines at our ports, and we know that they do not detect shielded, highly enriched uranium. But we use them anyway. We also know they alert on bananas, but we use them anyway.[7])

We should develop the mindset of linking the level of acceptable risk to the potential outcomes. For example, airline passengers expect that the planes they fly in have a 100% probability of landing after they take off. To ensure this criterion, there are rules for taking off and landing and planes have redundant systems and emergency systems, and we all gladly pay for that. In addition, federal aviation rules control whether a plane can fly given the weather conditions.

Similarly, the scientific community uses different confidence levels for different purposes. Therefore, if one is using a smart container to thwart thefts and hijacking of cargo, or for supply chain tracking information, one would likely use and be happy with a 95% confidence level. While the 99% false positive threshold is laudable, the requirement of obtaining near perfection is extremely difficult in the global container market, and more important, it inhibits the development and implementation of new ideas and practices.

All this talk of errors and of unexpected or improbable occurrences reflects some of the insights offered by Nassim Taleb, the so-called "skeptical empiricist," professional derivatives trader, and prolific writer on scientific and philosophical issues.[8] We operate within a world of probabilities, which in some ways contributes to the illusion of safety.[9] Taleb argues that we tend to underestimate the likelihood of a rare event occurring. But rare events happen, and when they *do* occur they are usually far more devastating that we might have imagined possible (see chapter 2).

SOME CONCLUDING THOUGHTS

It seems that a more reasonable approach would be to act as if our ports and our country were likely candidates for a particular debilitating disease or as if they were passengers on an airplane. We could use redundant devices and systems that would make the cost of using smart containers prohibitive, and we still couldn't control the container's use in bad weather. Thus, even if we were willing to pay, we could not have the reliability of the passenger plane. Maybe we could reach, at best, a 90% confidence level. With respect to being candidates for disease, the United States has the right mix of freedoms (like the right mix of genes), and living in our environment of global violence, which (like air quality) may not be always healthy, we become potential targets for sickness (violence) and death. So what should we do? We look around to find a test, an indicator of potential risk, and, in this analogy, a drug that can give us the best protection we can find. If our potential disease is cancer, and we can find a drug or procedure that only works 80% of the time, should we not accept it? Yes, it costs money, and yes, it is not a 100% sure thing, and yes, it may be even uncomfortable to take. So CBP doesn't like the remedies. They may cost them, inconvenience them, and even slow down port clearance. So does that mean we don't take these remedies? We certainly *can* inconvenience some CBP employees whose salaries we pay.

Another concept to consider is the "reasonable man theory" commonly used in judicial or quasi-judicial proceedings. What would a reasonable man believe or do? Said another way, it's the 75% level of probability, or "probable cause." The grand jury system is based on it and people's lives are affected by it, and the nation accepts it. Would it not be reasonable to have·a minimum of 75% standard of reliability instead of 99%?

Contrary to DHS opinion or policy, there should be an allowable failure rate that still gives us the best protection possible. The United States is dealing with creative, dangerous persons for whom it must have the best defense attainable, not the best defense possible. The United States cannot afford to have *no* defense because of a bureaucratic standard that simply cannot be met with our current and likely future technology, nor be developed because of unacceptable costs of added redundancies for sensors and communications. Even with redundant sub-systems, containers are victims of our climates, temperatures, rough handling, rough roads, and rough seas. Perfect mechanical and electronic functioning of container security systems capable of doing all that DHS expects of them are unattainable at this time with an unrealistic standard that actually increases risk—or, in this analogy, serious medical consequences. So do we have the luxury to wait for perfection? I think we all know the answer. The trading world cannot and does not equal a scientific laboratory in a scientific environment with scientists dedicated to scientific discoveries.

It is not enough to depend on government health care alone. The private sector, in most cases, knows more, can do more, and will offer a perspective that government often fails to see or simply ignores. DHS must alter its current treatment of securing the global supply chain.

NOTES

1. False positives are also known as Type I errors and false rejection errors—false rejection errors because they involve the incorrect rejection of the null hypothesis. To nonstatisticians, "false positive" is usually the preferred term because it is more understandable in words commonly used. A false positive occurs when one makes the decision that it is present in a sample that turns out to be erroneous or incorrect.

2. False negatives are also known as Type II errors and false acceptance errors. Again, to nonstatisticians, "false negative" is usually the preferred term. A false negative occurs when one makes a decision that it is not present in a sample that has been analyzed when, in fact, it is present at detectable concentrations.

3. The relationship can be much more complex depending on whether there is one distribution for both types of errors or two—one for each kind. In the case of medical testing, there may be one distribution that deals with the competence of the physician and another that describes the competence of a particular laboratory.

4. Alice Lipowicz, "More Woes for TWIC," *Washington Technology*, November 27, 2006, p. 1.

5. Charles Wilson, Patrick Grother, and Ramaswamy Ghandramouli, "Information Technology," Special Publication 800-76-1, National Institute of Standards and Technology, September 14, 2006, p. 26.

6. http://csrc.nist.gov/publications/drafts/800-76-1/SP800-76-1_draft.pdf, p. 32.

7. James Giermanski, "No More Excuses or Delays," *American Shipper*, October 2006, p. 2.

8. For a listing of his publications since 2004, see http://www.fooledbyrandomness .com.

9. We may know that the probability of a single engine O-ring or seal failing is one in 100 journeys, but when the engine has four of those seals then the probability of failure is one in 25 journeys. And it may not just be the engine that fails—the consequences could be substantial loss of life.

Index

About the Author

Dr. James R. Giermanski is chairman of Powers Global Holdings Inc. and president of Powers International LLC, an international transportation security company. He served as regents professor at Texas A&M International University and as an adjunct graduate faculty member at the University of North Carolina at Charlotte. He was director of transportation and logistics studies at the Center for the Study of Western Hemispheric Trade at Texas A&M International University.

Dr. Giermanski is co-inventor of a patent issued in the United States and in 35 other countries connected to transport container security. He is recognized as an expert in the global supply chain and container security by the World Bank and the World Customs Organization (WCO). He has frequently provided invited testimony on the North American Free Trade Agreement (NAFTA), transportation, and other international business issues before the U.S. Senate and House, the Texas Senate and House, the Environmental Protection Agency (EPA), and the U.S. International Trade Commission. He served as the co-chairman of the Texas Transportation Committee Task Force to prepare for NAFTA, sat for five years on the Texas Office of the Attorney General's Transborder Trucking International Working Group, and for three years was a member of the Research Advisory Committee on Management and Policy, Technical Advisory Panel, at the Texas Department of Transportation. He consulted on international transportation and transportation security, border logistics, and trade matters involving Mexico, and he has served as a border expert to assist the Arizona Department of Transportation in developing concepts and practices to improve the border-crossing activities on the Arizona-Mexico border. And at the request of the White House Council of Economic Advisors, he provided insight on trade issues and barriers on the southern border.

He has authored more than 200 articles, books, and monographs, with most focusing on container and supply chain security, international transportation, and trade issues, and for five years wrote the "International Insight" column in

Logistics Management. He has appeared as a special guest on the FOX News Channel's *Special Report with Brit Hume*, CNN, NBC, CBS, NPR, BBC, Voice of America, and the Canadian Broadcasting Corporation (CBC), in addition to many local and regional affiliates.

Finally, with his background as a former FBI special agent, an OSI special agent, and a colonel in the Office of Special Investigations (OSI), where he handled counterintelligence matters and supervised surreptitious U.S. base penetrations, he was selected as the first special agent of the Pennsylvania Crime Commission, where he specialized in organized crime.

Dr. Giermanski has a master's degree from the University of North Carolina at Charlotte, a master's degree from Florida International University, and a doctorate from the University of Miami. He is a graduate of Air Command and Staff College and the Air War College. While serving as a visiting scholar at the Center of Aerospace Doctrine, Research, and Education (CADRE), an Air Force think tank, he wrote a book on the counterintelligence training of Air Force Office of Special Investigations special agents, which was published by the Department of Defense.

Lightning Source UK Ltd.
Milton Keynes UK
UKOW05n0726221213

223469UK00007B/117/P